Parliament's
Generals

Parliament's Generals

Supreme Command and Politics during the British Wars 1642-51

Malcolm Wanklyn

Pen & Sword
MILITARY

AN IMPRINT OF PEN & SWORD BOOKS LTD.
YORKSHIRE – PHILADELPHIA

First published in Great Britain in 2019 by
PEN & SWORD MILITARY
an imprint of
Pen & Sword Books Ltd
Yorkshire - Philadelphia

ISBN 978 1 47389 836 3

A CIP catalogue record for this book is available from the British Library

Typeset in 10/13 & Sabon LT Std
by Aura Technology and Software Services, India

Printed and bound in UK by TJ International

Pen & Sword Books Ltd incorporates the Imprints of Aviation, Atlas, Family
History, Fiction, Maritime, Military, Discovery, Politics, History, Archaeology,
Select, Wharncliffe Local History, Wharncliffe True Crime, Military Classics,
Wharncliffe Transport, Leo Cooper, The Praetorian Press, Remember When, White
Owl, Seaforth Publishing and Frontline Publishing.

For a complete list of Pen & Sword titles please contact

PEN & SWORD BOOKS LTD
47 Church Street, Barnsley, South Yorkshire, S70 2AS, England
E-mail: enquiries@pen-and-sword.co.uk
Website: www.pen-and-sword.co.uk

Or

PEN & SWORD BOOKS
1950 Lawrence Rd, Havertown, PA 19083, USA
E-mail: Uspen-and-sword@casematepublishers.com
Website: www.penandswordbooks.com

Contents

Acknowledgements

My grateful thanks on this occasion for the advice and professional assistance generously given by Professor John Benson of the University of Wolverhampton; Dr Ismini Pells of the AHRC-funded project analysing maimed soldier petitions; Dr Mark Bainbridge, the librarian of Worcester College, Oxford; Simon Marsh of the Battlefield Trust; and the staff of the British Library, the National Archives, the National Archives Scotland and the Bodleian Library, Oxford. As in the past I owe a considerable debt to Charles Singleton, whose personal library makes up for deficiencies in my own.

This book could not have been written without the help of my family, and most particularly my son and daughter-in-law Jon and Julia, whose hospitality provided vital support for my visits to Kew. Norman their cat is also worthy of mention. Ministering to his needs at the drop of a hat when I was responsible for looking after him usually served to break my concentration, sometimes with bad effect, but he was also the unwitting instigator of new lines of thought.

Abbreviations

Bodleian	The Bodleian Library, Oxford
BL	British Library
HMC	Historical Manuscript Commission
NAS	National Archives Scotland
ODNB	Oxford Dictionary of National Biography
TNA	The National Archives, Kew

Definitions

Strategy: the overall objectives of a campaign or a group of campaigns being fought in parallel. This was normally the responsibility of government not of the generals.

Operations: the means by which strategy was put into effect. This could be a bone of contention between the government and its generals.

Tactics: the methods used by a commander in a confrontational situation, such as a battle, a siege, a standoff or an ambush, to inflict defeat on the enemy. In English armies this was acknowledged to be the responsibility of the senior military officer present.

List of Plates

The illustrations are owned by the National Portrait Gallery, and I am most grateful for permission to reproduce them. For consistency's sake they are all prints. Most are well known, but three deserve special mention.

The depiction of Fairfax and Cromwell on either side of Charles I is taken from a contemporary line engraving of the king's execution, in which they are portrayed as jointly presiding over events. The artist is not known, but he was probably Dutch. I could have chosen a similar engraving in which the portraits of the two generals are much larger and closer together, but the depiction of Cromwell is a grotesque caricature, fat in the face with an enormous nose.

The print of Cromwell and Lambert clearly dates from the mid-1650s, during the time of the First Protectorate (1654–7). It draws on two contemporary oil paintings attributable to Robert Walker. The original of John Lambert is well known, but Cromwell's is not in the public domain and may no longer exist.

Portrayals of George Monck in his pomp as lord general and Duke of Albemarle are numerous, but an oil painting in the National Portrait Gallery collection that was thought to be of him as a younger man is now believed to be of somebody else. The print reproduced as plate 8 is clearly taken from a portrait, now lost, that was almost certainly painted in Ireland c. 1648, as it describes Monck as major general, a rank that he did not subsequently hold. When restored to favour by Cromwell two years later he was successively colonel of foot, lieutenant general of artillery and general at sea. He was appointed governor of Scotland in 1654 where he remained until 1660. According to Sir Charles Firth, in *Scotland under the Commonwealth,* his rank at that time was general.

Maps and Battle Plans

Key to maps

Squares or oblongs indicate the position of bodies of horse and foot. Black is used throughout to represent parliamentary formations and white royalist ones. Cavalry are distinguished from infantry by the use of diagonal lines, but in the depiction of Dunbar I have not separated the horse from the foot because contemporary sources are not sufficiently informative.

This way of depicting how armies were deployed on the battlefield may be criticised as being too generalised and unnecessarily imprecise. However, it has always been my contention that splitting formations up into regiments, battalions and squadrons – the exact positions of which cannot be known from contemporary sources – is a misconceived practice, though sadly it is followed in many military histories of the British Wars.

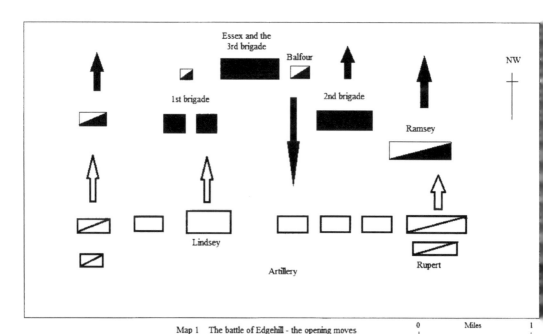

Map 1   The battle of Edgehill - the opening moves

0   Miles   1

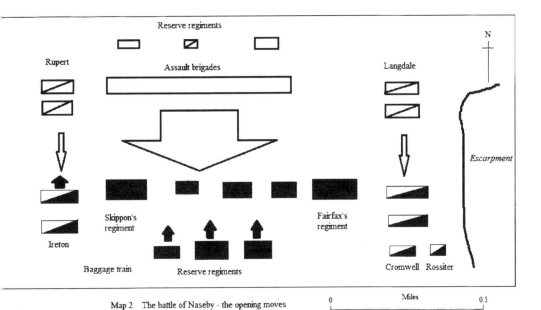

Map 2   The battle of Naseby - the opening moves

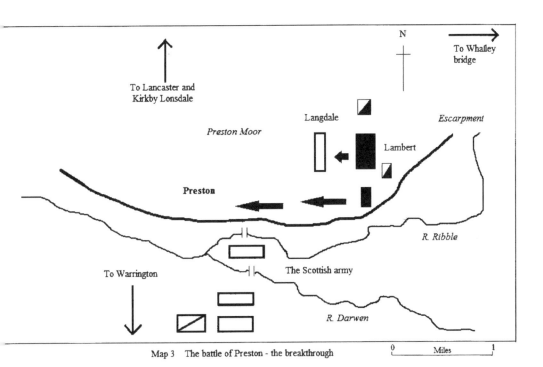

Map 3   The battle of Preston - the breakthrough

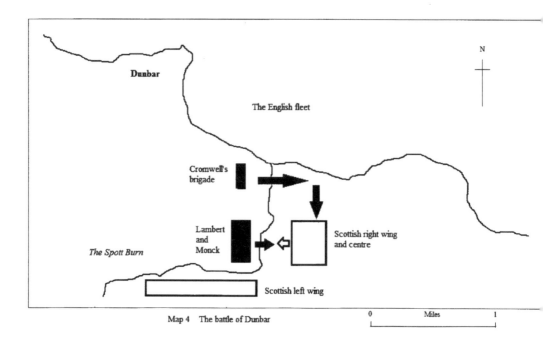

Map 4   The battle of Dunbar

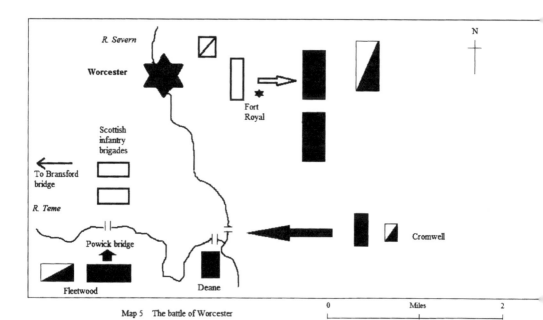

Map 5   The battle of Worcester

Prologue

It may seem excessively self-indulgent to write at length about the generals of the British Wars for the fourth time in fourteen years, but there are a number of sound scholarly reasons for making yet another journey through very familiar territory.[1]

First, the books I published between 2004 and 2011 focused primarily on what can be described as the purely military aspects of generalship, namely the successes and failures of army commanders in carrying out the orders of Parliament and its successive 'war cabinets', the Committee of Safety, the Committee of Both Kingdoms and the Committee at Derby House. I did not pay much attention to the politics of generalship, which covers such matters as establishing a good relationship with their political masters that would withstand setbacks and secure for them the resources needed to carry on the war; working with other army commanders with whom they were in competition for resources and reputation; seeing that the blame went elsewhere when campaigns did not go according to plan; and winning and then retaining the confidence of taxpayers, most particularly those in the city of London who also lent Parliament the money to finance the war.

These topics were not ignored in my earlier books, but when I did address them it was to provide background to the study of campaigns, sieges and battles. In some respects I made up for the neglect in journal articles, but in these the focus was very largely on the circumstances surrounding the birth of the New Model Army.[2] The purpose of this book is therefore to give due weighting to the political aspects of generalship over the entire length of the British Wars, but not to the exclusion of the battles, campaigns and sieges. Military and political aspects of generalship are mutually supportive in that success or failure in one contributed towards success or failure in the other.

In addition there are good reasons for revisiting the military aspect ten years after finishing writing *Warrior Generals*. Much has been published on the topic in the meantime; my own research interests have widened and deepened; and some essential sources previously only accessible by visits to British and American libraries are now easily available online. This book therefore gives me the chance to revise and occasionally to vigorously defend earlier assertions, judgements and critiques.

My other reason for returning to generalship in the British Wars is despair at the persistence of stereotypes. In history, a discipline that prides itself on its ability to deconstruct both primary and secondary sources, it is amazing how assertions made centuries ago are accepted without question, however suspect the evidence on which they are based. My campaign to do something about this began as an undergraduate, when I critiqued and then put the sword to S.R. Gardiner's claim that the king planned a three-fold attack on London in 1643. Ever since I have done my best to overturn received opinion in my lectures and publications, and being asked to write about Parliament's generals was an opportunity not to be missed, as many feature in the rogues' gallery of misconceived and ill-founded stereotypes.

However, the traditional subdivision in book-length studies of generals who fought in a particular war, the potted biography, would not provide the best framework for what I had in mind. Instead I have focused on the careers of Parliament's first three lord generals, around whom circled, like planets around a star, a number of other generals who were their rivals, associates or understudies, and sometimes all three. A discussion of the first lord general, the Earl of Essex, for example, runs side by side with that of his principal rival Sir William Waller, while Cromwell's rise to a position of dominance in the army is discussed within the military career paths first of the Earl of Manchester and then of Sir Thomas Fairfax. Later on in the book discussion of senior officers who were coming into prominence during Cromwell's first years as lord general are taken together rather than dealt with separately. This type of approach avoids one of the problems associated with excessive compartmentalisation, in that comparisons can be made between generals at leisure as the argument progresses, rather than hurriedly in the conclusion. It also gets round the potential trap of allotting a chapter to each and every general, which means that minor figures receive more attention than they deserve. Finally, a fine set of potted biographies of all of Parliament's generals already exists in the pages of the *Oxford Dictionary of National Biography*, many of which were written by the most eminent historians alive in the closing years of the twentieth century. However, the *ODNB* does have its limitations. Some biographies are guilty of hyperbole; others contain minor factual inaccuracies and those written by political historians sometimes provide only generalised information about military operations.

Breaking the mould of collective biographies and challenging long-standing stereotypes has its dangers, and I do not doubt that some of my conclusions will be seen as recklessly wrongheaded and even outrageous. Nevertheless, I maintain that it is important not to dumbly accept received opinion, but to think outside the box, most particularly by giving due weighting to sources that are usually disregarded because they conflict with or do not fit easily into the traditional sympathetic narrative of the rise and rise of Oliver Cromwell.

Part I

The First Lord General

Chapter 1

Robert Devereux, Third Earl of Essex

The factors that caused civil war to break out in England in the summer and autumn of 1642 can only be described as multi-causal and disputed, and it would go far beyond my remit to examine each in detail and weigh up one against another. From the military perspective only two aspects are truly significant. Unlike the kings of France and Spain, the early Stuarts did not command an army in peacetime that could be used to impose royal authority and serve as a deterrent to potentially rebellious subjects. Second, a war on English soil between the supporters of the king and the supporters of Parliament in 1642 would not have been a surprise to contemporaries. For two years before fighting began it had been intermittently on the cards as crisis followed crisis in relations between King Charles I and his English Parliament.

Potential causes of instability and tension in the body politic in England were long term, and originated deep in the sixteenth century – the democratic ideas latent in Protestantism absorbed by the growing numbers of ordinary people who could read the Bible; food shortages caused by a rising population; the growing expenses of government compounded by inflation; the difficulties of governing two and then three kingdoms with different social structures and different constitutions leading to more and more autocratic responses from central government; the threat posed to Protestantism in the British Isles and Europe by international Roman Catholicism; and just possibly the incongruity between political power vested for centuries in the Crown and the landowner and the growing economic power of the middling sort in the towns and the countryside. However, these in themselves were not enough to cause one group to take up arms against another. Inspired by the writings of Conrad Russell in the 1970s and 80s it is now customary to place much more emphasis on short-term causes dating from the accession to the throne of King Charles I in 1625.

A series of confrontations between the House of Commons in England and the king in the mid-1620s, mainly relating to a foreign policy that seemed to be driven more by pique than by the true interests of the kingdom, caused Charles I to attempt to rule the country from 1629 onwards without summoning parliaments to give him advice, pass laws and vote additional taxation. This forced his government to raise money by methods which, despite some legal precedents, were looked upon as illegal as they did not have parliamentary approval. Such actions, and the enforcement of the royal authority in various other ways, were widely seen as an affront to the liberties of the subject. At the same time royal encouragement of reforms in the church in England and Scotland that looked like a drift away from what had been achieved in both countries by the Reformation, caused disquiet in England and outright defiance in Scotland. Open warfare between the king and his Scottish subjects broke out in the summer of 1640. The speed with which the Scots got together their army compared with the difficulties the king faced in raising a force of similar size resulted in their army occupying the far north of England, with the only fighting being a skirmish at the crossing of the River Tyne in which numbers were decisive. A truce, which was negotiated in September to prevent a further Scottish advance followed by almost certain defeat in battle or an ignominious retreat, forced the king to summon an English parliament to vote taxes to pay for the upkeep of both armies.

A renewed outbreak of fighting had seemed possible, with two armies quartered in the north of England, and tension reached fever pitch on several occasions prior to a peace treaty being signed in August 1641, followed by the total disbandment of both.[1] But the lull that followed did not last. Two months later the outbreak of a Catholic uprising in Ireland made the issue of who controlled the armed forces – king or Parliament – of paramount importance. If the king relinquished this, the most fundamental of his prerogatives, England would change from a monarchy into an oligarchy; while if it remained in his hands Charles might use the army raised to reconquer Ireland to impose his will on his English subjects. Moreover, he was seen as still being surrounded by evil advisers, some of whom were Roman Catholics. The gap between the two sides was unbridgeable by political means, and the drift towards outright war in England accelerated from January 1642, but it was not until six months later that the supporters of the king and the supporters of Parliament were ready to take the final step of waging war against one another.

Raising regiments of horse and foot was all very well, but who was to lead them? Generals were in very short supply in the summer of 1642. Those of the Armada War generation were long dead, and so were their subordinates. The inglorious wars with France and Spain in the 1620s had not covered anybody in glory, and the best that could be said in favour of those in senior positions then who were still alive in 1642, such as the Earl of Lindsey, the king's lord general in the Edgehill campaign, is that the government of the time had not given them sufficient resources to accomplish the tasks they had been given.

However, in Robert Devereux, Third Earl of Essex and 15th Lord Ferrers of Chartley, who was appointed captain general on 14 July 1642, Parliament appeared to have a commander with all the qualities needed to bring the confrontation with the king to a successful conclusion, possibly even before the fighting began. In the preamble to his commission he was described in glowing terms as:

in every way qualified... a person of honour, wisdom and integrity, of noble birth, of great judgement in martial affairs, who had shown great competence as a servant of the state and steadfast loyalty to the cause of liberty as represented by Parliament.

Although this looks like lashings of hyperbole, it was not that far from the truth.[2]

First and foremost, Essex had a wider range of military experience over a longer period of time than anybody else in the English aristocracy. He had served in a senior capacity in the Cadiz expedition of 1625 and fought as colonel of an infantry regiment in Dutch service in the late 1620s. This brought an end to his service overseas, but thereafter he was lord lieutenant of Staffordshire, with responsibility for rearming and revitalising the county's trained bands in accordance with instructions issued by the king's Privy Council, and during the first military confrontations with Scotland in 1639 he was deputy commander of the English forces along the border.

Second, Essex came from a long line of military men dating back to the battle of Hastings and, as belief that qualities were inherited was common in the mid-seventeenth century, such an ancestry gave confidence in his powers of leadership. Moreover, his political stance since the summer of 1640 had been impeccable. He was one of the twelve peers who petitioned the king in August of that year to make a truce with the Scots and summon a parliament to redress the people's grievances. Once Parliament was in session his behaviour was that of a man determined to defend the liberties of the subject and to secure an enhanced role for Parliament in the constitution. Zeal for religious reform, however, was not a central, or indeed a peripheral concern to the earl, though he had misgivings about the baleful influence of some of the Anglican bishops, who had acquired important posts in government during the 1630s, and whose writings and sermons encouraged the king's authoritarian tendencies.

Finally, Essex's appointment as captain general of Parliament's forces seemed like a natural progression. He had served as lord general of the trained bands in the south of England in the summer and autumn of 1641, but this was only for the duration of the king's brief visit to his Scottish kingdom. His jurisdiction lapsed on Charles's return to London in mid-November, but there were rumours that he was to take charge of the army to be raised to put down the rebellion in Ireland, and when civil strife in London loomed early in 1642 he was appointed commander of an armed force to protect Parliament.[3]

However, Essex was not to be a free agent. His commission stated that he was to obey the direction and command of the two Houses, and this formula was repeated in the oath his officers were to take before being commissioned. How this was to be delivered was not stated, but soon after the beginning of his first campaign he was burdened with an advisory committee consisting of all the peers and MPs serving in his army. They were only permitted to discuss matters raised by him, but they were to act as the channel of communication between Parliament and the earl and could theoretically see their responsibility as being to ensure that orders from Westminster were understood and acted upon. Although a pale shadow of what was to follow, the committee was a reassurance to Parliament that the lord general would be under a measure of political control.[4]

The reasons why Parliament chose Essex as captain general are unremarkable, but the extent to which the appointment was a popular one is not so clear cut. Admittedly volunteers joined his army in their thousands, but the successful recruiting drive in London in July and August was presided over by a number of the leaders of the Parliamentary cause. It was not a solo effort on Essex's part.[5] There is also evidence that some people in London had doubts about him. In a speech to volunteers Captain Lloyd put words into the earl's mouth. His worry on taking up his command was that Parliament might listen to rumours that he was not as committed to the cause as his commission suggested. Such rumours probably stemmed from the fact that he had in the past been a courtier, but they were almost certainly scotched when news reached London a few days later that the king had denounced Essex and his fellow officers as traitors.[6]

But what was the state of mind of the lord general himself at the outbreak of war? The answer is that we know very little beyond the speeches he delivered at the time, and these were tailored to the audience he was addressing. His surviving letters for the first ten months of 1642 are uninformative;[7] he did not subsequently write his memoirs or keep a diary that survives; and his abject apology to the king, written immediately after the battle of Edgehill, was probably a contemporary fake.[8] We know the books he had in his library, but they do not necessarily tell us whether or not he read them, and the sole contemporary biography of the earl, written straight after his death in 1646, is nothing more than a tedious eulogy.[9]

What can be said with confidence, however, is that Essex was a man who had the fortitude that enabled him to live through the collapse of both his marriages in the most humiliating circumstances, and to move on to other things with his honour seemingly intact. In doing so he could be seen as drawing on strengths that came more easily to men of his caste than to those of a more lowly condition. In the words of Sir Thomas Smith, noblemen had the example of their ancestors 'which encourageth'; the experience of their education as a nobleman 'which enableth', and 'the love of their tenants and neighbours... which pricketh them forward' to follow in their forefathers' footsteps.[10] However, such influences not only encouraged the growth of what Smith described as virtues derived from 'ancient race' – honour, courage, self-confidence and so forth – but also pride and arrogance, inability to accept criticism, the expectation of instant obedience from their social inferiors, and the belief that because of their lineage and status they were entitled to hold one of the high offices of state, which were first in the king's gift and then, when war broke out, in Parliament's. But what Essex received did not live up to his expectations in the medium term and possibly from the very outbreak of hostilities.

The extent to which Essex failed to achieve what he expected of life may explain what Morrill has described as his prickliness and his propensity to take offence, which proved to be a major impediment in dealing with other generals and his political masters. This can be seen at its best and most damaging in his relationship with Sir William Waller, which hampered Parliament's war effort in the south of England for much of 1643 and 1644, but to be fair to the earl he was sorely provoked on several occasions. The first sign of the lord general's problems in dealing with other people, however, can be seen in his behaviour on 9 September 1642, when he was about to leave London to join his army headquarters at Northampton.

Essex was clearly in a grump that morning. His farewell speech in the Lords was terse in the extreme, and he made no mention of his regard for the members of the House of Commons, many of whom were standing at the bar of the House listening to him. They then went in search of him to give him their personal regards and in due course found him some distance away in the Palace of Westminster smoking his pipe. His only response was to rise to his feet, holding his pipe in one hand and his hat in the other, and to acknowledge their greetings in silence.[11] One possible explanation for his frostiness is that he had not been appointed Lord High Constable of England, which would have left him free to negotiate with the king on Parliament's behalf, but the evidence is no more than hearsay picked up by the Venetian ambassador's informants. Nevertheless, it has been repeated by many historians since, in some cases with considerable embellishments.[12] However, there is no mention of a discussion of the high constableship in the journals of the House of Commons or the House of Lords. Although anger at being rejected cannot be totally ruled out, as he may have thought he only had to drop a hint in private for his wish to be granted, a more likely explanation for what was an example of rudeness verging on contempt was the pressure that the two Houses were putting on him to join his army. This was expressed in an order that passed the two Houses on 27 August, directing him to advance with all possible speed to confront the enemy as the safety of the kingdom was at stake. The tone suggests that it was not the first time he had been asked, but it does end with what looks like a gesture of humility. The order was not issued because of concern about backwardness on the earl's part, but to scotch suggestions that Parliament was being slack.[13] An even more likely cause for Essex's behaviour is that Parliament had touched on a very raw nerve by its recent dealings with Sir William Uvedale, who had cuckolded him with his second wife, who had then given birth to a male child.[14]

Whatever lay behind the morning's dramas, Essex's reception as he left for his army headquarters should have done something to improve his temper. As he left Essex House, Lord Robartes addressed him on behalf of Parliament in a speech which pandered to the worst side of his personality:

> Your noble spirit which together with other virtues inherent in your soul renders you the most illustrious example of true nobility... your breast being pregnant with and swelling with the natural gifts of a complete and heroic general... the tongues of the Commons united together so with utmost strength of good will cry out Vivat Roy and Essex, God Save the King and Essex who goes forth for the safety of the king and the general good of the kingdom.[15]

Then, as he made his way by horse through the streets of London, he was apparently cheered by crowds of ordinary citizens, and his route to the top of Highgate Hill was lined by the city trained bands 'like a hedge'. It is difficult, however, to know how real or genuine the acclamation was. The fullest account his departure is in Chamberlain's hagiographic biography published in 1646, and the deployment of the trained bands must have been in response to an order from the lord mayor. It cannot have been a spontaneous act. Moreover, it is odd, if the spectacle was so impressive, that none of the London presses issued a pamphlet to describe it.

The circumstances of Essex's departure from London must also not be seen as evidence for Parliament's enthusiasm for armed conflict. Essex's remit was to do all he could to bring the king to his senses by a show of force, while his newly raised regiments under lesser commanders suppressed attempts by the king's supporters to raise troops and occupy territory in many parts of south and central England with a considerable measure of success. Indeed, when Essex left London all that was needed to clear the coastal counties as far as the Cornish border was to smoke out 300 or so royalist infantry and two troops of horse holed up at Sherborne in Dorset by the young Earl of Bedford, Essex's second-in-command. Most significantly, although the king's recruiting operations in north-east England had done quite well, Charles failed to persuade Sir John Hotham, the governor of Hull, to give him access to the vast quantities of military supplies left there after the end of the war with Scotland. He then moved south to Nottingham, but found little in the way of support in the east Midlands other than in Lincolnshire.

Soon after Essex arrived at Northampton the king's army was on the move again, heading for Shrewsbury, where it remained for three weeks. The lord general shadowed him forty miles to the south and set up his headquarters at Worcester, a convenient spot for threatening the flank of the enemy army should it march on London, or blocking its path if it moved down the Severn valley. There had, however, been one setback that probably had an impact on morale. While on the march Essex had sent on ahead a mixed brigade of cavalry and dragoons. Their orders were to intercept a convoy heading for Shrewsbury with large quantities of silver plate donated to the king's cause by the Oxford colleges, but Prince Rupert, charged with escorting it on its last lap, got to Worcester first and defeated Essex's cavalry at Powick bridge, just to the south of the city, on 23 September. However, it had not been a complete disaster. The dragoons lining the banks of the River Teme had sufficient firepower to stop the royalist pursuit in its tracks, and Rupert left the area with the convoy immediately afterwards, thus avoiding the rest of Essex's army, which made an unopposed entry into Worcester the following day.

Having occupied Worcester Essex sent units to Hereford and to Gloucester in the hope that they would be able to prevent regiments from the south-west and South Wales from joining the king. He also stationed a strong force of infantry at Kidderminster to keep a watch on the shortest route between Shrewsbury and London, which passed to the south of Birmingham.[16] But from then onwards, in the words of Morrill, it was 'downhill all the way', a valid comment given the way in which Essex's first year as lord general has been habitually described.[17]

The dominant narrative begins by noting Essex's defensive behaviour while at Worcester, despite his army heavily outnumbering the king's. Undisturbed, Charles's steadily increased in size, with regiments arriving from the north of England and from Wales, while those he had brought with him from Nottingham were extensively recruited. When it did set out for London on 10 October Essex was slow to react. Almost a fortnight later the first major battle of the war was fought close to Kineton in Warwickshire with many of Essex's regiments still lagging behind or on garrison duty. Both sides lost heavily, Essex in cavalry and the king's forces in infantry, in what is usually described as a draw, but when the parliamentary army fell back to Warwick the royalists resumed their march on the capital. It was only because the royalists took the slow route to London via the Thames valley, rather than over the Chilterns, that Essex was able to get to the capital first. Reinforced by the city militia regiments he faced them at Turnham Green, six miles to the west, in an eyeball-to-eyeball confrontation. In the event the heavily outnumbered royalists blinked, but Essex did nothing to cut off their retreat or to harass them as they fell back to Reading and so to Oxford, which became the king's headquarters for the rest of the war. Essex merely followed them at a safe distance, eventually establishing his own headquarters at Windsor.

For the next five months Parliament's field army remained in the Windsor area, ready to contest a new advance on London, but otherwise doing nothing of significance apart from antagonising the capital's citizens. Its upkeep in terms of pay, food and military hardware was a major grievance, as the burden fell almost entirely on Londoners. Unsurprisingly, their complaints were picked up in the House of Commons, with Essex's lack of drive being seen as largely responsible for the army's inactivity.[18] In April 1643, however, after the expiry of a short truce, the lord general set siege to Reading, which had provided winter quarters for a large brigade of royalist infantry. It had also impeded foodstuffs from Berkshire and south Buckinghamshire reaching the capital via the River Thames. After a short siege, during which the lord general frustrated an attempt by the king's army to relieve the town, the garrison surrendered, but his critics saw the terms as over-generous as they allowed the royalist troops to leave for Oxford, taking their weapons with them.

What followed was Worcester all over again. Essex remained motionless at Reading for six weeks, then advanced ineffectually along the western flank of the Chilterns to Thame in June and so to Great Brickhill in July, while the king received large reinforcements from the north and west and sufficient arms and ammunition to take the offensive. This resulted in the defeat of Parliament's army of the west at Roundway Down on 13 July, followed by the loss of Bristol later in the same month. To make matters worse, Essex's army was mouldering away through disease and desertion, and London was seen to be in greater danger than it had been in November 1642. Naturally the lord general got most of the blame in Parliament and in the capital, but he fought back, blaming his failure to make progress against the enemy on disobedient subordinates, inadequate resources and unrealistic objectives.[19]

In the event, the king decided that he was not yet strong enough to advance on the capital, and set siege to Gloucester so as to give time for more reinforcements to arrive from the north and west. Essex's army, once adequately resourced, marched to Gloucester's relief, reaching the city early in September, and on the way back to London Essex brushed off a serious attempt to stop him at Newbury on the 20th. However, as after Turnham Green, he did nothing whatsoever to exploit his success. Even worse, he abandoned his only conquest in the spring campaign, and for the second winter of the war Reading received a royalist garrison.

Chapter 2

The Lord General Under Attack

The charge of excessive caution verging on inertia was made vociferously by some of the Earl of Essex's contemporaries and has hung around his neck for centuries, though occasionally historians have shown a measure of sympathy. Sir Charles Firth, in the late nineteenth century, for example, tempered what he saw as Essex's incapacity as a fighting general with a recognition that the troops he commanded were 'never properly maintained or recruited', while Young and Holmes, though highly critical of Essex's campaigning throughout his career as commander-in-chief, congratulated him on retaining the loyalty of his troops.[1] Snow, his principal biographer, who might have been expected to have a more charitable view of his generalship, was non-committal but praised him for obeying orders and for not contemplating a military coup when attacked by his own side.[2] Others, however, have been totally negative in their comments, including Braddick and Gentles in the two most recent studies of war and politics in the 1640s.[3] If anything military historians have been even more hostile, with Essex's decisions while on campaign being variously described as crazy, folly, and the act of an imbecile.[4]

Admittedly the dominant narrative has taken some knocks, principally in studies of the battles the lord general fought.[5] Accusations of Essex's lack of drive, however, remain firmly in place, explained very largely in terms of his personality and his experience of fighting abroad in the 1620s,[6] but explanations that rely solely on such factors are dangerous as they are lacking in context. Decisions in military matters, as in other fields of human activity, are powerfully influenced by external circumstances such as the information available at the time and the restraints, often of a political nature, under which the army commander was operating.

One circumstance, for example, that has been almost totally ignored in assessments of Essex's generalship, is his position in Parliament's command structure which, as shown in the previous chapter, was a subordinate one. At all times he was subject to 'such instructions as he shall from time to time receive from both Houses of Parliament.'[7] It is therefore perfectly possible that the root cause of some of Essex's perceived inactivity can be found in the machinations of his political masters. By the same token, assessments of the actual military situation at certain crucial points in Essex's career often depend on narratives written in the late nineteenth century and are in serious need of deconstruction.[8]

For the last year of Essex's career as lord general it is comparatively easy to determine what external factors shaped his decision-making, thanks to the survival of the minute books of the Committee of Both Kingdoms and much of its correspondence.[9] Frustratingly, evidence of the orders that Essex received in the first eighteen months of the war is very far from complete. His personal papers no longer survive, and neither does the minute book of the Committee of Safety, Parliament's executive organ of government, which served as the intermediary between the legislature and its generals prior to the establishment of the Committee of Both Kingdoms. Admittedly the journals of the two Houses can be a great help in identifying the dates when instructions were first issued, and this is vital for establishing an accurate chronology, but it was the Committee of Safety that translated what were often generalized statements into clear and specific operational directives. Some of the detail can be found in the letters Essex and other generals wrote to Parliament that were copied into the journal of the House of Lords, but beyond that distinguishing between what the lord general was ordered to do, and what he did of his own volition, depends on the chance survival of single items in a wide range of documentary collections ranging from intercepted letters preserved among Prince Rupert's papers, through the numerous appendices to the reports of the Historical Manuscript Commission, and the even more numerous newspapers and one-off publications printed in London and Oxford during the war, to the incoming correspondence of William Lenthall, the Speaker of the House of Commons.

The difference in documentation is not the only reason why this chapter only focuses on the first eighteen months of Essex's lord generalship. In the spring of 1644 he underwent a metamorphosis. When his army emerged from winter quarters he immediately set out on a campaign of conquest in which he won back much of the territory in the west country and the Thames valley that had been lost in the previous year. No longer could he be accused of inertia, but instead he laid himself open to a charge of incompetence when it all ended in tears at Lostwithiel in Cornwall less than four months later.

* * * * *

The first charge against the lord general is that he should have tried to capture the king at Nottingham in August or early September 1642, when the royalist army was still exceedingly weak in terms of infantry.[10] This was the view of one of Charles's generals, but it does not take into account the fact that Essex's army was also quite slow in coming together, and that the first units raised were busy suppressing royalist activity throughout almost the whole of southern England until the end of September.[11] This was by command of Parliament, not the lord general, though he does not seem to have opposed a strategy based on principles that were centrifugal rather than centripetal. Moreover, a surprise attack on Nottingham, the only practicable way of capturing the king, would have been very difficult to mount given the distance involved and Essex's shortage of mounted troops, compared with those the king had managed to raise, and their lack of experience.

The next charge was that Essex should have advanced on Shrewsbury in late September or early October 1642 to do battle with the king's army while Parliament's forces still enjoyed numerical superiority. It can, however, be argued that this was the fault not of the lord general, but of his political masters. Although he had orders to fight the royalist army to free Charles from the clutches of his evil advisers, he also had orders to present a petition to the king. This was seen as a matter of the highest importance 'for the peace and good of the kingdom' and 'for the avoiding of blood.' The implication is that Essex was not to try and seize the king by force until all other possibilities had been exhausted. His superiors were also probably of the opinion that Charles would be unable to raise a large enough army to dare risking it in battle, and that as in the conflict with Scotland two years earlier he would ask for a truce before the real fighting began. However, the king played for time for as long as possible by making excuses as to why he could not accept the petition. Meanwhile his army grew until it was not far short of Parliament's in size. Essex's reaction to the final rejection, which came three days into the king's army's march towards London, is very interesting. He did not bewail the fact that the political initiative had failed. Instead he told Parliament that it had made a mistake in persisting so long with a stratagem that could only give advantage to the enemy.[12]

On 23 October the first full-scale battle of the English Civil Wars took place near Edgehill in south Warwickshire. It was technically a parliamentary victory, as the royalists withdrew from the battlefield at nightfall and turned down the chance of renewing the fight on the following morning, but in the afternoon, to the consternation of his officers, Essex turned tactical victory into operational defeat by marching north to Warwick, leaving the road to London wide open.[13] Possibly the earl experienced some kind of psychological crisis at this point, but if so he quickly recovered.[14] There are, however, two other explanations for the withdrawal that make good military sense. The first is that he thought the enemy were in no fit state to resume their march on London, and that they would try to return to the Welsh borderland, which would involve putting the River Severn between their army and his. As the nearest bridge not in parliamentary hands was at Bewdley, Warwick was an excellent place from which to intercept them and administer the killer blow before they got properly under way. The second is that on discovering the enemy were in better shape than he had thought, Essex decided not to seek another confrontation until his cavalry could be put in order. They had suffered badly in the battle and those who had escaped had fled far and wide. Warwick was the nearest safe place for a rendezvous where they would hopefully be able to recover from their ordeal.[15]

There were no complaints about the speed with which Essex marched his army to London after a few days' rest, or about his assembling a force of up to 24,000 men to block the path of the king's army towards the capital, but there was serious criticism of his tactics when the two armies faced one another at Turnham Green on 13 November. The two accounts of the circumstances describe a clash of opinion between the MPs and peers turned soldiers, who wanted the war to end as quickly as possible, and the professional officers, who had pecuniary reasons for wanting a more drawn-out affair. When the royalists boldly deployed in a cramped position near the Thames, Essex sent a brigade of several thousand men, including two of his crack regiments, to outflank them and cut off their retreat. The officers objected and Essex recalled the brigade. This behaviour fits neatly into a contemporary narrative that he was in thrall to his officers throughout his time as lord general, but there was a sound reason for ordering a recall. The infantry left at Turnham Green might prove unable to withstand a determined attack, despite outnumbering the enemy by a very large margin.[16] Most were either members of the London militia, who though well trained had no battle experience, or the Earl of Warwick's volunteers, who were not even well-trained.[17] The only possible trained and experienced reinforcements were regiments that had been guarding the bridge over the Thames at Kingston. Their presence there was no longer needed, as the brigade designed to block the enemy's retreat would be at Brentford, between Turnham Green and the bridge. However, despite setting out at first light, they had a twenty-mile march ahead of them. They were unlikely to arrive before nightfall, and even if the royalists held off until then they might be too exhausted to be of much use in a battle situation.[18]

The enemy retreated from Turnham Green without a fight, and there is no evidence that Essex did anything to harass them. His only immediate decision was to build a bridge of boats at Putney so as to enable him to quickly send troops south of the Thames should the king direct his army to march towards Kent, where there was considerable royalist support.[19] Instead it crossed the Thames at Kingston and headed towards Oxford, and Essex did nothing despite orders from Parliament that he should attack them.[20] No record survives of his reasons, but the order was not repeated. All I can suggest is that common sense prevailed. Cavalry and dragoons would be needed to take the lead in discomforting the enemy, but the royalists were even stronger in horse than they had been at Edgehill, and Essex dare not risk losing the few he had left to royalist counterattacks. He did, however, obey a second order which was to prevent the royalists plundering the country between his army's quarters and theirs.[21]

Kent remained quiet and the Surrey and West Sussex royalists were cowed by the capture and garrisoning of Farnham Castle and Chichester. London was thus secure from attack from the south during the winter months. Sir William Waller, who was to become the lord general's chief rival, deservedly got the glory, but correspondence concerning the surrender of both places shows clearly that his orders had come from the lord general rather than from higher up the food chain.[22] Essex in the meantime had not been totally idle. Fixing his headquarters at Windsor Castle, he was well placed to defend the western approaches to the capital and to keep a close eye on his neighbours at Reading, and in the depths of winter he edged closer to the latter by establishing a military presence at Wokingham and Henley-on-Thames.[23] He was also planning how to capture Berkshire's county town when the weather improved.

The lord general's case against MPs like Henry Martin, who wanted more action and compared summer in Devonshire and Yorkshire with winter in the London area, was that his army was ill-provided for active campaigning and required more in the way of resources. It was also dispersed and difficult to reassemble.[24] There were doubts in the House about the first point, given that other commanders were winning successes on a shoestring while Essex's army swallowed up resources at an alarming rate.[25] But there is considerable truth in the second. Although his infantry had been strengthened by five infantry regiments raised by the Earl of Warwick to defend London in October 1642, his cavalry were fewer than ever. No new regiments had been raised since Edgehill, and two whole regiments that had fought there together with a number of additional troops had been sent to provincial commands, presumably on the orders of the Committee of Safety.

By early March Essex was ready to take the field, with Reading as his most likely target, but he was stopped in his tracks by the first substantive round of peace negotiations, the so-called Treaty of Oxford. These did not progress as far as an actual truce, but the terms for a cessation of hostilities in the Thames valley were so close to being agreed that the Committee of Safety probably ordered Essex to abide by them, as no military actions took place in the Thames valley theatre of war until discussions at Oxford ended without agreement on 14 April. The lord general was consulted about the terms of the truce, but the extensive changes he advised suggest that he was unhappy with the whole idea.[26]

When the ceasefire ended, Essex immediately marched on Reading. It quickly surrendered on generous terms, in that the soldiers were not taken prisoner but allowed to march to Oxford with their pikes and muskets, but he did nothing to follow up his success despite knowing the shortage of gunpowder at the king's headquarters. He knew their only hope of remaining there was the arrival of munitions from the north of England, which the queen had recently obtained from the Netherlands, but there was nothing he could do to stop the convoy for the same reason he had not harried the retreating royalists in November. Instead he ordered cavalry regiments that had been raised during the winter in East Anglia and the East Midlands to rendezvous to the south of the royalist staging post at Newark to block the convoy's path, but they took too long to assemble and the convoy got through to Oxford unscathed on 13 May.[27]

Essex's critics in the Commons nevertheless focused on the fact that the main field army did not stir from Reading in the fortnight following its capture. His response was that the troops would not move without pay, putting the ball firmly back in Parliament's court. However, what really held him back was politics conducted at the highest level. Members of the Committee of Safety were trying to persuade the queen to put pressure on the king to reopen peace negotiations, the pledge of their sincerity being a guarantee that Essex would not march on Oxford while Henrietta Maria was consulting her husband, a process which she deliberately dragged out for as long as she could.[28] Essex's inactivity is therefore scarcely surprising.

The next charge against Essex was that in the early summer he allowed the king's field army to be massively reinforced by regiments raised in the north and the west of England. Those from the north were the escort for a second convoy of munitions that was due to arrive in Oxford in June, accompanied by the queen. On this occasion too Essex was dependent on a rendezvous of provincial forces, which were to stop the convoy getting any further south than Newark, and it worked for a time, but the disorganized and poorly led body fell apart for reasons discussed elsewhere, and the convoy and its escort arrived at Oxford in mid-July.[29]

In the case of the king's western army it was widely claimed that Essex had more of a case to answer. After its Pyrrhic victory at Landown near Bath on 5 July, and the destruction of much of its small supply of gunpowder in an unplanned explosion, the royalist army of the west had split in two. The cavalry had ridden to Oxford looking for help, while the infantry were bottled up in the town of Devizes in Wiltshire by Sir William Waller and Parliament's army of the west, some 6,000 strong. Waller was concerned about the threat to his siege operations of cavalry belonging to the king's field army, and he clearly thought that Essex should do something about it.[30] On 10 July, three days before the battle of Roundway Down, at which the Oxford cavalry did indeed destroy his army, Waller wrote to the lord general asking him either to send reinforcements, or to create a diversion by threatening to attack Oxford. At the same time he also wrote to Parliament asking for cavalry support. However, Waller's other reports about what was going on at Devizes were of a very positive nature, and Essex's informants visiting Oxford had seen no sign of an expedition being prepared to go to the aid of the western army.[31] Moreover, it is highly likely that both Essex and Parliament received news from Waller soon afterwards that in a night attack he had scattered a cavalry brigade bringing a supply of ammunition from Oxford to Devizes.

So the lord general did nothing, having dismissed Waller's request as alarmist, and reaped the consequences when Sir William and his supporters in London, and also Waller's principal biographer, blamed him for what happened at Roundway Down.[32] However, their accusations lacked context. There was nothing Essex could have done that would have been of any help. The first problem was the distances involved. On 10 July the lord general and his army were at Great Brickhill in north Buckinghamshire, which was thirty miles from Oxford and ninety from Devizes. Then there was the military situation in Essex's immediate environs. The king's forces were massed in the Cherwell valley waiting for the arrival of the munitions convoy from Newark, and were thus ideally placed not only to block any attempt to move troops from Great Brickhill towards Devizes, but also to intercept an advance on Oxford well before it reached the royalist headquarters. Moreover, Essex's army was in no fit state to fight anybody in mid-July 1643, and Parliament knew that full well. On the day before Waller's request for cavalry was read in the Commons the House had responded positively to an urgent plea from the lord general for more horses and horse equipment for his army, without which it could not engage with the enemy. Unsurprisingly the response to Waller's request was that the Committee of Safety should order regiments stationed in Dorset and Hampshire to ride to Devizes as quickly as possible, but the lord general's regiments were not mentioned.[33]

However, if Essex had a very good case for arguing that he could not be held responsible for Waller's misfortune, the same cannot be said of his inactivity following the safe return of his army to London in late September after relieving Gloucester and fighting off the king's forces at Newbury in masterly fashion. The field army regiments, unlike some of the London trained bands, had not suffered heavy casualties, but they immediately went into winter quarters, and their contribution during the winter towards frustrating royalist attempts to occupy more territory in the counties to the north and south of London was minimal. An advance by a corps of the royalist western army into Sussex was stopped by Sir William Waller at Arundel without any help from Essex's army, while the abandonment of new garrisons at Newport Pagnell and Towcester was brought about by pressure from a brigade drawn from the London trained bands supported by a single regiment of Essex's cavalry.[34] However, under instructions from the Committee of Both Kingdoms a brigade of Essex's cavalry under Sir William Balfour, stiffened by musketeers on horseback, joined Waller in mid-March 1644 and helped him win the battle of Cheriton against Hopton's corps of the army of the west and some regiments from the Oxford army. Allegedly this was against Essex's wishes, but I have found no evidence of this. In fact the brigade reached the rendezvous at Petersfield before Waller did, which suggests a measure of enthusiasm.[35]

Thus some of the criticisms of Essex's conduct are unfounded, as they are lacking in context or just plain wrong, while others are red herrings, but there is a strong sense of his resting on his laurels after the battle at Newbury. However, to get a fully rounded impression of Essex's generalship during his eighteen months or so in command it is necessary to look at his performance on the battlefield. The focus must be on Edgehill rather than Newbury, because at Newbury his options were limited by the need to fight a grimly defensive battle against a multiplicity of royalist attacks spread over some twelve hours of daylight. All that was reported was that he inspired his troops with his presence close to the fighting, which he signalled rather dangerously by wearing a large white hat, that he rotated his infantry regiments when those in the front line began to tire, and possibly that he personally led his own infantry regiment forward to recover lost ground.[36] Throughout he appears to have displayed his customary stoicism and unflappability, which were particularly necessary in battles that were no better than slogging matches, but they were not the qualities to attract the enthusiasm of the proto-journalists who reported on the battles for the London journals.

* * * * *

At Edgehill the royalists were not ready for battle until after midday, so Essex was able to deploy his army as he wished a mile or so to the north-west of the escarpment and parallel to it.[37] The formation he adopted was an orthodox one for a battle fought in open country: that is, infantry in the centre and cavalry on the wings. It is also clear from what followed that Essex intended to allow the enemy to take the initiative, but this was not because of his allegedly defensive mind-set. To have attacked the king's forces as they came down from Edgehill would have prejudiced Parliament's claim that it was the king's supporters who were the aggressors, a sentiment that is very apparent in the language used in the petition the king had refused to receive earlier in the month. He might also have thought that deploying in full sight of the enemy would be the last chance of avoiding further bloodshed, as the sheer size of his army compared with theirs could be enough to persuade them to ask for a truce.

To make his defensive deployment as effective as possible, Essex made good use of the ground. The small force of cavalry on his right wing was protected to some extent by furze bushes interspersed with small patches of boggy ground. In the centre the infantry were drawn up in one of Kineton's open fields. This would cause problems for the enemy horse and foot as they advanced, if the ridge and furrow was as pronounced as it is today in the pasture immediately below Edgehill. To make matters worse, the effectiveness of the artillery barrage accompanying the enemy attack would be reduced by the heavy clay soil causing the cannonballs to sink in rather than ricochet.[38]

The left wing, however, had no natural defences, but it did not quite present an open flank to the enemy, as at least one royalist cavalry unit had to negotiate several hedge lines in order to get at the enemy. However, as they jumped them they cannot have been formidable obstacles.[39] Essex also tried to blunt the enemy charge by lining one of the hedges with musketeers to fire into their flank as they rode forward to attack, but in the event they were driven from the field by royalist dragoons before the battle proper began. He also massed his own cavalry on the left wing as the king had stationed most of his horse on that side of the battlefield.[40] However, to blame the parliamentary cavalry remaining stationary to meet the royalist attack is misguided.[41] It was logical in the light of the political considerations described above, but the strength in depth it required to be effective proved impossible, as the commander on the spot was obliged to extend his line by orders from above in response to the royalists' deployment of most of their cavalry facing him.[42]

The twelve infantry regiments under Essex's personal command were in three formations. The first brigade, which was to bear the brunt of the initial royalist assault, was deployed on the right, facing two of the five royalist brigades, its right flank guarded by cavalry and dragoons and the difficult ground described above. A second brigade was positioned to its left facing the fourth and fifth royalist brigades, leaving a considerable distance between it and the first brigade. Behind the first line was the third brigade, placed in such a position as to assault the third royalist brigade should it attempt to launch an oblique or flank attack on either of the brigades in the first line as they grappled with the enemy.[43]

Essex's most imaginative decision was to establish a reserve of as many as nine troops of horse. The exact position of these units when the fighting began has been uncertain for many years.[44] But the matter is resolved by a source printed a month after the battle to clear up misunderstandings that had arisen, but which is frequently ignored by historians because it is not in the volumes of the Thomason Tracts containing the rest of the parliamentary accounts of the battle. This states quite clearly that the reserve cavalry were drawn up in two formations flanking the third infantry brigade, a position that makes complete sense given that the third brigade was itself a reserve.[45] Moreover, the fact that they were under the command of Sir William Balfour, Essex's lieutenant general of horse, suggests that they were deliberately there, not that they were an ad hoc body of fortunates who happened somehow or other to avoid being caught up in the fighting on the wings. In fact it was almost as if Essex foresaw how the battle might develop, with the royalist cavalry routing both his wings and then following them over the horizon, leaving him in possession of the only cavalry units left on the battlefield.[46]

The lord general took up a position close to the third brigade, which included his own regiment of foot, and once battle was joined he did all that was possible to shape the course of events. First, it was the best place from which to decide where and when to commit the reserves, and once they had been committed he was close to the actual fighting, inspiring the soldiers by his bravery. Second, he did not lose his nerve when his horse on both wings and one of his infantry brigades streamed off the field a quarter of an hour into the battle pursued by enemy cavalry.[47] Finally, he seems to have masterminded the counter-attack on the second brigade of the king's infantry, the turning point of the battle that changed near certain defeat into a type of victory. The second (and strongest) royalist infantry brigade, led by Charles I's lord general the Earl of Lindsey, attacked Essex's first brigade and put two of its regiments under great pressure until Essex brought up the other two and both sides withdrew for a breather. He then resumed the attack with two regiments from the reserve brigade, aided by Balfour's troops and his own lifeguard, and the enemy were defeated and driven back, sustaining hundreds of casualties in the process.[48] Earlier in the battle, given his position with the reserves,

Essex is most likely to have ordered Balfour's regiment to charge the third royalist brigade in the flank as it wheeled to attack the flank of his first brigade of infantry in the struggle between it and the strongest of the king's infantry brigades. The decision to continue the charge into the royalist artillery line, on the other hand, seems to have been taken by Balfour on his own initiative, but he then returned to the reserves, probably as originally ordered in time to take part in the destruction of Lindsey's brigade.[49]

Thus at Edgehill and Newbury Essex showed himself as a hands-on battlefield commander, not a mere observer from a distance. He did not allow the battle to develop of its own volition relying on instructions he issued beforehand which became increasingly irrelevant, nor did he become engrossed in the fighting in one part of the battlefield to the neglect of the others. However, although his undoubted skill in managing an army before and during a battle saved Parliament's skin in both battles, when all is said and done they did nothing to bring outright victory any closer.

Chapter 3

Essex's Rivals

Any general who failed to accomplish the aims set by his political masters ran a high risk of being sacked. Alternatively, he might choose to resign of his own accord, blaming them for his lack of success. Twice during 1643 Essex offered his resignation, but in very different circumstances. In June when he was at his most reviled the reason was despair at inadequate resourcing. In October when his reputation was higher than it had been since Turnham Green it was because of a limitation on his authority as commander-in-chief. On both occasions he got his way. He set out for the relief of Gloucester in late August with an army that was fit for purpose in terms of numbers, pay and equipment, and by the end of October Sir William Waller had lost his operational independence. A third opportunity for Parliament to take Essex at his word came six months later, though on this occasion the threat was implicit rather than explicit. The lord general stated that he had not quitted his post in the past despite the humiliations inflicted upon him, but after two months of talk there had been no agreement as to how his army was to be resourced for the 1644 campaign. The only step taken by Parliament had been to reduce the size of his army, while the army of the Eastern Association under the Earl of Manchester's command was larger by some 4,000 men and adequately funded. It was also independent of his jurisdiction.[1] Essex got nowhere with regard to Manchester's army, but satisfying his army's immediate needs so that it was able to take the field a month later was sufficient to stop him turning a hint into a formal resignation.

Essex's success in keeping his position and winning points with threats of resignation was not only because he had a strong body of support in the Commons provided the cost of maintaining his army was kept under control. It was also because his opponents were caught on the horns of a dilemma. They dare not give Essex unlimited financial and political support for fear that he might win the war and, from a position of strength and in the interests of reconciliation, make a weak accommodation with the enemy. On the other hand, if they deprived his army of resources and he led it out to fight the king he would lose the war, whereas if it was allowed to moulder away in its quarters the king's forces would merely walk over it on their way to London. Their preferred option was therefore to try and set up an alternative army, which was to fail in the summer of 1643, and after a hopeful start it failed in 1644 with the army of the Eastern Association. To make matters worse they were not able to take Essex at his word. Although during the first twenty months of the war there were at various times a number of potential lords general, at the precise moments when Essex offered or appeared to offer his resignation they were either out of the running or experiencing a dip in their own fortunes.

If an army commander needed to be replaced, for whatever reason, the logical choice was his second-in-command, but this was not an option for Parliament from the second half of 1643 onwards. The Earl of Bedford, who had been general of horse at Edgehill, changed sides in August 1643. Below him in the lord general's army were Sir John Meldrum, the major general of infantry, and Sir William Balfour, the lieutenant general of cavalry, but Meldrum was transferred to the Trent valley theatre of war in June 1643, while Balfour was elderly and suffering from indifferent health. Moreover, it may have counted against both of them that they were Scots. A final possibility was Phillip Skippon, Meldrum's successor as major general, who came into contention after acting as Essex's second-in-command at Newbury and forcing the royalists to evacuate Newport Pagnell and Towcester in the ensuing winter campaign in the Ouse valley.[2] Although very experienced in warfare on the Continent and extremely popular in London, whose militia he had commanded since the autumn of 1642, Skippon's career from beginning to end suggests that he lacked the ambition for the highest command. It may also have counted against him in late 1643 and early 1644 that he was not a member of the aristocracy. Although a gentleman by birth, his landed estate was no more than a single manor in Norfolk.

An alternative to Essex would have been another army commander, and theoretically there were several available. Robert Rich, Earl of Warwick, had been briefly in command of a reserve army raised in the autumn of 1642 to defend London in the event of Essex's army being annihilated or the king's forces managing to reach the capital before Essex did.[3] He issued commissions for at least five new infantry regiments which, if not ready in time for the stand-off at Turnham Green, were receiving pay for the third and fourth weeks of November. But before the end of the month Warwick had resigned. Essex and his army were defending the westward approaches to London, and it therefore no longer made military or financial sense for Parliament to continue resourcing a second army.[4] Also, Warwick was a naval officer first and foremost, having operated as the Earl of Northumberland's deputy for much of 1642, and in the following February Parliament appointed him lord high admiral. For the rest of 1643 and 1644 he devoted himself to the fleet with a considerable degree of success,[5] but given that in the English armed forces army and navy officers were interchangeable until well into the second half of the seventeenth century, I see Warwick as Essex's natural successor should the need have arisen, but at no time did he show any sign of wanting to be lord general.

A man with longer experience of commanding an army was Ferdinando, Lord Fairfax, lord general of the North, who from December 1642 to early June 1645 enjoyed independent command over Parliament's forces operating on the far side of the River Trent. With no pre-war military experience himself he was very reliant on that of his son Sir Thomas and the inspiration provided by his deceased father, uncles and cousins, whose involvement in fighting in Europe from the 1580s onwards was second to none. The achievements of the two Fairfaxes won the admiration of the radicals in Parliament and the city, but the switchback ride that had marked their encounters with the king's forces from December 1642 onwards experienced a sharp downturn with their army's defeat by the Marquis of Newcastle at Adwalton Moor in June 1643. What was left of the Fairfaxes' army retreated to Hull and, having been resupplied by sea, was raiding as far as the outskirts of York by mid-August.[6] This deterred Newcastle from joining the king in the south of England. Instead he set siege to Hull, but the younger Fairfax's success at Winceby and his father's impressive sortie from Hull in mid-October began a significant recovery, culminating in their joint destruction of the Yorkshire corps of Newcastle's army at Selby in mid-April 1644. But it did not foreshadow things to come. Less than three months later Fairfax's army fled from the battlefield at Marston Moor, taking their general with them.

There is, I suppose, some merit in seeing Lord Fairfax as a latter day Fabius Cunctator.[7] However, his most positive qualities, stoicism in the face of defeat and the ability to bounce back, were mirror images of those of the Earl of Essex, and were certainly no guarantee that he was capable of bringing the war to a quick and successful conclusion. In addition there was no evidence that he had the qualities needed to manage a large army on campaign or on the battlefield. Until his victory at Selby in April 1644 he had never had more than 5,000 men under his command.[8]

The same caveat also clearly applied to the commanders of small armies or brigades that were taking shape in the provinces from the winter of 1642 onwards. Of these the one who would have enjoyed the greatest support from the radicals among Essex's critics in Parliament, because of his outspoken views, was Robert Greville, Lord Brooke, who campaigned in the central Midlands, but he had been killed at the siege of Lichfield in the following March.[9] Almost as unfortunate was Henry Grey, Earl of Stamford, who lost his honour rather than his life.

Left behind in command of the garrisons at Gloucester, Worcester and Hereford by the lord general in October 1642, when the field army set off in pursuit of the king, Stamford's hunger for promotion shines through the letters he wrote to the House of Lords over the next couple of months. In December he got his reward when he was appointed major general with jurisdiction over Herefordshire, Shropshire and Worcestershire, but he quickly transferred to a command at the same rank in Devon and Cornwall, which was probably more prestigious. After a false start caused by an over-ambitious subordinate confronting the enemy in Cornwall before he arrived with reinforcements, Stamford formed a substantial army around a nucleus provided by one of the regiments of foot Essex had left behind at Worcester. Cunningly using a localized truce to build up its strength, he was in control of the whole of Devonshire by late April and followed up victories at Modbury and Sourton Down with an invasion of Cornwall. He then made the fatal error of underestimating the enemy's military experience and determination. Instead of keeping his army together, on 16 May he sent his cavalry off on a wild goose chase to break up a supposed royalist rendezvous at Bodmin. While they were away, the Cornish infantry under Sir Ralph Hopton evicted him and his infantry from a supposedly impregnable position at Stratton near Bude, inflicting many casualties. Stamford managed to reach the safety of Exeter, which he defended in a siege lasting over three months, while sensibly sending his cavalry eastwards to help in the defence of Bristol and its environs. Their destruction in Sir William Waller's disastrous campaign in Somerset, Wiltshire and Gloucestershire in June and July 1643 was not Stamford's fault, but he surrendered Exeter prematurely in the opinion of his political masters, and then became involved in an unseemly quarrel with one of the Cornish MPs over the circumstances surrounding the defeat at Stratton.[10] That and allegations of cowardice marked the end of Stamford's military career, and he was subsequently employed only on diplomatic missions. The best that can be said of him is that his ambition exceeded his abilities.[11]

Stamford's military career had been full of incident, if nothing else, but even this could not be said of Lord Grey of Wark. Commissioned as major general of an army to be raised in East Anglia he led it to the siege of Reading in April 1643, after which it mouldered away through disease and lack of pay.[12] He was dismissed in July and was immediately replaced by the Earl of Manchester, whose only experience of a military nature was his regiment of foot running away at Edgehill before coming to grips with the enemy.[13] His siege of King's Lynn against determined opposition in August and September 1643 was a success, but he arrived too late on the battlefield to claim any credit for Sir Thomas Fairfax and Oliver Cromwell's victory at Winceby in October. Indeed it was not until he had stormed Lincoln in early June 1644 that he began to establish a military reputation. However, given the size of the army he was successfully managing, he looked like a potential successor to the lord general, but Essex's luck held. Manchester's role in the battle of Marston Moor in July was decorative at best, and from then onwards his reputation plummeted.[14] He did not have sufficient strength of character to control his quarrelling subordinates, Lawrence Crawford and Oliver Cromwell; he disputed and disobeyed operational commands from Parliament and the Committee of Both Kingdoms (though in my opinion for good reason); and his tactics at the second battle of Newbury were questionable at best.[15] But what really destroyed him was the argument put forward by Oliver Cromwell after the Newbury campaign that he had no wish to win the war outright and that he had done all he could to ensure that it did not happen.

The last of the first round of major generals to be appointed in the winter of 1642 was Sir William Waller, a landed gentleman belonging to a Kentish family.[16] Waller was to be the most formidable of Essex's rivals, and like the earl he had a distinguished military ancestry and some experience of fighting in Europe in the wars of the 1620s.[17] His principal biographers claim that Sir William played no significant part in the opposition to the Crown's wars with Scotland, which brought about the collapse of the Personal Rule and the summoning of the Long Parliament.[18] However, there is some circumstantial evidence that he had some contact with the junta headed by John Pym, John Hampden and various peers that conspired with the Scots to sabotage the king's preparations for war in 1640, and were to dominate proceedings in Parliament down to the outbreak of the Civil War and beyond. He may also have purchased a share in the Providence Bay Company, which would have brought him into contact with the same set of men.[19] However, when Waller appealed against the result of a by-election at Andover in March 1641, which he had lost, the junta was not inclined to use its influence in the House of Commons to set aside the result, probably because the man returned was a cousin of the Earl of Essex. But Vernon, the successful candidate, turned out to be a disappointment. By early 1642 he was displaying distinct signs of royalism, and on 3 May 1642 the Commons overturned its previous ruling and declared Sir William the rightful member of parliament for Andover.

Once he had secured a seat in Parliament, Waller's rise was very rapid indeed, such that within three months he became a founder member of the Committee of Safety. Adair attributes this partly to an inflated opinion of his military experience,[20] but although Sir William was adept in blowing his own trumpet my hunch is that he had performed some significant service for the king's opponents prior to May 1642. However, whatever the reason or reasons for his sudden appearance in the front rank of the king's foes, he entered the civil war determined to establish a military reputation.

Commissioned by the Earl of Essex as commander of a troop of horse, Sir William had raised it within days. Newly promoted to colonel soon afterwards, his first mission was to recapture Portsmouth and its large magazine of military and naval supplies, the governor having unexpectedly declared for the king. By force of personality Waller persuaded the local militia and a newly raised regiment of foot to obey his commands, and in a series of combined operations lasting several weeks, involving infantry and artillery, he browbeat the garrison into surrender. In its letter of thanks Parliament recognized Waller's personal contribution, but also acknowledged that the operation had been a cooperative effort.[21]

At the battle of Edgehill neither Waller nor his regiment distinguished themselves. Stationed on the left wing, they were swept from the field with the rest of Ramsey's command. Waller's horse was shot, but he managed to make his escape, and it is highly likely that the regiment had come together again by the time of the stand-off at Turnham Green three weeks later. They are not mentioned as being present, and so it is possible, given Waller's family connections with Kent and his recent military experience in Hampshire, that he and his men were part of the brigade defending Kingston bridge which, like the force that had captured Portsmouth, included county trained bands as well as army units and was commanded by James Ramsey, who had been Waller's superior officer at Edgehill.

As the king's army withdrew from the outskirts of London, Parliament's primary concern was to prevent the royalists obtaining a lodgement in the counties to the south and east of London, and Waller was chosen to head up the military operation. Within two months he had snuffed out a royalist uprising in Surrey by capturing Farnham Castle and placing a garrison there. He followed this up by destroying two regiments of royalist horse at Winchester and then frustrating the efforts of the West Sussex royalists to establish a military base for the king at Chichester. With Kent secured by other officers before Edgehill, Essex's army in winter quarters to the west of the capital, and Lord Grey of Wark raising his brigade in East Anglia, the capital was surrounded by a ring of friendly forces protecting the areas from which it obtained the bulk of its food supplies. To Londoners the visual evidence of Waller's achievements was not only well-stocked market stalls, but also columns of prisoners arriving in town. It is not surprising that they began calling him William the Conqueror in recognition of his military achievements, and along with that came popularity.

The House of Commons had promised Waller some mark of favour in due course in the letter thanking him for capturing Farnham Castle, and on 11 February he received his reward when he was promoted to major general of five counties in the west of England from Somerset and Wiltshire in the south to Shropshire in the north with Bristol, the second city in the kingdom, as his headquarters. But it was not an independent command.[22] Like the rest of the major generals he was subject to orders issued by the lord general, and like the lord general to those issued by Parliament and the Committee of Safety. The destruction of the Committee's minutes and most of its letters to Parliament's generals creates difficulties in understanding exactly what was going on in the chain of command. However, the chance survival of a letter to Waller written by John Pym on 14 March, presumably on the Committee's behalf, required him to relieve the isolated garrison at Gloucester and, if possible, to clear the counties of Somerset and Wiltshire of the enemy while on his way to Bristol.[23] By then Sir William was just a day short of reaching his headquarters, having passed through Salisbury and Bath and organized Parliament's supporters among the landed gentry in Wiltshire and Somerset. Once again he had shown his get-up-and-go attitude towards campaigning, and a passage in Pym's letter can be read as a sideswipe at the lord general's low level of activity.

For the next month Waller focused as instructed on the central part of his command and the string of his successes lengthened. He occupied Malmesbury in north Wiltshire and put in a temporary garrison. He then dispersed several thousand infantry raised by Lord Herbert in Monmouthshire, which were threatening Gloucester from a fortified camp at Highnam, just outside the city. What followed was a ding-dong campaign for the control of Gloucestershire to the west of the Severn, fought against a similar sized force from the Oxford army under Prince Maurice's command, which ended when the prince was called away to assist his uncle in the relief of Reading. Waller then occupied the disputed territory and established a garrison at Tewkesbury to keep an eye on it. The capture of Hereford, which had been in royalist hands since Stamford's departure in December, ensued. Such had been William the Conqueror's achievements in less than six weeks that a Gloucester parson had no hesitation in describing him as being worth a thousand soldiers to the parliamentary cause.[24]

Chapter 4

London's Favourite

So far Waller had done everything his political masters had asked of him. He had also displayed the kind of martial qualities that Essex appeared to lack, but success seems to have gone to Sir William's head. He began to exhibit signs of brusqueness and arrogance towards others in the chain of command. By the end of June Nathaniel Fiennes, the governor of Bristol, Sir Walter Earle, Parliament's commander in Dorset, and the Earl of Stamford all had reason for taking offence at the ways in which they had been treated. Waller drew on the second city's garrison for troops for his field army without considering how this might affect its ability to defend itself; when Earle met Waller on 22 May he was given fair words about military support against a royalist incursion, but nothing happened for a month and by that time it was too late; while Stamford's offer to set up a meeting in April to discuss how best they could combine to defeat the Cornish met with a curt refusal because of Waller's more pressing commitments elsewhere in his command.[1]

The Conqueror had no compunction about treating the lord general in a similar manner. The first occasion was in the third week of April 1643 when he ignored Essex's orders to leave his command and assist him in the siege of Reading. This was not because of the security situation in the Severn valley, as Prince Maurice had returned to Oxford. He also does not seem to have received orders from the Committee of Safety to remain where he was that would have superseded Essex's, though he may have used Pym's letter as an excuse. The real reason was his plan to capture Hereford, which looked like an easy picking as the Oxford brigade had left and Lord Herbert's men had not recovered from the drubbing they received at Highnam. Moreover, the glowing reports in the London newspapers would enhance his reputation at a time when it might be overshadowed by Essex's capture of Reading. Waller stormed Hereford the day before Essex persuaded the Reading garrison to surrender, but it was three-day wonder as the army of the west did not have sufficient spare infantry to establish a permanent garrison there as well as at Tewkesbury.

Thus the first case of Waller's disobedience did no damage to the parliamentary cause. The second, however, was the first step towards Parliament losing control of Bristol and almost the whole of south-western and south central England. Immediately after the first munitions convoy from Newark reached Oxford, the king ordered a brigade of cavalry commanded by the Marquis of Hertford and Prince Maurice to enter the counties that formed the southern part of

Waller's command. Their task was to rapidly raise new regiments of horse and foot there and in Dorset. They were then to join forces with the Cornish infantry who, having defeated the Earl of Stamford at Stratton, were marching across Devonshire towards the county boundary, and escort them to Oxford. Essex knew what Hertford and Maurice were up to and ordered Waller to disrupt their recruiting operations.[2] But Waller did nothing for six weeks, despite having accurate intelligence from Sir William Earle concerning the enemy's whereabouts and their initial lack of numbers. Instead, as in April, he was about to make a move against a royalist garrison in the north of his command. Worcester was his target this time, and he and his army arrived outside the city walls on 29 May.[3]

Waller may, of course, have received an order from the Committee of Safety countermanding the lord general's, but it is highly unlikely. The Committee knew from captured correspondence that the king intended the Cornish infantry to join him at Oxford, and would have seen the seriousness of a royalist push into the counties through which it would have to march. There is also no hint of a recent change in orders in a letter written by the civilian administrator Sir Robert Cooke to the Speaker of the House of Commons from Tewkesbury on 2 June explaining what the army of the west had been doing for the past fortnight, and there is no doubt that Essex believed that Sir William was on his way to disrupt the recruiting operation. Finally, when Sir Walter Earle had his face-to-face meeting with Sir William it is most unlikely that he did not pass on the bad news, from correspondence with Exeter, about the battle at Stratton six days earlier.[4] To be fair, Waller probably did not know of Hopton's exact whereabouts on 22 May, but he knew of Hopton's instructions and a man of Waller's perspicacity ought to have been able to put two and two together.[5]

If Sir William had nipped the royalist recruiting expedition in the bud in late May, which he could easily have done, the Cornish advance would have ground to a halt at the county boundary. For the infantry to have taken the shortest route from Devon to Oxford across the open downland of South Dorset and Wiltshire would have been suicidal given Waller's strength in horse. A more northerly line through the Somerset levels looks superficially more attractive for infantry operating without horse, but the risk of being trapped there and forced to surrender was almost as bad. Waller had only to bar their passage at one of the river crossings and then use his mounted troops to cut off their retreat. However, thanks to Waller's insubordination the Oxford cavalry met the Cornish infantry at Chard on 4 June, and the two brigades then enjoyed a quiet three weeks to shake down into an army before he confronted them. In the meantime he had failed to take Worcester by storm while they had captured Taunton and Bridgewater and overrun Somerset as far north as the Mendip Hills.[6]

During June Waller increased his strength in infantry by adding the garrison at Tewkesbury to his army.[7] He also took more foot soldiers from Bristol, and when at the end of the month he felt bold enough to risk a battle he had with him a force of between 5,000 and 6,000 men. This was very similar in size to the king's new army of the west, but the royalists were stronger than he was in foot though weaker in horse. In the complicated jockeying for position along the borders of Somerset, Wiltshire and Gloucestershire that followed Sir William displayed his customary skills in surprising and routing small detachments of the enemy, and at Lansdown to the north of Bath on 5 July he showed considerable promise as a battlefield commander. Deploying his army on top of a steep-sided hill he drove off some cavalry attacks and then inflicted heavy casualties on the Cornish infantry as they made repeated attempts to gain a foothold on the crest. As night fell they succeeded in doing so, and his troops fell back to a prepared position behind a stone wall that ran across the downs several hundred yards to the rear, but before dawn he made a tactical withdrawal into Bath.[8]

Waller's army had suffered very few casualties during the battle, thus reducing the imbalance in infantry between the two armies. The royalists, on the other hand, were dispirited by their losses, which included the death of their senior infantry colonel Sir Bevil Grenville, and the serious injuries suffered soon after Lansdown by Sir Ralph Hopton, when a wagon-load of gunpowder exploded. Waller then used his superior strength in horse first to block their eastwards march towards Oxford, and then to harry them as they drifted south to Devizes.

Waller's optimism was slightly dented when he heard on 10 July that there were Oxford army horse in the vicinity, and it was at that time that he wrote to the lord general and to the House of Commons asking for assistance, but on the 11th, in the first successful night attack of the war, his regiment captured wagons carrying gunpowder approaching Devizes from the east and routed the cavalry brigade escorting them. The following day his confidence had returned in full measure. In a letter written to the Speaker of the House of Commons he took divine support for granted: 'we have such experience of God that we doubt not to give you a good account of Sir Ralph Hopton'. In his memoirs he cited another letter written at about the same time: 'so sure was I of victory that I wrote to Parliament to bid them to be at rest for that I would shortly send them an account of the numbers taken and the numbers slain'.[9] But pride comes before a fall.

On the 13th a second relief expedition made its appearance on the hills to the north of Devizes, and the battle of Roundway Down followed. In the opinion of all but his most ardent supporters Waller should have won easily. In the first place he had a significant numerical advantage over the enemy. Second the relief force consisted entirely of cavalry armed with nothing more dangerous than swords and pistols. It was thus significantly lacking in firepower for anything other than a cavalry-on-cavalry engagement.[10] Nevertheless, Waller deployed his army in textbook fashion with the infantry massed in the centre and the cavalry on the wings as if he were facing a conventional army.[11] What he should have done was draw up his cavalry regiments in a defensive formation with his musketeers positioned such that they could inflict heavy casualties on the enemy just prior to the moment of impact. As it was his infantry faced the front with a gap between them and their horse. All they could do, therefore, was fire a single volley in the general direction of the enemy as they charged, in the hope of hitting something. However, this would not necessarily have mattered had Waller managed the battle in a different manner.

Waller's second and ultimately fatal mistake was to take command of one of the wings. This meant that he was personally involved in the cavalry action almost from the start. As a result the rest of the army was left to its own devices. Yet with five regiments of foot and seven of horse, comprising between 4,000 and 5,000 men, facing a force under half its size, Waller should have stationed himself with his uncommitted units, as Essex had done at Edgehill, ready to feed them into the fighting at the most appropriate moment. He could thus have deployed or redeployed his infantry such that they could pour musket fire into the enemy's flanks and rear while they were engaged in the mêlée or discomfort them with a pike charge. Instead they remained motionless, mere spectators of the engagement, until their cavalry had been driven from the battlefield and the enemy horse turned on them using captured artillery pieces.[12]

The only argument that can be made in Waller's defence is that his cavalry were unfit for battle because of their intensive campaigning over the past fortnight, but it does not stand serious scrutiny.[13] Five of his seven regiments had not seen action for three days prior to the battle and should have been thoroughly rested. The royalists, on the other hand, had ridden from Oxford to Marlborough on 11 or 12 July, some thirty miles or so, and from Marlborough to Devizes on the day of the battle, a distance of well over ten miles.[14]

* * * * *

Roundway Down ended in an outright royalist victory. Almost all Waller's infantry were killed or forced to surrender, while the few who did eventually reach the safety of Bristol were unarmed, having thrown away their weapons in the interests of speed and anonymity.[15] More of the horse escaped, but with Bristol denuded of foot by Waller's two earlier requisitions it was abundantly clear that he could not assemble a marching army with which to continue the campaign. After consulting his council of war he decided not to take charge of the defence of his headquarters, which might soon be besieged, but to ride to London in search of help, taking with him only a few hundred mounted men and a disproportionate number of officers.[16] In the circumstances this was probably the best course of action, but it failed in its purpose because of the speed with which the royalists responded to his defeat.

On arriving in the capital Waller found that his popularity had increased rather than diminished. On receiving news of the battle the London journals controlled by the lord general's radical opponents put up a smokescreen to conceal what had really happened. First they blamed Stamford's horse for the defeat, and then the lord general, in a more indirect way, for doing nothing to take the pressure off Sir William.[17] In addition they suggested very strongly that Waller had suffered a setback, not a disaster. Well over a week after the battle it was reported in the press that his supporters had regrouped, with 4,000 and then 6,000 men under arms in the west country awaiting his return with reinforcements.[18] Moreover, Parliament's reaction was supportive rather than condemnatory. Instead of instantly sacking him, it responded positively to a petition circulated by the London radicals asking for a new army to be raised under a new general, who would be Essex's equal not his subordinate, the nucleus being provided by what it was led to understand was a substantial part of Waller's army.[19]

The high point in the campaign was a rally at the Guildhall on 27 July to raise money and to recruit volunteers, which followed immediately on the Commons appointing Waller as commander of the new army. It also ordered Essex to issue him with a commission that made it clear that henceforth he was to take his orders only from Parliament or the Committee of Safety, which was ironic, given that disobedience to orders had been the root cause of his losing his first army. When Sir William appeared at the rally the rapturous Londoners greeted him as the city's saviour, which is not surprising given the way he was introduced by the radical MP Henry Marten. Under Waller's command the new army would end the war rapidly via a *levée en masse,* beginning in London, which would spread to the provinces. Not only would this ensure that the king's armies were swept into oblivion by sheer force of numbers, it would also serve to separate the sheep from the goats by revealing in their true colours civilians who were merely paying lip-service to the parliamentary cause, and officers and soldiers who saw the army as a cash-cow, and who had been responsible for the war continuing for so long. Moreover, the outright victory that the new army won would serve to permanently safeguard the citizens' religion, laws and liberties and what little was left of their wealth, Essex's army having consumed so much of it.[20]

The hopes of the radicals in the Commons and the city that the new army would swiftly bring the war to a close were soon dashed. To succeed it needed Parliament's and the Committee of Safety's total and unconditional support, but their interest was instrumental not ideological and varied with the military situation, which changed from day to day. In mid-July 1643 another royalist advance on London looked highly likely. The second munitions convoy, which had arrived in the Oxford area on 13 July, had an escort of 4,000 veterans of the campaigns in the north. On the same day, the victory at Roundway Down meant that Charles had another 5,000 or more soldiers from the south-west and south-central England at his command, with experience gained in the campaigns against Stamford and Waller. Admittedly, Essex, still stationed at Great Brickhill, was blocking the king's quickest route to the capital via Watling Street, but if the lord general engaged him in battle as his honour required and was soundly beaten (which the latest report on the state of his army suggested would be the most likely outcome), looking to London's defences was essential, and Waller's new army, supported by the London trained bands, would be all that stood between the king and outright victory.

However, the immediate crisis passed within days, after what was probably the worst strategic mistake made by the royalists in the entire war. The king was persuaded to divide his forces, with most regiments being assigned to the siege of Bristol, where they suffered very heavy casualties when it was stormed on the 26th, and then to the sieges of Gloucester and Exeter. But unlike Warwick's army after Turnham Green, the second reserve army was not immediately discontinued. Instead Parliament put it on the back burner, with priority being given to Essex's army. Nevertheless, it continued to back Waller most particularly in his struggle to obtain a commission from the lord general that would make him truly independent. This may merely have been a tactic to keep the radicals quiet, but continued interest in the second army can also be seen as a sensible precaution given another change in the military situation. Essex's army, supported by two brigades of London trained bands and some provincial regiments, was heading for Gloucester and the near certainty of a battle with the king's forces besieging it.

This determination not to keep all its eggs in one basket can also be seen in Parliament's treatment of Essex's army in late July and August. When the enthusiasm for the second army was at its height, it did enough in terms of resources to ensure that the field army did not deteriorate any further, and when it became clear that the king was not yet ready to march on London, it released more to enable the lord general to go on the offensive.[21] However, Essex in his turn made sure, as a politically aware general, that Parliament was kept fully informed about the state of his army and its future needs, even when it was Waller's army that was in the limelight.

The first move was a plea from the lord general's council of war received by the House of Lords on the 22nd, couched in the most deferential language but stark in its message. If not immediately supplied with resources, the army would cease to exist as a fighting force within a week. Nine days later Essex presented Parliament with a realistic estimate of what it required to be able to campaign effectively, and on that day the Commons passed the first resolution releasing resources.[22] At the same time Essex made his own political position clear, winning some favour as a result from some of those MPs who had backed the new army at its inception.

A strong body of opinion in both Houses favoured a new round of peace negotiations in late July and early August, in which substantial concessions would be made on matters concerning the royal prerogative, and this caused the radicals in the city to think in terms of a coup to expel moderates from Parliament. Those in favour of negotiations, who were to become the core of the future 'peace party', clearly hoped for Essex's support, given that he had mentioned a treaty with the king or a trial by battle involving his and the king's army in a letter written when he was in the greatest despair a month earlier. However, he took the wind from their sails by declaring that he was opposed to negotiations taking place at a time of weakness. This appeared to be a complete *volte face* from the pessimism he had expressed on 11 July, but as I have argued elsewhere his letter was probably an ill-judged ploy to bring Parliament to its senses about resourcing that spectacularly backfired.[23]

* * * * *

When Essex left the London area for Gloucester on 26 August, having, with extreme reluctance, granted Waller his commission, the new army should have taken wings and flown, but it did not. The most optimistic assessment of the size of the force Waller managed to assemble to the west of London in mid-September to go to Essex's aid should he get into trouble was 6,000 men, and at least half of these belonged to London trained band regiments on temporary loan. Unsurprisingly the House of Commons was getting impatient with the slow progress, and this was expressed in resolutions passed on the 11th and the 20th.[24]

In the event the new army's services were not required, as Essex did not need to be rescued, but when Sir William did set out to campaign as major general of the counties of Kent, Surrey, Sussex and Hampshire in late October, with an army containing some units intended for the July army, only his own dragoon regiment and possibly his cavalry regiment were up to strength. So also were two other cavalry regiments, the nuclei of which had survived Roundway Down and accompanied him to London. However, his new infantry regiment, the original having perished at the storming of Bristol, was only 300 strong, and of the twenty new regiments that he himself had commissioned in August, only four of the foot and none of the horse were still in existence by the time he handed in his commission in early October. Moreover, two of the four, Haselrig's and Potley's, were not ready to join him on campaign until December.[25]

The contrast between Waller's experience of recruiting and Warwick's ten months earlier is astounding, as the latter had managed to raise six new infantry regiments from scratch in less than six weeks. Waller's supporters blamed Essex for taking a month to grant him his commission. In other circumstances the loss of momentum would have been important, but not, it seems, in this case. He had been raising men in the city and its environs to repopulate the regiments of his old army, as these did not require new commissions, but his success had been mixed, with his own regiment being less than half complete in late October. It therefore seems likely that from the start he was scraping the bottom of a barrel that was nearly empty.

The pool of potential volunteers in London and its immediate environs had largely shrunk for reasons that had nothing to do with Waller or the concept of a new army. In the first place the county of Essex, which had been a valuable source of recruits in November 1642, was out of bounds as it was part of the Eastern Association. At first its army commander, the Earl of Manchester, was willing to be flexible about recruiting, but the cross-county committee that met at

Cambridge and ran the Association politically and administratively was much less keen and the door was soon firmly shut.[26]

Of greater importance was the fact that London had been drained of potential volunteers by the eight months of fighting that had followed Warwick's resignation. In addition, the number of city trained band regiments had increased from six to sixteen, and the conditions for ordinary soldiers serving in such regiments were more attractive than for those serving in Parliament's armies. Although the trained bands fought in the armies of Essex and Waller from the siege of Reading onwards, it was on a rota system and during 1643 and early 1644 only for limited periods of time agreed in advance.

There was, however, one factor for which Waller had some personal responsibility: the false propaganda that had accompanied the birth of the second army in late July. At the time a volunteer had every reason for thinking that his period of service would be short. He would be joining a force which was already several thousand strong and would quickly grow to such a size that the enemy would be overwhelmed by sheer numbers or frightened into suing for peace, but the speed with which Bristol surrendered, taken together with its governor's claim that its defenders were largely citizens rather than Waller's soldiers, clearly showed that the nucleus around which the radicals had promised to create the new army had always been a fiction. At the time only the Venetian ambassador expressed the view that Waller's promises had been empty and mendacious, but he would not have written in such terms to his political masters had his informants not heard similar language being used in the streets and markets of the capital.[27]

By the time the lord general returned to London after giving the king's forces a bloody nose at Newbury, Waller's moment had passed, but he claims not to have been that concerned. He had lost most of his enthusiasm for the new army when he came under pressure from his radical allies over the appointment of officers. They expected him to choose religious zealots with little or no military experience. He, on the other hand, was determined to appoint men of proven military ability, and the names of his new colonels suggest that it was his wish that prevailed.[28] This caused the radicals to look elsewhere for an alternative to the lord general, but Waller continued to have his uses as a rod for chastising Essex when he fell short of Parliament's expectations. Nevertheless, Waller could still have succeeded as lord general in 1644 had Essex become physically incapable of commanding his army in the field, or upset Parliament to such an extent that he had been sacked, but from September 1643 onwards Sir William did little to show that he was the man for the job.

Although still capable of exploiting his enemy's mistakes, as he did very effectively in Sussex and Hampshire in the winter of 1643/4, Waller's surprise attacks were becoming increasingly predictable, and as a result the enemy were able to turn the tables on him, as they did in the manoeuvring that preceded his victory at Cheriton in Hampshire in March 1644 and again during the encounter at Cropredy Bridge in Oxfordshire in late June.[29] He was also becoming cautious in operational matters. Having won an uninspiring slogging match at Cheriton, in which numbers determined the outcome, he did not immediately push forward into territory he had lost the previous summer. Instead he wasted time in ill-coordinated raiding from Christchurch in the south to Newbury in the north and in trying to browbeat the governor of Winchester into surrendering. This lack of focus gave the royalists the chance to regroup. Outnumbered as a consequence, Waller was back at his army base at Farnham within a fortnight, to the consternation of his political masters, while in September and October, to Essex's ill-concealed delight, he did nothing to delay the king's armies eastward march after Lostwithiel, despite having the means to do so with his superior numbers of cavalry and dragoons.[30] The rendezvous of Parliament's forces in the south organized by the strategists at Westminster to stop the royalists' forward progress therefore took place not at Salisbury, as intended, but at Basingstoke fifty miles to the east.

In late October the lord general's illness at last gave Sir William the chance to show what he could do on the battlefield in command of a force of well over 10,000 men, but the outcome of his attack on the western flank of the king's armies at Newbury was disappointing from beginning to end.[31] His plan of attack was uncoordinated, probably because, as at Roundway Down, he led his cavalry into the attack instead of remaining in the rear with his extensive reserves, to exploit weaknesses in the enemy line of battle as they occurred. Later in the battle, having reached a position from which he could exert tactical control, he allowed a breakthrough by Essex's infantry in the centre to be halted because it was getting dark, while a hopeful attempt to outflank the enemy position on the right was allowed to go ahead with insufficient infantry support. Finally, in an act of supreme caution, he did nothing to prevent the enemy withdrawing from the battlefield under the cover of darkness, even though he was fully aware of what was happening and had units well placed to exploit the situation.[32]

Chapter 5

Essex's Last Campaign

Bringing Waller to heel by the threat of resignation in early October 1643 was the high point in the revival of the lord general's reputation. The decline that followed was slow at first, occasioned as in the previous winter by his inactivity compared with Waller in the counties to the south of London and Sir Thomas Fairfax in the north of England, but from February 1644 it gathered pace, with humiliation followed by humiliation. Part of the problem was that Essex was becoming more isolated. John Pym, who had managed the House of Commons, the rulers of London and provincial interests in such a way as to protect Essex against his critics, died in December.[1] Insofar as anybody filled his shoes it was Sir Henry Vane the Younger, the Treasurer of the Navy, and Oliver St John, the Solicitor General. However, Vane had been the severest of Essex's critics from the spring of 1643 onwards, while St John, though initially in a friendly relationship with the lord general, began to follow in Vane's footsteps through, it seems, their wish for religious reform that went beyond a Presbyterian Church of England.[2]

Pym's death also allowed two parties that were beginning to take shape within the Commons to grow, namely the peace party and its apparent opposite, the war party.[3] Put simply the first wanted the war to end through negotiation with the king, the second in outright victory. However, neither was ever any more than a substantial minority, and neither managed to dominate decision-making in the House of Commons or the Lords for an extended period of time. Moreover, the label 'peace party' is slightly misleading. The terms its leaders expected the king to agree to were impossibly severe, such that the only peace initiative to get off the ground, the so-called Treaty of Uxbridge of February 1645, made no progress whatsoever. Thus the only hope of gaining Charles's consent to the limitations on royal power they wanted was to destroy his means to resist, and even then there was no guarantee that he would agree to cooperate. The lord general is normally associated with the peace party, as its members almost invariably supported his interests in Parliament, while the war party wished him to be replaced or, at worst, to reduce his power and his independence, but he was always careful to preserve his neutrality by refusing to have anything to do with peace feelers from the king that were sometimes addressed to him personally.

The lord general's authority was also challenged by the alliance Parliament concluded with the Scottish government in September 1643, the so-called Solemn League and Covenant. First, his army would lose its military primacy, as the force the Scots agreed to deploy in England would be twice the size of his own. Second, the Scots saw Sir Henry Vane, who had negotiated the alliance, as their principal political friend. Third, they had nothing but contempt for the casual way in which the war had been waged in England in 1642 and 1643, and held Essex, or at least some of his leading officers, directly responsible.[4] Finally, the Scots had a more hands-on approach towards managing their armies. While on campaign they were accompanied by government ministers and other leading politicians who could overrule the generals' decisions, and there was a risk that Parliament would in due course copy them.[5]

The Scottish government's involvement in the fighting in England was driven entirely by self-interest. Between 1637 and 1641 the Scottish people, led by a powerful section of the Scottish nobility and clergy, had carried through a revolution in which a pure form of Presbyterianism replaced the hybrid imposed on the country by kings James and Charles. At the same time royal authority over the Scottish church was abolished and the royal prerogative reduced to the level that those who had sided with Parliament rather than the king wished to see in England. In the summer of 1643, however, it looked as if Charles was coming close to winning the war in England, and having done so there was nothing to prevent him using force to restore his authority in Scotland. To ensure that the king was defeated in England was therefore essential for the security of the revolution, but to be totally confident about its future it made sense for the Scots to work hard to establish Presbyterianism as the state religion in England. However, there was cause for alarm. The power of the English bishops and church courts to keep a lid on religious radicalism had ended in the crisis of the summer of 1640. One result had been the growth in support for more liberal and less structured forms of Protestantism, as practised by Independents, ancestors of the Congregationalists, and by Baptists. To the Scottish government these were new enemies who were more dangerous than the bishops. To ensure that their second war aim was achieved, it was essential for the Scottish government and church to have a powerful political and religious presence in London, and so from late January 1644 onwards Scottish commissioners, led by Lord Chancellor Loudon, were accommodated in a residence close to the Palace of Westminster, from where they took an active part in the day-to-day management of the war through membership of the Committee of Both Kingdoms, which could not conduct business without a Scot being present. As important was shaping the English church once the war had been won, and from November 1643 onwards Scottish clergy and laity attended the Westminster Assembly, which had been charged by Parliament with preparing proposals for the post-war government and doctrine of the church in England.[6]

The decline in regard for the lord general was in part a consequence of the recovery of Waller's reputation as William the Conqueror following his successes in Sussex and Hampshire from December 1643 onwards, which encouraged his supporters in the Commons to try and enhance his military authority. Matters came to a head during the Cheriton campaign, when the House passed an ordinance putting the South-East Association of Kent, Surrey, Sussex and

Hampshire on a firmer financial footing and giving it and its general the right to refuse to accept Essex's orders unless they were backed up by a Parliamentary decree. The House of Lords were unhappy with the wording, but gave way on news of the victory. They did, however, secure an amendment which placed Waller firmly under Essex's command should Essex's army and Waller's army happen to campaign together in the future.[7]

Earlier Essex had lost the powers of command over another major general. Complaints about his taking military resources from the Eastern Association to supply his army led to the addition of a clause to an ordinance passed on 20 January concerning the Association's finances that gave the Earl of Manchester and the committee at Cambridge greater independence. Their forces were to be 'kept entire and not drawn forth without the knowledge and joint consent of the earl and the committee or one of them if they are apart' unless the order had the approval of Parliament, but unlike Waller's ordinance it did not place Manchester under the lord general's authority if at any time the two armies were obliged to make common cause against the enemy.[8]

There is no doubt that losing control over men who were supposed to be his subordinates irked the lord general, not only because it was a criticism of him, but also because it was an act of disobedience on Waller's part that had lost Parliament the south west and the greater part of south-central England. In addition, Essex had to agree to his army being reduced in size as an economy measure, and as a result it was smaller than the Earl of Manchester's.[9] Moreover, he was only allowed to advise Parliament on the officers who were to be retained, not to select them himself.[10] However, he went along with the reform measure, as he attended the House of Lords on the day the ordinance was approved and did not vote against it.[11] Possibly this was in the expectation that a slimmer army would be properly financed and properly supplied with military hardware. In the event, in order to get his army fully financed he had to suffer the further humiliation of going cap in hand to the Corporation of London meeting in the Guildhall, accompanied by his political enemy Sir Henry Vane and three other members of the Lords and the Commons, but it was worth it. Despite a lack of harmony in the joint presentation, with Essex attributing the victory at Cheriton to Balfour first and Waller second, and Vane not mentioning Balfour at all, it was sufficiently convincing to loosen the purse strings and by mid-May Essex's army was ready to take the field.[12]

These real reductions in the lord general's authority have been noted by historians, but they have not attracted much attention. Far greater interest has been shown in the ordinance establishing the Committee of Both Kingdoms that was to determine strategy, oversee military operations and allocate military resources. Essex is supposed to have bitterly opposed its establishment,[13] but it is difficult to see how it diminished his authority. In the first place it was he who introduced the measure in the House of Lords on 1 February 1644. Trouble did not begin until a week later, when the Commons approved the ordinance and returned it to the Lords with amendments. The Lords' objection was to a clause that only slightly modified the wording of the original and in a way that seems uncontentious. Instead of authorising the committee to 'order and direct whatsoever concerns the managing of the war' it was 'to advise, consult, order and direct concerning the carrying on and managing of the war.'[14] However, just over a week after the Lords took umbrage the lord general formally proposed the third reading of the ordinance in the House, even though the new wording had been retained.[15] What is surprising is not that the Lords backed down and passed the ordinance, but that Essex, who must have been behind the Lords' disquiet, should have been initially unhappy with the amendment and then changed his mind. To be advised and consulted seems innocuous, while to carry on does not seem to enhance the committee's power to manage the war to his detriment. Moreover, Essex had plenty of experience of being managed. The few letters of the Committee of Safety that survive show that it was giving Essex operational orders from November 1642 at the earliest until late December 1643 at the latest, six weeks before it surrendered its powers to the new committee.[16]

The most likely explanation of the lord general's behaviour was given at the time by Robert Baillie, a Scottish minister resident in London who sat in the Westminster Assembly. Peace party members of parliament, incensed that they could be outvoted in the new committee by Scots and their war party allies, tricked the lord general into thinking that his powers would be diminished by the changed wording,[17] but in the end he came to his senses having presumably discussed the matter privately with his leading officers.[18]

* * * * *

On 8 May 1644 the Committee of Both Kingdoms instructed Essex and Waller to march together against the king's forces wherever they appeared in a body in the south or the west of England.[19] At the time the prospects for a highly successful campaign looked very good indeed. Even though Hopton's corps, defeated at Cheriton, had been absorbed into the king's field army, the armies of Essex and Waller still outnumbered it by a considerable margin, and both were strong in cavalry as well as infantry. When they joined forces the lord general assumed the role of commander-in-chief, as he was empowered to do by Waller's most recent commission, and the decision was taken to advance on Oxford in the hope of provoking the king into fighting a battle. Although Essex's army was to the north of the Thames and Waller's to the south at the start of the campaign, both armies approached Oxford along the south bank, a sensible precaution against the royalist generals using interior lines to defeat one and then the other.

As Essex's and Waller's armies advanced, the king's forces fell back, abandoning first Reading, an open town with its fortifications having been dismantled in advance, and then Abingdon, which had been garrisoned by the royalists since late 1642. Essex's army then crossed to the north bank of the

Thames, while Waller's continued along the south bank, the purpose being to prevent the king and his forces leaving Oxford by surrounding the city, though this created a new risk of the enemy using interior lines. The Committee of Both Kingdoms did nothing to interfere with the operation other than present the generals with a distraction. On 30 May they were separately ordered to send forces to the relief of Lyme in Dorset under siege from Prince Maurice's army of the west, but the letter to Waller included a back-handed criticism of Essex: 'we shall not need to recommend this further to you having always had experience of your forwardness.'[20]

By 3 June the two armies had almost surrounded Oxford and a confrontation with the enemy was expected hourly, but for three days Essex was held up by royalist defences on the far bank of the River Cherwell to the north of the city, and the Committee seems to have decided that the cautious Essex of the 1643 campaign had returned. It therefore sent John Crewe, one of its members, to make sure that a new set of orders was obeyed. If a battle had not taken place by 8 June, Waller's entire army was to march to the relief of Lyme, while Essex was to keep the king in check in the Oxford area, calling on local forces from Gloucester and the central Midlands garrisons should reinforcements be needed. If these were still insufficient, he was to take up a defensive position covering Reading and Abingdon to prevent central Berkshire being overrun and await further orders.[21] However, the Committee's instructions were based on the presumption that if a battle did not take place the king would remain in the Oxford area. In the event he did not and the rumpus that followed illustrated the difficulties of trying to conduct military operations from a distance.

On 4 June Essex crossed the Cherwell and advanced to Woodstock, thus cutting all the escape routes to the north and the north-west. In the meantime Waller had advanced to Newbridge on the Thames near Faringdon, thus cutting the road from Oxford to Bristol, but although he now controlled the river crossing crucial to completing the ring around the king's headquarters, he did not cross it and move towards Woodstock as the bridge was not strong enough to bear the weight of his train of artillery. As a result there was still a gap of a couple of miles between the two parliamentary armies, which effectively widened when a threat to Abingdon from Oxford on the afternoon of the 4th caused Waller to withdraw most of his forces from Newbridge, leaving behind just enough men to defend the bridge. The royalists seized their opportunity. On the night of 4/5 June the king, accompanied by his cavalry and several thousand musketeers riding piggy-back behind the troopers, rode through the gap between Newbridge and Woodstock and so into the Cotswolds. Two days later days the 'flying army' reached safety on the far side of the River Severn at Worcester.[22]

Essex and Waller set off in pursuit, but almost immediately gave up the chase. A crucial council of war then took place at Chipping Norton on 6 June to decide how best to proceed, as their earlier instructions did not allow for the king's leaving Oxford with half his army. The strategic imperatives were first to prevent the king joining Prince Rupert, who was busily recruiting in Lancashire in preparation for crossing the Pennines, and confronting the allied armies besieging York.[23] The second was to relieve Lyme. Letters sent by the Committee to the army commanders in late May and early June had been sufficiently ambiguous for Essex to make an operational decision that was not in accordance with the spirit of the letter of 30 May. Waller, with the more mobile of the two armies, should keep tabs on the king, drawing on the assistance of regiments currently in the west Midlands and Cheshire as required, while Essex headed for Lyme.

In a letter to the Committee on 7 June, Waller and Sir Arthur Haselrig, his lieutenant general of horse and one of the war party leaders in the Commons, appear to have agreed that this was the best course of action, probably because it would give them the chance of capturing the king and bringing him to London in triumph. So initially did Parliament,[24] but within two days Haselrig had changed his mind. Returning to Westminster he consulted other war party leaders and was persuaded to denounce the decision in the Commons and to demand Essex's dismissal, but this was going too far. Instead, prompted by the Committee the Commons ordered Essex to stop at the Wiltshire/Dorset border until such time as Waller's army arrived, and then to return to the Midlands. In the meantime he was to send cavalry to the relief of Lyme.[25]

Essex's response was a very well-argued defence of his actions based on military logic, which included a strong hint that the new instructions showed the Committee's basic ignorance of how campaigns should be conducted. He also warned the members that if he obeyed his army would revolt, and ended the letter with the ominous words 'you will repent too late and I too soon'.[26] The Committee's reaction was to wash its hands of the whole matter, leaving it to Parliament to discipline the lord general. For the next fortnight the only letter they sent him concerned the delivery of pay for his army.[27]

The lord general's outright refusal to obey orders might have ended his military career, had he not again shown the strength of purpose he had displayed in the expedition to Gloucester. Marching quickly across Wiltshire and Dorset he forced the royalists to abandon the siege of Lyme on 17 June and to surrender Weymouth three days later. Soon afterwards Taunton Castle fell easily into his hands, while the citizens of Barnstaple, emboldened by the withdrawal of most of its garrison to strengthen Prince Maurice's army, abandoned the king's cause and declared for Parliament.

Essex's two bullish letters to Parliament following the relief of Lyme asked for permission to advance further into the west of England, but if ordered to return as per his earlier instructions he would resign and sit in the Lords, being no longer 'fit to be trusted any further in the business', while his letter to the Committee of Both Kingdoms on 21 June mixes confidence born of success with a spoonful of sarcasm. Parliament, however, was reasonably conciliatory. In a draft letter written on 19 June he was allowed to reconquer the west, but he must in future obey orders. It would have been better for all concerned if he had done so in the first place. He was also criticized for using unnecessarily offensive language in his letters to the Committee, which he probably now regretted.

The war party in the House of Commons then began to have second thoughts. Some of Essex's officers and staff had connived at the plundering of goods at Weymouth that belonged to the state, and there were signs of lethargy. One senior officer had been heard to say that the capture of Exeter, the next probable objective, was work for the following year. Essex countered with a letter signed by his senior officers supporting his conduct of the campaign, while Waller blotted his copybook when the tactics he used to attack the king's army at Cropredy Bridge on 30 June led to heavy casualties and the loss of several pieces of artillery. But it was not until 6 July that the two Houses agreed on the final wording of a letter to be sent to the lord general drawing a line under the whole business. His political masters allowed him to remain in the west, but refused to admit that they had been in the wrong. If he had obeyed his original instructions even more could have been achieved.[28]

Having relieved Lyme, Essex set about raising new regiments in Somerset and north Devon and putting garrisons into Barnstaple, Weymouth and Taunton. Seeking a battle with Prince Maurice was out of the question, as he was in west Cornwall having escorted the queen from Exeter to Falmouth, the safest port in royalist hands, from where she set sail for France on about 12 July.[29] While Maurice was away Essex did contemplate setting siege to the city, but instead decided to complete the conquest of Devonshire by providing succour for the besieged garrison at Plymouth, which he hoped would assist him in destroying Prince Maurice's army. However, before he had marched many miles beyond Exeter the chance was lost. The royalist army of the west had returned to Exeter by a circuitous route that avoided a confrontation.[30]

Having chased away the enemy forces surrounding Plymouth, Essex was persuaded to move into Cornwall (possibly against his better judgement, or so he claimed subsequently). He had been convinced that supplies and recruits would be forthcoming from a county that had been fairly evenly divided between royalists and parliamentarians at the start of the war. In the meantime the king's army, having escaped the attentions of Sir William Waller, was marching at full speed into the west of England to rendezvous with Prince Maurice. Uncle and nephew met at Honiton on 25 July. They then followed in Essex's wake, intent on trapping his army and forcing it to fight or surrender.[31]

What followed was, in Essex's words, 'the greatest blow that ever befell our party'.[32] Trapped in a narrow peninsula in south-east Cornwall between Lostwithiel and Fowey, Essex's infantry were pushed back into a smaller and smaller perimeter in a series of engagements. They were forced to surrender on 3 September after the last defence line covering Fowey had been breached, but the lord general escaped to Plymouth by fishing boat on the grounds that the parliamentary cause would suffer more if he was made a prisoner. The only bright spots had been the escape of the cavalry through a poorly defended section of the royalist perimeter, and the king's decision to allow Essex's foot soldiers to return to Parliament's quarters. At this point Parliament would have had good reason for depriving Essex of his command, but it did nothing of the sort. Instead it commiserated with him and promised to recruit his infantry in preparation for the inevitable eastwards advance of the king's army. There were three points in Essex's favour. First, most of his infantry and nearly all his horse survived to fight another day, and there would be no problems in re-equipping them.[33] Second, although the royalists made several attempts to persuade Essex to join the king in issuing a joint plea for peace, culminating in a letter from Charles himself that addressed the lord general as Dear Friend, he stuck to his previous resolve not to get involved with such matters. Peace-making was a matter for Parliament. Thus he had, as in August 1643, proved his commitment to the cause, though some of his officers had talked to the enemy and in due course they were to be called to account. Third, he had not lost his confidence, as was shown by his very professional appraisal of his army's needs, but this was how a great nobleman with a distinguished ancestry was expected to behave in the face of adversity.[34]

The lord general's resilience was not just a matter of character. He was sure that he had been betrayed by his enemies on the Committee of Both Kingdoms, who should have ordered Waller to do something to intercept royalist supplies heading for Cornwall or cause mayhem in the Oxford area, either of which would have forced the king to return hurriedly eastward. Sir William later claimed in conversation with Sir Simons D'Ewes that he had been ordered not to stir. Some attempts have been made in the past to discredit D'Ewes's allegation, but there is some evidence to back it up.[35] On 15 July Waller informed the Committee that the king was heading for Bristol, and that he was determined to follow him, but would wait for orders to that effect before leaving his army's encampment at Buckingham. The response was that he was not to move to Bristol, but south into Berkshire to protect the territory he and Essex had conquered in May and June. He was also to send 1,000 horse into Dorset to strengthen Parliament's hold on Weymouth and its environs, but all that Essex was told in a letter written by the Committee on the following day was that the king was at Bristol and that Waller had no more than 2,500 horse and 1,500 foot. Much later he learned that Waller's orders had been changed, as he was sent a copy of the Committee's letter to Waller, but it was not accompanied by any intelligence about the movements of the king's army.[36] On 18 July he sent the Committee a letter from Tiverton, just before he set out for Cornwall, in which he stated that his council of war had some concern about the king's army being in the Bristol area, but that it had decided to march further west 'hoping that Sir William with his army and additional forces will take care of the king's army'.[37] This surely required a response containing up-to-date information about the enemy's movements, but nothing of the sort was sent by Parliament or the Committee before 9 August, by which time the lord general and his army were surrounded.[38] That his army was starved of intelligence in late July is clear from a letter written by Lord Robartes, one of his generals, on the last day of the month to Colonel Robert Bennett, who was raising a regiment in North Devon: 'you will use your best endeavours to understand of the king's movements and Prince Maurice's and also where Sir William Waller is, and that hereof you advise me as soon as you get any certain information'.[39]

There was also a distinct lack of urgency on the Committee's part compared with the way it had reacted on previous occasions when one of its armies was under threat, and this continued until almost the end of August. On the 2nd Sir Phillip Stapleton, one of Essex's senior officers, who had just arrived in the capital from Cornwall, passed on the lord general's request for an order to be given 'for seconding the army by a considerable force' to the House of Commons, but the Committee of Both Kingdoms did not take it seriously.[40] A letter it wrote to the Essex a week later was full of news about the war elsewhere, but promised nothing other than that Waller had 2,000 horse at Dorchester, 'which is all could be done in the present state of his forces'. The following day it promised to reinforce the brigade with 500 dragoons and to order it to disrupt supplies going to the king's army. It was also thinking about sending 'greater forces westwards', but considered that by cutting off food and fodder 'the enemy will be reduced to greater straits than you... having the sea open'.[41] Later in the month the Committee ordered Waller to get his infantry ready to march and to send his cavalry from Dorset towards Lostwithiel, but it was too little too late.[42] When the army in Cornwall surrendered, Waller's foot were still at Farnham and the horse had yet to cross the River Tamar.[43]

Chapter 6

The Earl of Essex and the Newbury Campaign

Although what happened at Lostwithiel had neither ended the lord general's career nor destroyed his army, it has been widely seen as facilitating the creation of the New Model Army. According to Snow, after the humiliation in Cornwall Essex was too war-weary and too disillusioned to resist Parliament taking away his powers one by one over a period of eight months until, all authority gone, he resigned as lord general on 3 April 1645, just as the New Model was coming into being.[1] Adamson, however, has seen Essex's loss of authority as a precursor to army reform. He had been the principal stumbling block and Lostwithiel provided the opportunity to supersede him. In early October 1644, therefore, Parliament passed an ordinance combining Essex's, Waller's and Manchester's forces into a single entity under the direct control of a sub-committee of the Committee of Both Kingdoms. Thus the New Model Army existed in all but name four months before the ordinance authorising it became law.[2]

In contrast, an older view saw little connection between the downfall of the Earl of Essex and army reform, for which it was a concomitant not a precursor. Sir William Waller planted the seed in a letter to the Committee of Both Kingdoms eight weeks before Lostwithiel when his army began to disintegrate in the midst of chasing the king around the south Midlands. Until Parliament had an army entirely under its control, he wrote, 'it is in a manner impossible to do anything of importance'. However, for the seed to germinate an accelerator was needed. This appeared on 19 November when the committee at Cambridge informed the House of Commons that it could no longer raise sufficient funds to keep the Earl of Manchester's army in the field. It was thus a financial crisis that forced Parliament to confront the messy and contentious business of army reform.[3]

On the other hand, it has been argued that the idea for a new army came late on the scene and in response not to the Earl of Essex's downfall, but to the failure to get rid of him. In December 1644 the House of Commons passed the Self-Denying Ordinance, by which all MPs and peers would be forced to resign their commissions in the armed forces. This would end the lord general's military career and that of other members of the Upper House, but in other respects command in the armies might remain much the same. MPs who were officers, like Oliver Cromwell and Sir William Waller, had only to resign their seats to be reinstated. However, on 13 January the House of Lords rejected the ordinance.

The upshot was that the only sure way of getting rid of Essex was to merge the best parts of the three armies in the south of England into one. If Parliament then refused to vote money to pay those regiments that were not chosen for the new army, what was left of Essex's (and also Manchester's and Waller's) would disappear like morning mist in the rising sun.[4]

Surprisingly, nobody has considered that the lord general might have been thoroughly in favour of wide-ranging military reform. Time and time again the under-resourcing of his army had curbed its ability to take the field, and when it did the lord general had been frustrated by his political masters and by overlapping or competing jurisdictions that gave commanders of provincial armies excuses for not providing him with assistance when he needed it.[5] There is little doubt that, if he had been asked, he would have opted for three fundamental changes: first, for the army to be financed by a national tax that brought in sufficient funds to obviate the need to go cap in hand to the mercantile elite of London asking for a loan; second, for a commission from Parliament that enabled him to issue mandatory orders to commanders of the provincial armies; and third, for a ruling from Parliament that his operational decisions would not be subject to day-to-day interference. The first two were to be enshrined in the New Model Army Ordinance of February 1645, with independence from the operational commands of the Committee of Both Kingdoms being granted to his successor as commander-in-chief four months later during the Naseby campaign. And even though it was Sir Thomas Fairfax who was the beneficiary in terms of command and control, there was every chance that he would meet with misfortune. In such circumstances it would be difficult for Essex's enemies to prevent him being reinstated as lord general.

The only way of unravelling this tangled web is to test the various hypotheses against both an accurate chronology of the army reforms themselves, and an up-to-date appraisal of the military context at every stage in the process. The starting point must therefore be Waller's flash of inspiration in July 1644, but this can be quickly dismissed as it has been taken out of context. He was not complaining about the behaviour of the mix of provincial forces that made up the core of his army, but about London trained-band regiments serving with him on a temporary basis, which had upped sticks and marched home carrying the body of their colonel, who may have died of exhaustion.[6] But these were troops over which neither the Committee of Both Kingdoms nor Parliament had any direct control. They were only attached to Waller's army because the city authorities had given their consent.[7] However, transferring control of the city militia from the Corporation to Parliament or its general was not part of the programme of military reform carried through in the winter of 1644–5. Waller's pronouncement is therefore irrelevant to a discussion of such reforms.

Equally irrelevant to the birth of the New Model Army was the ordinance of 2 October, brought out of obscurity by Adamson.[8] It is just possible that the war party saw it as the thin end of a very long wedge for removing Essex from his command, but if this was its intention it was quickly overtaken by events. The context of the ordinance was that in order to block the westwards advance of the king's forces after Lostwithiel, the three generals commanding armies in the south would have to work together. Its purpose was two-fold: first to ensure that Essex, Manchester and Waller obeyed the orders of the Committee of Both Kingdoms, and second that the campaign was not sabotaged by rivalries and quarrels between them. It referred back to the disobedience that had marked Essex's behaviour during the summer and Manchester's during the autumn, and the ill-feeling between the three men and some of their officers – long-standing between Waller and Essex and more recent between Waller and Manchester.[9] The solution was for the campaign to be run by a steering group consisting of soldiers and civilian members of the Committee. The phrase 'preserved in unity' that appears in the ordinance merely refers to the need for the army group to behave as one if it was to be effective. It had nothing to do with combining the three armies into one, as they were treated as completely separate entities in all the documents referring to, or emanating from, the steering group.

In addition, there was nothing particularly new in the ordinance. The right of the Committee of Both Kingdoms to give binding instructions to commanders in the field was embodied in the ordinances establishing it.[10] The only substantive change was to introduce civilians into military decision-making in the field. As such it reflected the practice in the Scottish army, and it is interesting that immediately after the remit and the membership of the steering committee had been approved, the representatives of the Scottish government in London were patting themselves on the back for resolving all the problems of managing a potentially fractious army group as it prepared to face the enemy.[11] Moreover, the instructions most emphatically do not provide a management structure for a reformed field army. First, the steering group was not to continue indefinitely, as Adamson strongly implies. Indeed, it was wound up on 4 November, a fortnight before the autumn campaign came to an end.[12] It also did not form a model for the subsequent management of the New Model Army. Admittedly it was revived on a single occasion in the spring of 1645, but then it lasted for no longer than three days.[13] Second, the instructions never referred to the three armies as a single entity. Indeed, they specifically state that 'the forces joined with his Excellency being distinct forces are to be commanded by their respective officers', and as such they retained their independent existence until a month after the New Model Ordinance became law. Admittedly, units were moved from one army to another during the autumn and winter as the Committee of Both Kingdoms saw fit, but this had been happening long before the October ordinance came into force as, for example, when Balfour's brigade from Essex's army joined Waller's for the Hampshire campaign of March/April 1644.[14]

Finally, unleashing the tensions that would accompany the remodelling of the three armies might be both exceedingly foolhardy and quite unnecessary given the military context. In early October 1644 battle with the last of the king's armies was imminent, and in the words of Sir William Waller victory would bring the war to a swift conclusion: 'Destroy but this army and the deed is done'.[15]

* * * * *

From the time of his arrival at Portsmouth on or before 11 September, the lord general focused on refreshing, recruiting and rearming his infantry, but when the king's forces crossed the Devon/Somerset county boundary late in the month he began to take interest in what other generals were doing in response to the Committee of Both Kingdoms' resolve to bottle the king's army up in the west country for the winter.[16] There was the occasional sideswipe at the Earl of Manchester, who was making very slow progress, but unsurprisingly it was Waller who came in for the most criticism. Sir William should have used his superiority in mounted troops to delay the royalists' progress as they marched from the enclosed countryside of Devon into the open chalk downs of Dorset and Wiltshire. Instead he had fallen back as they advanced, thus imperilling the Committee's efforts to bring about a rendezvous of the three armies. By deliberately avoiding contact with the enemy, he had also made it difficult to obtain first-rate intelligence of their movements and intentions.[17] Essex also suggested that he should join his cavalry, which were temporarily under Waller's command after escaping from Cornwall, but the Committee told him to remain where he was. Relations between the two generals were bound to be icy, despite Essex's promises to overlook previous provocations.[18]

In early October, as the Committee of Both Kingdoms debated the instructions for managing the army group, it became increasingly apparent that the royalists were intent on a battle. They were not heading for Bristol and the Severn valley, where they might manage to spin out time until wintry conditions brought the campaigning season to an end. Instead they were making for their besieged garrisons of Donnington Castle and Basing House on the Hampshire/Berkshire border, in precisely the area where the army group was due to rendezvous. Moreover, the odds were heavily stacked in Parliament's favour. Intelligence provided by the deserter Sir John Urry revealed that the armies of the king and Prince Maurice were inferior in numbers to the forces that the Committee of Both Kingdoms was assembling, and that many of the rank-and-file were recently impressed men with little training and possibly even less motivation.[19]

Essex duly led his infantry to the grand rendezvous with his horse, Waller's cavalry and dragoons, Manchester's army and six regiments of the London trained bands.[20] This happened at Basingstoke on 21 October, by which time the enemy had reached Whitchurch on the present-day A34 between Newbury and Winchester, only twelve miles to the west. With contact imminent he and the other army commanders agreed on how best to deploy their forces covering the siege works around Basing House, but the rendezvous itself was sufficient to deter the royalists. They responded by marching due north and drawing up in a very strong defensive position just to the north of Newbury, in the angle between the rivers Kennet and Lambourn and defended by artillery positioned in their garrison at Donnington Castle. There, amply supplied with provisions for man and horse, they could bide their time until either Prince Rupert arrived with reinforcements from the Welsh borderland and a battle ensued, or shortage of provisions forced the enemy army group to disperse.[21]

The lord general played no part in the campaign that followed. An infection of the bowels, which began before he left Portsmouth, was exacerbated by the rapid march across country, and by 24 October he was in great pain and confined to bed at Reading, some fifteen miles behind the army group headquarters at Thatcham, just to the east of Newbury.[22] Three days later the remaining commanders forced the royalists to fight a battle earlier than they had wanted by an adroit pincer movement. Waller, with the bulk of the army group, attacked the enemy position from the west where there were no natural defences, while Manchester, with the rest, pinned the enemy in place on the banks of the River Lambourn. Reports written the following day claimed that all the generals and the troops had performed well and that casualties had been light. The royalists, on the other hand, having suffered heavy losses, had fled in panic in three different directions.[23]

On 31 October, however, a less optimistic account reached London, written by Phillip Skippon, Essex's major general of foot. This hinted that the battle had been poorly conducted. Also, it made no mention whatsoever of the pursuit stage, in which the heaviest losses would normally have been inflicted on a defeated enemy.[24] Skippon's silence is not surprising. There had been no pursuit. The steering group, though aware that the royalists were retreating under the cover of darkness, did nothing to impede them and by dawn they were too far away to be caught.[25] Even so, a determined pursuit by the whole army group on the following day might well have prevented the enemy forces from regrouping. This did not happen because the generals had very different views about the army group's best line of advance. As a result they did nothing more adventurous than pushing their cavalry forward to the edge of the Berkshire downs, fifteen miles to the north of battlefield, and there they remained for the next nine days.[26]

By the end of October, Essex was well enough to be concerned about what was not happening in the army group in his absence. He may or may not have been aware that the generals were in dispute about what to do next, but he certainly knew that they were not in hot pursuit of the enemy from the contents of a letter he had read written by Richard Browne, garrison commander at Abingdon. To have followed up its victory, the army group would have needed to pass through the town or close by, but Browne's patrols were still encountering bodies of enemy horse in the area some days after the battle.[27]

Doubtless perplexed, the lord general wrote on 1 November to Crewe and Johnston, the two civilians on the steering group, asking what orders it had received from London. His letter does not survive, but in their reply they informed him that the Committee of Both Kingdoms had instructed the generals to advance past Abingdon to the far side of Oxford to prevent the king's forces being reinforced by Prince Rupert.[28] Quite clearly they had not done so. The lord general's reaction to the news is not known, but his mind-set at the time is revealed by his reply to a letter from a royalist general concerning the exchange of prisoners. The latter had seemingly made some humorous comment about the mishandling of the pursuit stage of the battle. Essex's response was that 'had he been present the king's forces would not have drawn off so quickly'.[29]

The Committee of Both Kingdoms was also concerned about the inactivity of the army group. On the morning of 4 November it took action.[30] A letter was composed, to be endorsed by the two Houses of Parliament, which, while praising the officers and soldiers for their bravery in the battle, warned of an impending rendezvous of the king's forces in the Cotswolds. The generals were therefore to advance at once to prevent this happening. The fact that Denzil Holles, Essex's most influential political ally in the Lower House, carried the letter from the Commons to the Lords for signature suggests very strongly that the lord general, who by then was convalescing in the comfort of his London residence, was in full agreement with its contents.[31]

Within hours, however, the situation changed. Crewe and Johnston arrived unexpectedly at the afternoon meeting of the Committee with news that the council of war had agreed unanimously that it was too late to scatter the king's forces before they regrouped. Instead it recommended a tactical withdrawal. The enemy, strengthened by Rupert's brigade, were unlikely to remain to the west of Oxford. Their most likely move would be to try to recover their artillery train, which they had left behind at Donnington Castle. If the army group returned to Newbury it would be in the best place to pounce on them as they approached. It would also be in better fettle, having enjoyed several days' rest and recuperation billeted in the surrounding villages. This would not be the case if it remained any longer in an exposed position on the downs waiting for the enemy to advance.

The Committee, convinced by the unanimity of the senior officers, recalled their letter before it left London. The new orders were for the army group to return to the Newbury area if the generals thought it best and to wait for the enemy to arrive.[32] This it did, but what followed was an unpleasant surprise, most particularly to their political masters. First, the royalists recovered their artillery train from Donnington Castle without a blow being struck, and then, when they offered to fight a third battle of Newbury on the site of the second battle and again two miles further to the north, the generals refused to be drawn.[33]

It took some time for news of what had happened to reach London, but rumours were soon circulating that all had not gone well. On the 10th the Committee of Both Kingdoms, meeting untypically on a Sunday and with the Earl of Essex present, framed a letter to the army commanders asking for accurate information. The fact that this was the only matter of business recorded in the minutes, and that the letter was not sent, suggests that the meeting was an acrimonious one in which the lord general is most unlikely to have remained silent, given the criticisms for inaction to which he had been subject in the past.[34] A revised version was sent on the 12th in response to two cheerful but cunningly phrased communications from Newbury that put the best possible gloss on what had happened. The tone was one of disappointment, with just a hint of sarcasm: 'We have received your letters concerning the relief of Donnington Castle by the enemy, and are very sorry that they met not with that opposition expected from an army which God hath blessed lately with so happy a victory against them'.[35]

On the following day, with Essex present, the Committee's language was more forthright. The generals were informed that they had brought dishonour on themselves and, by inference, on their political masters and on all who had fought for Parliament against the king. What a contrast to the language used in the letter sent to the lord general after Lostwithiel![36]

The House of Commons, however, was more indulgent. Waller's second-in-command Sir Arthur Haselrig, who had returned from Newbury to plead the generals' case, convinced the MPs that the enemy could not have been prevented from reaching Donnington Castle, and that the decisions not to fight them subsequently were based on sound military reasoning.[37] The lord general, on the other hand, was far from happy and sought some clarification from Phillip Skippon. Skippon responded by exonerating himself and Essex's regiments from blame, thus suggesting that others were responsible for the missed opportunities of 8–10 November. However, though pressed, he would not name names.[38]

Holmes, uniquely, has noted that Essex's military prospects were improving during the course of November, but the evidence he cites is not convincing, comprising wishful thinking on the part of the lord general's friends and an observation by the Venetian ambassador, whose intelligence was often as bad as it was good.[39] As a result the hypothesis has largely been ignored, but a careful reading of the papers of the Committee of Both Kingdoms puts it on a much firmer footing. Almost invariably it met at Derby House, but on the only two occasions when the lord general was present in the latter part of November it met at Essex House. This may have been a mere courtesy in view of the lord general's slow recovery from his illness. More likely it was because listening to his advice on military matters was regarded as essential, given what had happened in the recent campaign.[40]

There were also signs that, instead of being little more than first among equals, as had been the case during the life of the steering group, Essex was now regarded as de facto commander-in-chief of Parliament's armies in the south. On 18 November, and again on the 21st, for example, he was empowered to issue orders to officers in all three armies in the army group.[41] Later in the month it was he rather than Manchester who was authorized by the Committee to take charge of the last military operation of the year, supplying the Abingdon garrison with food and munitions, even though it was largely carried out not by his own troops, but by a brigade of London trained bands and regiments belonging to Manchester's army.[42]

For the lord general such regard was a novel experience, as hitherto his relations with the Committee of Both Kingdoms had been characterized by mutual dislike and distrust, reaching a peak in July and August 1644. Essex's pride had a lot to do with it, but it takes two to tango and its membership was heavily slanted in favour of his critics, even though Waller and Haselrig had been absent on campaign for much of the time. This pattern had prevailed into the autumn with a spat over the funding of Essex's army occurring as late as 8 November,[43] as the Scottish representatives, if not openly hostile towards the lord general, were still reluctant to let go of the idea that men like Sir Henry Vane and Oliver St John, who had negotiated the Solemn League and Covenant, were no longer their friends.[44] But it was not the field commanders' mishandling of the events of 8–10 November that brought about the Committee's change of attitude. The Scottish representatives had turned from being critics of Essex to being his friends, and this was largely due to the Independent stalwart Oliver Cromwell, who had run political rings around them after Marston Moor, as described in Chapter 8. However, the straw that broke the camel's back was probably rumours that Cromwell had deliberately prevented the army group winning an outright victory at Newbury on 27 October, because it was not in the interest of the Independents for it to do so.

Chapter 7

The Birth of the New Model Army

With the lord general's reputation on an upward trajectory, Parliament began the business of army reform. On 19 November the House of Commons ordered the Committee of Both Kingdoms 'to consider the state and condition of all the forces under the command of Parliament and to put them in such a posture as may make them most useful and advantageous to the kingdom'. However, although it was probably the first tentative step in the reform process, it was no more than a general statement of intent, and may have been concerned primarily with ensuring that during the winter the generals quartered their troops in the best places for protecting parliamentary controlled territory against raiding.[1] Gardiner, however, linked it with the Eastern Association's plea for help. Admittedly, the reading of the Association's petition took place immediately before the order to the Committee, but this does not necessarily suggest cause and effect. First, the petition was not a bombshell to bring the house to its senses, as Gardiner implied.[2] The Association's finances had been a matter of serious concern in early October, with Parliament on one occasion switching pistols intended for Essex's army to Oliver Cromwell's regiment of horse.[3] Moreover, the Commons did not treat the petition as something that required immediate attention and a radical solution. It was not until a full fortnight later that the House responded, and then it merely recommended that the Association should increase its income by weeding out corruption.[4]

What almost certainly did push the Commons into more direct and specific action was yet another military embarrassment that occurred a few days later, and one in which its orders had been disregarded not only by Manchester and Waller, but also by their deputies Balfour, Cromwell and Skippon. From 17 to 21 November the Committee of Both Kingdoms received no intelligence whatsoever from the army group, but rumours were circulating that the king's forces were on the move, intent on relieving Basing House, and possibly threatening Windsor Castle, where the garrison had mutinied a few days earlier. Local forces from all over southern England were therefore ordered to converge on Basing to join Waller and Manchester, but instead of the generals stationing their armies in a convenient position for a rendezvous, they gave orders for them to retreat via Reading to the north bank of the Thames prior to dispersing into winter quarters. Unsurprisingly, the provincial regiments, including those in the siege works at Basing, fell back into Surrey and Sussex for fear of being annihilated. A day or so later the royalists completed Parliament's discomfiture by resupplying the garrison using a single brigade of horse which, to its commander's surprise, encountered no opposition whatsoever.[5]

Within hours the MPs had bitten the bullet. The Committee of Both Kingdoms was 'to consider the state and condition of the armies as now disposed and commanded' within the context of the devising of 'a frame or model of the whole militia... as may be most advantageous to the service of the public... notwithstanding any former ordinances'.[6] This expanded on the earlier resolution in two ways. First, it focused on remodelling. Second, it tore up all previous ordinances relating to the armies of Essex, Waller and Manchester.

Two days before the second resolution was passed, Sir William Waller and Oliver Cromwell returned to London, leaving Manchester to supervise the dispersal of the army group into its winter quarters. They immediately went to a meeting of the Committee of Both Kingdoms, which was discussing what reply it should make to a demand from the Commons that it should explain why the autumn campaign had come to such an abrupt and ignominious end.[7] The evidence its members supplied showed that it was the generals, not the Committee, who were responsible for the royalist relief of Basing, but that was not enough. The Commons demanded that Waller and Cromwell should give an account of all the 'proceedings of the armies since their conjunction'; that is, 20 October. It also seems highly likely that the generals informed the Committee that they intended to place most of the blame on the Earl of Manchester. Otherwise it is difficult to explain why Sir Phillip Stapleton, the lord general's principal ally on the Committee, agreed to act as the messenger taking the Committee's evidence to the Commons. This is not surprising, as it was not in the lord general's interest to defend Manchester. He was bound to defend himself, and Cromwell to respond, and in the process new revelations might be made that would further discredit both of them and Waller as well, thus strengthening Essex's claims to be the commander of the reformed militia.[8]

By the end of November, however, the tide had turned once more. The order of events was as follows. First, the return to Westminster of the three commanders in the field who were members of the Committee of Both Kingdoms – Waller, Cromwell, and Haselrig – ended the brief period when Essex and his supporters enjoyed a majority.[9] Second, Essex's opponents in the Commons opened up a new front against him on 28 November by claiming that Captain Anthony Buller, one of his officers, had recruited Roman Catholics into his troop of horse. Adamson makes much of this, but there are no real grounds for thinking that it was anything other than a three-day wonder.[10] At the same time Essex had heard of efforts by his political enemies to implicate him in an earlier, and as yet unresolved, scandal concerning contacts between his officers and the king's in Cornwall, but he met with a stone wall when he enquired about them.[11] Third, the Scottish representatives on the Committee seem to have lost interest in supporting the lord general when he failed to produce lawyers willing to endorse their proposal to sue Cromwell as an 'incendiary' for trying to undermine the Anglo-Scottish alliance.[12] Instead they turned their attention to a new round of peace negotiations with the king. Finally, on 9 December,

Zouch Tate, the chairman of the Commons committee investigating both the
debacle at Lostwithiel and Cromwell's charges against Manchester, proposed the
disenabling principle by which members of both Houses were to give up their
commissions in the armed forces.[13]

The fatal impact of the disenabling principle on Essex's career should it become
law is self-evident, but at the same time his position was being weakened by the
behaviour of his senior infantry officers. Some had come under attack because
of alleged underhand dealings with the royalists during the early stages of the
Lostwithiel operation, and of the collapse of defences along the road to Fowey
at its conclusion. One, Colonel Butler, was under arrest; others were kept in
London as witnesses and not allowed to return to the army; yet others, who were
on the fringes, did return and redeemed their reputation by their conduct at the
second battle of Newbury. Their integrity was, however, attacked by Cromwell,
presumably because three of his infantry color were potentially capable of
strengthening Manchester's case against him by giving evidence critical of his
conduct during the autumn campaign.[14]. His gambit was to blame Essex's men 'in
a roundabout way' for the mishaps of the autumn campaign (which presumably
means in general terms) and also to criticize them for their irreligious behaviour.[15]
However, he soon came to regret his words when it transpired that he was pushing
at an open door. The outcome of the debate was such as to make his position
unassailable, with the MPs firstly accepting his defence against Manchester's
accusations, and then blocking any further action against him by the House
of Lords by raising a procedural issue.[16] A few days later he received a further
assurance of his impregnability when he learned that Scottish efforts to label him
as an incendiary had fallen at the first hurdle.[17] He therefore used his speech in
the debate over the disenabling principle on 9 December to offer an olive branch
to Skippon and his fellow officers in Essex's army, whose military expertise would
be very useful in the future.

Cromwell's words were reported as follows:

> I recommend to your prudence, not to insist upon any complaint or oversight
> of any commander-in-chief upon any occasion whatsoever; for as I must
> acknowledge myself guilty of oversights, they can rarely be avoided in military
> matters.[18]

This has been misread by some of his contemporaries and by a number of
historians from Firth's day onwards as being a peace offering towards the Earl of
Manchester.[19] This is clearly incorrect. On the following day he repeated on oath
the allegations he had made against the earl on 25 November.[20]

A key to understanding the notion Cromwell was articulating lies in the
meaning of the term 'commander-in-chief', which in England in late 1644 was
applied not just to Essex, Manchester and other army commanders, but to
anybody in independent command of a body of men. Thus on 10 October the

Committee of Both Kingdoms used the term when referring to the commanders of the London brigade marching to the army group rendezvous, on 16 November to the commander of a garrison, and soon afterwards to the three lieutenant generals of cavalry in the southern armies.[21]

The other key lies in the clause 'oversights that can rarely be avoided in military matters'. Cromwell was only offering an amnesty to those guilty of mistakes of a tactical nature. There can be no quarrel with this, given the errors that occurred due to ambiguous orders or faulty intelligence, and the difficulties officers had in understanding what was going on outside their immediate surroundings once the fog of black gunpowder had descended on the battlefield. However, at the same time it was an argument that would enable him to escape from the charges levelled against his conduct during the autumn campaign. Manchester might also have been forgiven for the tactics he had used at Newbury on 27 October, but the principal charge against him – deliberately sabotaging the war effort in the interest of a negotiated peace – was on a higher plain altogether as it laid him open to a charge of high treason.

In the event the conciliatory gesture worked. Two of the three colonels who had witnessed the failure of Cromwell's horse to disrupt the royalist retreat at the second battle of Newbury, Skippon and Barclay, did not say a word, and they duly received their reward. Skippon became major general of infantry in the New Model Army and Barclay was named as senior colonel of foot. The third officer, William Davies, did not do so well. His name was put forward as governor of the Isle of Ely, but he was not chosen.[22] Not long afterwards Essex's friends were accusing Skippon of having betrayed his general at Lostwithiel.[23]

But that is not quite the end of the story. The principals had been won over, but nothing yet had been done to satisfy the troop and company commanders whose honour had also been besmirched by Cromwell's accusations. On 21 December a petition was addressed to the House of Lords, signed by forty-six of Essex's lieutenant-colonels, majors and captains and some of his staff officers. It may possibly be seen as a defensive reaction to the loss of their protector and advocate, but it was only four days since Essex's men of business had lost the fight to exempt him from the disenabling provision, which seems a remarkably short period for the petition to have gained so many signatures. The document was concerned primarily with the lord general's army's honour. It claimed that Parliament's failure to provide for the army had caused its members to seize food by force, thus ruining its reputation. In addition the lack of pay had caused army chaplains to quit the army, resulting in the spread of licentiousness.[24] Next came a plea for the settlement of arrears of pay, but also a request, with one eye to the remodelling that was about to take place, that in future something must be done to ensure that armies were paid regularly and on time.[25]

The response is interesting. The Lords sent the petition to the Commons, where after a considerable delay it was debated at length. Some MPs saw it as a breach of parliamentary privilege for soldiers to petition in that manner, but nothing of this nature was recorded in the Journal of the House. Instead, on the following day the sum of £6,000 was voted for the supply of Essex's army.[26] Moreover, signing the petition did not have an adverse effect on the careers of most of those who had signed it. Twenty-six out of the forty-six were offered and accepted commissions in the New Model Army.[27]

* * * * *

The two pieces of legislation that provided the framework for the military reforms were the Self-Denying Ordinance and the New Model Army Ordinance. The former gave legislative force to the disenabling principle; the latter established the new army and the financial arrangements that would underpin it. The first, having passed the Commons on 19 December 1644, was rejected by the Lords on 13 January 1645. The second passed the Commons on 27 January and the Lords on 17 February, while a new self-denying ordinance was passed by both Houses on 3 April.[28] The timeline of both pieces of legislation shows that Gentles was clearly wrong in suggesting that the reformers' priority was to remove Essex and Manchester via the Self-Denying Ordinance, and then to leave the armies in the south much as they were.[29] First, the Committee of Both Kingdoms completed the draft of the military aspects of the New Model Ordinance in meetings held on 31 December and 6 January, including the size of the new army, the number of regiments and how much it would all cost.[30] Thus initially the two ordinances progressed in parallel, not in sequence. Second, it can be inferred from the Committee's minutes for the 6th that the New Model Army was to be a replacement for the three southern armies. While some consideration was given to the money needed to pay garrisons and provincial forces in counties in the south and the Midlands only partly under parliament's control, nothing was said about the ongoing costs of the armies of Essex, Manchester and Waller. Moreover, given the language used in the committee at Cambridge's petition to parliament of 19 November 1644, the collection of £30,000 a month for the New Model Army on top of the levy to maintain the Eastern Association army would have been utterly impossible.[31]

The process by which the military reforms gained parliamentary approval has been portrayed by Snow and others as the remorseless grinding down of the body of opinion hostile to the New Model Army, led in the Lords by the Earl of Essex and in the Commons by his men of business.[32] This is no more than a half-truth. There is no evidence whatsoever that the lord general was opposed to army reform in principle or indeed to the New Model Army Ordinance. Although not as regular a participant in the day-to-day business of the Committee of Both Kingdoms as Manchester or Waller, he attended the two most crucial meetings mentioned above. He was also present on 1 and 7 January, which suggests very strongly that he had not been unhappy with the outcome of the previous days' meetings. Moreover, he sat in the Lords' chamber on 4 and 13–17 February when the New Model Army Ordinance went through its principal legislative stages, and did not register a protest against any of the concessions made by the Lords to the Commons to secure its passage.[33] Admittedly, on 21 January Essex's supporters in the Commons had tried to prevent Sir Thomas Fairfax, lieutenant general of horse in Parliament's army of the north, from being named as the new army's commander-in-chief.[34] However, once the vote on the amendment had been lost nothing further was said about the worthiness of Fairfax's candidature in either House.

What Essex did oppose once the New Model Ordinance had passed both Houses were many of the captains and field officers named in the list that the new commander-in-chief delivered to Parliament for its approval in late February. Stoyle has argued that it was part and parcel of the lord general's ongoing alliance with the Scottish leadership, the objective being to safeguard the careers of many Scottish officers serving in the English armies who had not been selected for the New Model.[35] The word in London was that this was Essex's rationale, and his political associates were indeed describing the New Model officer-list as anti-Presbyterian,[36] but there were other considerations. Almost all the changes the Lords proposed in regiments that had previously fought in Essex's army were designed to do what they claimed, namely to keep experienced and battle-hardened officers in charge of their existing troops and companies.[37]However, Essex lost this battle. The peers, under remorseless pressure from the Commons and from the Corporation of London, which refused to lend money until they relented, accepted Fairfax's list in its entirety in mid-March.[38]

It is now necessary to review the progress of the disenabling principle from start to finish. The original Self-Denying Ordinance was far less complex than the New Model Army Ordinance and it quickly passed through its various stages in the Commons, with an amendment exempting the lord general only failing to pass by seven votes in a House of almost 200.[39] The Lords' subsequent rejection of the ordinance, however, was not merely a kneejerk reaction to the Commons' laying-aside of the Earl of Essex. Gardiner claimed the peers were determined that one of their members should lead the new army into battle, but although the peers argued that they and their forbears held 'the chiefest commands' in English armies, which in the past had fought in defence of liberty, they did not state that the role had been exclusively theirs.[40] They said they were more worried about removing so many experienced members from the armed forces,[41] but I would nevertheless agree with Gardiner that they dug in their heels because of a matter of principle. Unlike MPs, peers could not continue in military service by renouncing their titles. It was also a matter of honour. The terms of the ordinance implied that unresolved issues surrounding the behaviour in Cornwall of Colonel Butler, who commanded Essex's regiment of foot, and the Earl of Manchester's conduct as army commander made it unsafe to entrust members of the peerage with the task of winning the war.

Essex was one of the eight-man committee nominated by the Lords to examine the Self-Denying Ordinance and comment on its contents, but he kept a low profile. It was Manchester who presented the committee's report to the

House, and who also reported on the two meetings with representatives of the Commons held subsequently with the aim of achieving a compromise.[42] However, while discussions were taking place the Lower House tried to apply pressure on the Lords by accusing the two noble generals of disobeying the orders of the Committee of Both Kingdoms concerning the quartering of their troops. Essex replied in typically robust fashion. He excused himself by pleading military necessity and blaming Sir William Waller.[43]

With only four peers registering their disapproval when the Lords rejected the ordinance in mid-January, the Commons took the matter no further until the New Model Army Ordinance had passed both Houses, but no sooner had it done so than a new ordinance embodying the disenabling principle received its first reading in the Lower House. On this occasion, however, it took five weeks to receive its third reading.[44] This was almost certainly because members at the committee stage struggled with a formula that would be acceptable to the Upper House, but not be seen as a climb-down by the Commons. Such discussions almost certainly took place informed by hints that the peers would accept a solution which left the disenabling principle in place, but did not cast doubt on their collective honour.

The Upper House's behaviour since 13 January had showed that it was not opposed to the disenabling principle. On the following day, for example, the peers made an important gesture of goodwill by setting up a committee to frame a disenabling ordinance covering members of the two Houses who had been appointed to non-military offices since 1640.[45] They also did not register a protest against the list of colonels for the New Model Army passed by the Lower House on 22 January, which did not include a single member of either the Lords or the Commons. It can be argued that this shows that the peers were already losing the will to fight their corner, but it is also clear that the list addressed the Lords' concern about the lack of experience among the senior officers in the new army if peers and MPs were excluded.[46] The colonels of horse and foot were all men who already held that rank and almost all had been in command of their regiments on campaign.[47]

The House of Commons finally passed the new Self-Denying Ordinance on 31 March. Members of the two Houses were to resign their commissions in the armed forces within forty days of its becoming law, but the crucial element was that it did not stipulate that peers could not be subsequently appointed to military commands. Sadly its wording cannot be compared with the ordinance rejected by the Lords in January, as no copy of the latter exists. Gentles believed that the two ordinances were identical.[48] However, if there had been such an obvious loophole in the first, it is impossible to understand why so many peers were so hostile towards it. The satisfaction of the Upper House with the new ordinance must also be emphasized. It took only four days to pass through its various stages, during which time the peers did not alter a single word. Moreover, no objections were recorded in the Lords' Journal, a remarkable contrast to the peers' behaviour during votes on the first ordinance and on Fairfax's officers' list.[49]

The civilized way in which the reform process ended meant that Essex and the Commons parted on very good terms. When he surrendered his commission on the day before the Lords gave the Self-Denying Ordinance its third reading, his words were gracious in the extreme. The Lower House responded in a similar manner. Nothing more was said about his conduct in the Lostwithiel campaign, and he was voted very substantial compensation for the financial losses he had suffered as a result of his Welsh Borderland estates being in enemy hands since the start of the war.[50] There is, however, no doubt that the lord general still had anxieties about how the war would progress. In his valedictory message to Parliament he wished the new army well, but feared it might not 'prove as good an expedient to the present distempers as some will have it believed'.[51] He was also almost certainly the 'great person', who had spoken in stronger words, but sorrowfully, to Sir Thomas Fairfax in late April 1645, just as Fairfax was about set out on campaign, to the effect that the New Model Army was facing defeat.[52] Such words would have been unsurprising. A third of the colonels approved by the House of Commons on 22 January had resigned during April and some of their replacements were more junior officers.[53] However, Essex had the reassurance that Parliament would be able to call on him (or one of his fellow peers) should the New Model Army suffer a defeat or should Fairfax, with his many war wounds, be no longer physically capable of commanding it in the field.[54]

Part II

The Second Lord General

Chapter 8

The Politician as Army Officer: Oliver Cromwell 1642–44

It may seem incongruous to write about the early military career of the third lord general before that of the second, but there is a very good reason for doing so. From the beginning there are hints that Cromwell was more than Sir Thomas Fairfax's deputy, and from the summer of 1647 onwards it is clear that the role of commander-in-chief was shared, with the former taking the lead in the political aspects of generalship, while the latter had overall control of military operations, but there are signs of a duumvirate being in place from the start. For example, Cromwell sent to Parliament his own accounts of the battles of Naseby and Langport and of the capture of Bristol, and when, in October 1645, the House of Commons endorsed the operational independence the Committee of Both Kingdoms had given Fairfax in June, Cromwell was given the same authority. Finally, note should be taken of the way in which Cromwell wrote about his general to William Lenthall, the Speaker of the House of Commons, in his Naseby letter. In what can best be described as an assessment of Fairfax's performance, the language he uses is patronising and redolent not of a second-in-command, but of one of the young general's political masters, which of course he was by virtue of his seat in the House of Commons and membership of the Committee of Both Kingdoms.[1] Indeed, it could almost be said that Sir Thomas as commander-in-chief of the new army was the creation of Cromwell the politician, through his passionate support for the disenabling principle, and his sponsorship of the motion in the Commons confirming Fairfax's appointment as general. It is also possible that contained in the words he used in the Naseby letter is a reminder to Lenthall that the young general had performed in ways in which he had promised he would in discussions between them before Fairfax's name was first put to Parliament.

The first paragraph briefly describes the battle and its aftermath, and in it Cromwell uses the first person plural throughout. He then remembered that if he wished to avoid committing the sin of pride he must attribute success entirely to God, and this takes up much of the second paragraph, combined with the hope that Fairfax was of the same opinion, but in the middle is a telling short passage that puts Fairfax in his earthly rather than his heavenly place: 'The general served you with all faithfulness and honour'. Clearly politicians were the masters, generals the servants.[2]

Another reason for discussing Cromwell's early military career in detail at this point is that it is such a powerful illustration of the politician as army officer. I use this phrase not simply because in terms of chronology he was politician first and soldier second, but rather because, for Cromwell, achieving a position of military primacy was the means to an end not an end in itself, and that was to achieve his aspirations for religious liberty. This is the theme of the third paragraph of the letter to Lenthall, which was deleted before Parliament allowed it to be published.[3] In this respect he was the antithesis of Sir Thomas Fairfax, for whom being a successful general was an end in itself, and also possibly of the Earl of Essex while he was lord general, if we discount his ambition to be lord high constable. It should not therefore be surprising that Cromwell drew on skills he had acquired as a politician to smooth his way up the military chain of command. During the first year or so, when he was learning how to be an army officer, these were used to conceal his mistakes, to see off potential critics and rivals, and to ensure that his successes received more credit in the media than was their due. However, his use of the dark arts during the climb from captain to general in the army of the Eastern Association, and its mirror image from keen but second-ranking member of parliament to a political mover and shaker during the remodelling of the southern armies, has been concealed by the shimmering image of Cromwell the man that emerged during the course of the nineteenth century.

From the restoration of the monarchy in 1660 Cromwell had been commended by some but vilified by many, with Lord Clarendon's description of him as a 'bold bad man' being probably the consensual medium. However, at precisely the time when the newly developed techniques of textual analysis were being applied by historians to the traces of the past surviving into the present, and challenging ancient stereotypes, a new stereotype appeared which served as armour formidable enough to protect Cromwell from criticism, other than from Roman Catholics and the odd eccentric advocate of King Charles the Martyr.

Thomas Carlyle laid the foundations in *Letters and Speeches of Oliver Cromwell* (1845). His depiction of Cromwell as superman received scholarly clout in S.R. Gardiner's *History of the Great Civil War* and *History of the Commonwealth* (1893, 1903), and secured a wider audience with C.H. Firth's full-length popular biography *Oliver Cromwell and the Rule of the Puritans in England* (1900). Their message was that, although Cromwell failed to achieve the Puritan revolution he had wanted, as a champion of religious and political liberty against absolute monarchy, as the founder of the British Empire, and as the first person to unite England, Scotland and Ireland, he shaped the future of the lands he had conquered and then governed as lord protector. Moreover, he embodied a set of values that were universally admired. To Carlyle he was 'not a man of falsehoods but a man of truths'; to Gardiner he was among the noblest of men with the noblest of motives; and to Firth his acts showed the 'plain heroic magnitude of his mind'.[4] Thus, having been effectively canonized, any shortcomings or inconsistencies in his behaviour could be explained away or dismissed as sad necessity.

A hundred years of research and the passing into oblivion of the second and third historical developments for which he was given credit have necessarily dented the late-Victorian image of the man, but historians continue to lean over backwards to give Cromwell the benefit of the doubt, even in relation to his treatment of the Irish. Typical is his entry in the *Oxford Dictionary of National Biography* in which John Morrill, having noted how he abandoned ally after ally during the course of his career, still managed to sum him up as 'a man of towering integrity'.[5] Four years later things had moved on a little. In a speech commemorating the 350th anniversary of his death, Cromwell was declared guilty at times of 'cynical, low, political cunning, and sheer military muscle and legal chicanery', but even so this had to be weighed in the balance against his achievements and aspirations, some of which were for the good of his country.[6] However, there are now stronger signs that the traditional stereotype is losing its power to deflect criticism.[7] However, Cromwell's reputation need not necessarily suffer, as regard for him as an army commander has, if anything, been enhanced by recent publications.[8]

But why not begin the study of Cromwell in 1645 rather than 1642? The reason is that the first two and a half years of his military career provide excellent illustrations of his modus operandi at a time when he was not influential enough to hide the evidence.

* * * * *

In late August 1642, Oliver Cromwell, at the age of forty-two and with no known military experience, received a commission from the Earl of Essex to raise a troop of horse for Parliament's field army.[9] He had done so in time for the battle of Edgehill two months later, but it arrived late on the battlefield and then withdrew, possibly before coming to grips with the enemy. Like a number of other troops in Essex's army, Cromwell's was seconded in December or January 1643 to one of the newly established major-generalships as part of Parliament's strategy to establish control over as large a geographical area as possible. In his case it was Lord Grey of Wark's Eastern Association, which included Cambridge, his Parliamentary constituency, and soon afterwards he was commissioned as colonel.[10]

If his seizure of plate being sent by the University of Cambridge to the king in August 1642 is discounted on the grounds that he was still to all intents and purposes the local MP leading an ad hoc posse, Cromwell's first experience of independent command was in Norfolk in early 1643 where he first secured Norwich and then forced the surrender of the principal gathering of royalists in East Anglia at Lowestoft a few days later.[11] There is little doubt that so far Cromwell had been in contact with royalist sympathisers that were even less well organized than those Waller was facing in the south of England at exactly the same time. By April, however, he had moved his operations to the Fenlands, where he was acting as Lord Grey's deputy, but after overrunning a small royalist garrison at Crowland in south Lincolnshire he fixed his quarters at Peterborough.[12] There he received orders from the lord general to join forces with troops of cavalry stationed in Lincolnshire, Leicestershire and Derbyshire, to intercept the first convoy of munitions from the north of England on its way to Oxford, the safe arrival of which was vital to the king's continued presence in the Thames valley. However, several attempts to agree on a place of rendezvous failed, and the convoy reached Oxford without incident.[13]

The Lincolnshire men blamed Cromwell for taking his time, while Cromwell blamed Lord Grey of Groby for worrying too much about the fate of Leicester, his headquarters, if he strayed too far from the town. Grey's concern is not surprising given that Cromwell expected them to join forces at Spalding, forty miles to the east, but conveniently close to Cromwell's troops, who were less than fifteen miles away between Crowland and Peterborough. Moreover, Spalding was a long way from the royalist convoy's route to Oxford, which was likely to be from Newark to Banbury. It suggests that Cromwell saw Grey's troops as providing an escort for East Anglian troops heading towards a larger rendezvous with troops from north Lincolnshire and east Yorkshire somewhere near Grantham. This hints at timorousness, but it can be viewed as common sense given the aggressive raiding carried out in south and central Lincolnshire during April by royalist horse based at Newark. There would be no risk of Grey's force being attacked, as it would be approaching Spalding from the south via Stamford. But if so, why did Cromwell not offer to join Lord Grey at Leicester using the same route?

Alternatively, Cromwell may have been putting Lord Grey off because he had unfinished business in the Fens. This was what the Lincolnshire officers thought, and the future turncoat Sir John Hotham junior provided a possible motive, in the jest that Cromwell was 'still kept eating up the fat clergy of Peterborough', and despite Hotham's reputation for sarcastic language combined with arrogance, there may be some truth in it. Cromwell's men spent their time at Peterborough pillaging the cathedral and destroying images, vestments and stained-glass windows.[14] To be cynical, this was just the sort of behaviour to stoke up the religious zeal Cromwell wanted to see in his troops, as evidence of ideological commitment to the parliamentary cause, and at the same time doing it would destroy any vestiges of superstition that such behaviour would immediately be followed by divine retribution.

Nevertheless, there was compensation on 13 May when a scrap at Grantham between royalist horse from Newark and parliamentary horse from Yorkshire, Lincolnshire and East Anglia gave Cromwell's regiment its first serious victory, which it achieved by charging the enemy 'at a pretty round trot'. Charging the enemy was not a move initiated by Cromwell. It was a collective decision, taken after considerable discussion, as he freely admitted in his own account of the engagement. Another account, however gives the credit to Lord Willoughby of Parham, who had fought in the Edgehill campaign as a colonel of horse, and who would have been as aware as Cromwell of what Sir William Balfour had achieved by charging the enemy. Interestingly, the only accounts of the engagement to get into print were written by Cromwell himself and by three men he had previously rescued from Crowland, who unsurprisingly had nothing but praise for the colonel.[15]

There followed an operational faux pas, from which Cromwell was lucky to escape with his honour and military reputation intact. The force that had triumphed at Grantham hung about in the Newark area for several weeks, where it was joined by mounted troops from Leicestershire, Nottinghamshire and Derbyshire. They were ordered to go to the aid of Lord Fairfax, the Parliament's lord general in the north, who by storming a royalist brigade quartered at Wakefield had won a major victory against the odds. As a result he had brought down on himself the wrath of the king's general in the north, the Earl of Newcastle, and desperately needed reinforcements before he was overwhelmed. However, the commanders of the various contingents remained where they were in the Nottingham area and then broke up on about 28 June. As a result Fairfax's army was destroyed at Adwalton Moor on 30 June. To make matters worse, a second munitions convoy held up at Newark for weeks by the combined force was able to march to Oxford unmolested when Cromwell and his fellow commanders returned to their respective bases. The final blow fell when Sir John Hotham junior, one of the commanders in the combined force, was brought down by clear evidence that he had been in treasonable correspondence with the Earl of Newcastle in the hope of gaining generous enough terms to change sides. According to John Hutchinson, the Nottinghamshire commander, he and Cromwell became suspicious and alerted the Committee of Safety. An order duly came for Hotham to be arrested. Accompanying it was the very experienced Scottish officer Sir John Meldrum, who then took charge of military operations in the middle Trent valley.

Oliver Cromwell further redeemed himself by a military success, but one that was seemingly not his alone. Back in Lincolnshire in late July he and Meldrum were ordered by Lord Willoughby, the local commander-in-chief, to relieve the besieged garrison at Gainsborough. There followed a cavalry engagement on 28 July with some of the Earl of Newcastle's crack regiments of horse, in which Cromwell handled his regiment in a consummate manner. The long letter in which he described the engagement shows him displaying great tactical skill in the handling of his reserves and in regrouping and redirecting units such that they were able to perform more than one task during a battle, but there are some inconsistencies in the narrative compared with the official report of the battle, which gave more credit to the Lincolnshire cavalry. In addition Cromwell makes no mention of Meldrum, who seems to have been in overall charge of the engagement.[16] But although the fight at Gainsborough was a clear success, it was followed by operational disaster. At the approach of much larger royalist forces, Cromwell and his comrades were forced to retreat, abandoning first Gainsborough and then Lincoln, with Willoughby's infantry finally finding refuge in Boston on the coast and at Spalding, while Cromwell's cavalry returned to Peterborough sixty miles to the south.

The fortunes of Cromwell and his regiment improved with the reorganisation of the Eastern Association army under its new commander, the Earl of Manchester. Cromwell was charged with organising the defence of the Lincolnshire coastline from the Humber to the Wash, an easier task than had been anticipated, as instead of marching south Newcastle set siege to Hull. Nevertheless, he had to contend with several brigades of the earl's cavalry and the regiments based at Newark, which outnumbered him, but in late September odds moved in his favour when he was joined by Sir Thomas Fairfax and the Northern army cavalry, shipped across the Humber estuary from Hull, and then by the Earl of Manchester with the Eastern Association infantry. On 11 October Cromwell and Fairfax won what was probably the largest engagement in the Civil Wars involving cavalry and dragoons alone, at Winceby to the north of Boston,[17] but Cromwell's personal role in the victory was limited. He was dismounted early in the mêlée and lucky not to be killed, while the routing of the royalists was the work of Fairfax's cavalry rather than his own. Nevertheless, he got most of the praise in the London journals.[18]

Cromwell was militarily inactive during the winter months, but very busy at Westminster fighting political battles on behalf of the Eastern Association army. First, as mentioned earlier among the lord general's misfortunes, Parliament decided that it should be an independent command and thus need no longer obey Essex's orders. Second, the Association was permitted to raise a much larger army of 14,000 men. Next Lord Willoughby of Parham, who had been senior commander in Lincolnshire as Essex's deputy, was made subordinate to the Earl of Manchester instead, and, unwilling to accept what he saw as a demotion, he resigned. Finally both Cromwell and Manchester were chosen to serve on the parliamentary alliance's new executive body, the Committee of Both Kingdoms.[19]

Cromwell's record as a skilled political operator was significantly enhanced by his work in revealing Lord Willoughby's incompetence and piloting the Eastern Association ordinance through the Commons. His reward was to be commissioned as lieutenant general of cavalry in Manchester's army, but whether or not political gains were part and parcel of a wider scheme by religious radicals to turn the Eastern Association army into a counterweight to the Scottish army, which crossed the border into England on 19 January, is by no means certain. Nevertheless, the baleful consequences of aspirations for religious freedom if the Scottish army quickly won the war for the coalition must surely have been at the centre of Cromwell and his associates' minds in the fledgling war party in the winter of 1643/4. It would not therefore have been surprising for them to have taken counter-measures, but for these to be effective they needed to be sure of the Earl of Manchester, and it is almost certainly this that fixes in time the comments Manchester used in his defence against Cromwell at the end of the year, namely that he hated the Scots more than the royalists, and that he would prefer an army that contained no Presbyterians. Alarmed by this kind of pressure, Manchester, who was a senior and experienced politician and a great admirer of the achievements of the Scottish revolution, appointed Lawrence Crawford as his major general of infantry. As determined an individual as Cromwell, and as convinced in his religious opinions as his fellow Scots, he quickly put the cat among the pigeons by persuading Manchester to dismiss Lieutenant Colonel Packer from his own regiment of foot because he was a Baptist. Cromwell protested, but bided his time. For the moment he concentrated on building up military muscle. In this he was helped by the fact that the increase in the size of the army meant that he could increase the size of his brigade from under 2,000 to about 4,000 horse, divided into several regiments. In addition a new infantry regiment was raised, many of whose officers were convinced Independents.[20]

At Marston Moor Cromwell's cavalry did very well in routing the wing of the enemy army facing them, and then in taking a major part in the destruction of the rest of the royalist army. Immediately afterwards Major Thomas Harrison galloped off to London with news of the victory. The Eastern Association army had won the battle, while the Scottish army had fled the battlefield, and this was taken up in only a slightly less extreme form in accounts written by Thomas Stockdale and Manchester's chaplain Simeon Ash. The Scots were incensed, and rightly so, as there is little doubt that a brigade of Scottish horse under Lieutenant General David Leslie, described patronisingly by Cromwell as 'a few Scots in our rear', also played an important part. A more balanced view emerged in later accounts, such as those written by Major General Lumsden and Captain Stewart, but Cromwell continued to take almost all the credit, and his enhanced military reputation brought with it political gains. When he arrived back in London in September the Commons thanked him profusely, declaring in good providential language that he was God's special instrument in obtaining 'that great victory at York'. Earlier in the day it had passed a resolution that there should be a measure of toleration for Independents in the new state church, who could not fully accept the rigid structures of Scottish Presbyterianism.[21] The devil turned out to be in the detail, but it was a first step towards what Cromwell and his fellow war party members wanted from the war.

There remains, however, the possibility that the rapturous media coverage concealed an incident during the battle that did not put Cromwell in a good light. There is no doubt that after his regiments had routed the first line of royalist horse, he sustained a wound when his regiment was charged by Prince Rupert's reserves. He left the battlefield for treatment, but he returned and there can be little doubt that he and David Leslie masterminded the final stage of the battle in which the remaining royalist units were snuffed out one by one, but there are conflicting narratives as to how success on the left wing was transformed into outright victory.

Historians in general accept that the wound Cromwell sustained was slight, that he was not off the battlefield for long, and that he was heavily involved in the attack on the royalist centre and left wing. However, General Crawford, who had routed the enemy infantry facing him on the left of the allied infantry line at the same time as the left wing of the allied cavalry routed the horse, claimed that Cromwell, seeing the enemy cavalry in flight, was uncertain what to do next, but that his preference was to disengage, presumably to cover the retreat of the rest of the allied armies, who were clearly suffering at the hands of the royalists. Crawford, however, insisted that he should not remain stationary, but charge the enemy units to his right. Cromwell replied that he could not do so because of his wound, whereupon Crawford took charge of the Ironsides, led them into the attack, and the battle turned decisively in the allies' favour. We only have Crawford's word for this at second hand, and it has been almost universally dismissed on the grounds that Crawford and Denzil Holles, who reported it, were bitter enemies of the lieutenant general. But this is a clear case of leaning over backwards in respect to the traditional stereotype of Cromwell. I would not discount Holles's testimony, given the utter conviction with which he narrated the incident. Three times he had heard Crawford make the accusation, and on the fourth occasion it had been within Cromwell's hearing.[22] What should have followed was a duel. This clearly did not happen, or Holles would have mentioned it. The inference is therefore that Crawford was telling the truth.

The circumstances were such that the fourth incident could not have occurred any earlier than September 1644, when Manchester, Crawford and Cromwell were in London for Holles to have observed it. However, if Crawford had been saying the same thing immediately after the battle it would help to explain the rumpus that threatened to tear Manchester's army apart during August. For several months after Marston Moor the Eastern Association cavalry was inactive while the infantry set siege to and captured various royalist garrisons in Derbyshire and south Yorkshire. In Crawford's absence supervising the sieges Cromwell began an intrigue against him, which Manchester successfully quashed, but his successful defence of Crawford created a breach between him and his lieutenant general that was to have profound consequences. Cromwell decided to use all his political skills to bring about Manchester's downfall, with the object presumably, as his second-in-command, of taking his place.[23] This was probably what he was hinting in late September when he assured John Lilburne that his hope for revenge on Manchester for humiliating him in an incident that happened two months earlier would soon be realised.[24]

* * * * *

It could be argued that the story so far has only chipped away at Cromwell's honour and accomplishments, and that some of the evidence is circumstantial or possibly prejudiced, but from August 1644 errors and inconsistencies in his and his supporters' accounts of events can be found in the unprecedented levels of disinformation they included in their effort to discredit the Earl of Manchester, which can be shown to be such because it can be checked against independent sources. In addition there was an unprecedented level of opportunity for the man to incriminate himself, because he was forced to be his own advocate on five separate occasions between the speech in the Commons on 25 November, and a lengthy written denunciation of the Earl which can be dated to mid-December as it addresses some of the charges Manchester made against him.[25]

However, it was Cromwell, not Manchester, who was believed. MPs uncommitted to the war or the peace party, and citizens of London who were worried by the course of events in the second half of 1644, were eager receptors of a simple explanation. Others, who may not have believed Cromwell's narrative, were willing to go along with it to punish what Parliament and the Committee of Both Kingdoms saw as his arrogance during the four week preceding the grand rendezvous, while for Cromwell's fellow senior officers in the Newbury campaign Manchester was a convenient if fortuitous scapegoat for their own mistakes and misdemeanours.

Cromwell's first accusations relate to the period between the three allied armies going their separate ways in late July 1644 after the surrender of York, and before the news of the disaster at Lostwithiel reaching Manchester's army headquarters at Lincoln on or before 8 September. During August the earl failed to obey the Committee of Both Kingdoms' orders to march on Chester to disrupt Prince Rupert's attempt to create a new army after the losses sustained at Marston Moor. He had also refused the suggestion of the East Midlands county committees that he should set siege to Newark. In fact it was Manchester's cavalry commanders who had rejected the idea of a march on Chester, while the Committee had turned down Manchester's request that his army should besiege Newark.[26]

The first two allegations were merely illustrations of Manchester's reluctance to vigorously pursue the war after Marston Moor. Much more serious, and much more convincing, was the allegation that he deliberately slowed down the pace of his army's march south. As a result the king's armies were able to progress as far east as Winchester before the Committee could put in place an army group large enough to fight them. Not only had the chance of pinning the king in the West Country until the end of the campaigning season been lost, but he had also then gone on to relieve several of his garrisons that were on the point of surrendering. Here Cromwell was on firm ground, as there was plentiful evidence of Manchester's procrastination in the letters that passed between him and the Committee of Both Kingdoms. Moreover, Sir William Waller, who had come under some criticism for doing nothing to impede the king's armies' march eastwards, would back him up, and did so in his speech to the Commons on 25 November and in the evidence he subsequently gave to the Commons committee investigating Cromwell's allegations. However, Manchester had good reason for thinking that he and Waller were not strong enough in infantry to face the king's armies until reinforced by a strong brigade of London trained band regiments and the Earl of Essex's regiments still busy recovering from their ordeal in Cornwall in south

Hampshire.[27] Additionally, there is strong circumstantial evidence that Cromwell had agreed with him, or at least kept his mouth shut, but whether this was because he believed Manchester was right, or because it would help incriminate him, is unclear. However, he was cunning enough to cover his own tracks by making sure, through his war party allies, that letters which incriminated him were not copied into the Committee of Both Kingdoms' letter book.[28]

Cromwell's subsequent take on the events of late September and early to mid-October 1644 in the evidence given to the House of Commons' investigating committee was that if the Eastern Association army had marched westwards immediately after he and his general had visited London in mid-September, the army group that came together in Dorset would have been strong enough not only to confine the victors of Lostwithiel to Devon and Cornwall, but also to defeat them in battle if that was necessary. Manchester, however, had dragged his feet to such an extent that by 14 October the bulk of the Eastern Association army was no further west than the Kennet valley between Newbury and Reading, whereas Waller, too weak to take on the royalists alone, had fallen back into Wiltshire. Yet Cromwell's behaviour points strongly towards his being convinced at the very least that there were more important priorities than joining Waller as quickly as possible. The only evidence that he was passionately committed to a swift advance into the West Country in the month before the grand rendezvous is in a letter written in early September.[29]

The first sign that Cromwell had lost his enthusiasm for an aggressive move against the king's armies can be seen in the Glenham scare. On 25 September the Eastern Association horse, under Cromwell's command, were quartered to the east and north of Oxford, on the orders of the Committee of Both Kingdoms, covering the siege of Banbury. On that date, in a letter to the Committee, Manchester questioned the wisdom of doing so. All that remained with the main body of his army, at that time in the Uxbridge area, was sufficient horse to guard his infantry from attack. If he sent these to join Waller, as he had been instructed, it would be dangerous for him to advance any further towards a rendezvous with Sir William.[30] The clear implication is that the Banbury brigade was in the wrong place. It should be either speeding towards Waller's army, or with Manchester so that he could send westwards the horse that he had with him.

While the Committee of Both Kingdoms was considering this, it received a letter from Cromwell that no longer survives, to the effect that Sir Thomas Glenham, the former royalist governor of York, had left Newark with a powerful body of horse and was on his way south.[31] What Cromwell would not have said was that the news was a month out of date. In late August Sir Samuel Luke, in his capacity as Essex's scoutmaster, had reported Glenham's arrival at Newark, but it soon became clear that the information was incorrect. Prince Rupert had sent Glenham in the opposite direction to serve as governor of Carlisle.[32] The only thing that can possibly have breathed new life into the false intelligence report was the return to Newark in late September of weak cavalry regiments which had fought at Marston Moor and subsequently gone to Chester with Prince Rupert.[33] Nevertheless, Cromwell managed to convince the Committee of Both Kingdoms that they were Glenham's brigade, and he duly ordered a general rendezvous of mounted troops in the south Midlands to take place at Towcester, just to the south of Northampton.[34]

The Glenham threat was known to be false by 1 October.[35] Two days later the Commons ordered Manchester to withdraw all his forces from the Banbury area apart from 500 cavalry and dragoons. The remainder were to join the rest of the Eastern Association army, which by that time was quartered in the villages between Reading and Newbury. On the 7th the order was changed. Cromwell, who had remained at Banbury, was to immediately join Waller in Dorset with all the Eastern Association horse, whether he had received instructions from Manchester or not, apart from 500 that were to act as an escort for the Eastern Association infantry as it too marched westwards.[36]

What followed indicates at best a lack of urgency on Cromwell's part, at worst a deliberate refusal to be drawn any further west than the Kennet valley. Instead of heading for a rendezvous with Waller, Cromwell remained where he was. It took a second order to get him moving, but he headed not for Salisbury, where Waller was then quartered, having fallen back before the king's forces as they advanced, but for Reading, and by a most circuitous route through the Chilterns and so over the Thames at Henley. In consequence Cromwell did not join his general until the 13th, while his cavalry and dragoons did not arrive until the following day.[37] There is no evidence that they then rode westwards following other Eastern Association horse, which Manchester had already sent to join Waller a day or so earlier.[38] Instead the Banbury contingent remained near Reading until the grand rendezvous of Essex's, Manchester's and Waller's forces with the London brigade at Basingstoke on the 21st.

In connection with this episode it is interesting and possibly significant that a letter written by Manchester to the Committee on the 16th no longer exists. Although ordered to be read in both Houses of Parliament, it was not, and neither was it copied into the Committee's letter book. Its place in the letter chain means that it would almost certainly have provided information about Cromwell's movements, and possibly explained why he had disobeyed clear instructions from the Committee to join Waller.[39] Its disappearance, and also that of the letter of 26 September which had revived the Glenham scare, meant that the narrative Cromwell and his supporters gave to the world on 25 November and afterwards would be difficult to dispute. All that remained on record was a paper trail that pointed to Manchester singlehandedly protesting against orders to assist Waller in halting the royalist armies' advance and then neglecting to carry them out.[40]

Once the army group had come together, Cromwell and his supporters argued that he consistently recommended attacking the enemy, but was frustrated at every turn by Manchester, who chaired the council of war after Essex's departure due to illness. However, evidence dating from the campaign itself rather than from the ensuing inquest provides plentiful evidence of Cromwell's caution and his direct involvement in decision-making that caused good opportunities to be missed. During the battle at Newbury Cromwell's cavalry did next to nothing, and when the royalists began leaving the battlefield under the cover of darkness his regiments, which were close by, refused to attack them. There is no doubt that Cromwell and his fellow commanders knew that a retreat was taking place, but despite the entreaties of Essex's three officers, who had first raised the alarm, they received no orders to disrupt the proceedings. At first the two civilian members of the steering committee were keen to do something, but in the end they were dissuaded, presumably by the three generals with the main body, Waller, Haselrig and Cromwell.[41] Manchester bore no responsibility for the decision as he was two miles away on the far side of the enemy army with the rest of the army group.

Cromwell hinted that fear of fighting in the dark was the reason the steering committee decided to do nothing, but this is difficult to understand given that there was a bright moon until about 11 o'clock.[42] Moreover, night attacks, if not an everyday occurrence during the English Civil Wars, were not uncommon. Colonel Chudleigh had discomforted half of the king's Cornish army in May 1643 while it was on a night march across Sourton Down,[43] and only five days before the second battle at Newbury Waller's Captain Fincher managed, under the cover of darkness, to beat up some royalist horse and capture or kill sixty of them.[44]

The next charge against Manchester was that he was reluctant to follow the enemy to prevent them regrouping in the days immediately after the battle. The army group certainly took its time, and there were strong logistical reasons for it, but there was also a division in the steering committee as to how to proceed, which caused a delay. Two of the six members, Waller and Haselrig, wrote an impassioned letter to the Committee of Both Kingdoms registering their protest against the decision not to vigorously pursue the enemy to prevent them regrouping. They clearly did not have Cromwell's support, or they would surely have mentioned it.[45]

From that point until the end of the campaign on 20 November Cromwell and his supporters on one side, and Manchester's and his on the other, give very different narratives of events. Cromwell blamed Manchester for not fighting a third battle of Newbury when the king's forces returned to the battlefield on 9 November, and for abandoning the siege of Basing House eleven days later. Manchester blamed Cromwell for withdrawing his patrols from the Berkshire downs, which would have given early warning of the king's advance, and then refusing to fight because his cavalry were worn out by the campaign and the bad weather. My inclination is to believe Manchester rather than Cromwell, as there are two independent pieces of evidence in his favour that pre-date Cromwell's speech of 25 November and Manchester's response. First, Major General Skippon, writing to the Earl of Essex on 10 November about the failure to fight a third battle of Newbury, blamed the cavalry for arriving too late in the day to attack the enemy. Second, the order from the army group commanders ordering the withdrawal of their troops covering the siege of Basing House was signed by Oliver Cromwell. It would have disappeared from the record had Sir Simons D'Ewes not copied it in his diary.[46]

Such machinations achieved their purpose in one respect. Manchester defended himself with gusto, backed by a majority in the House of Lords, but he was in disgrace for the next six months and the case against him was never closed. Fear that it might be reopened may explain some anomalies in his behaviour in the late 1640s when he was speaker of the House of Lords. However, if Cromwell's purpose in attacking the earl was purely to gain command of the Eastern Association army, it was overtaken by events, namely the reform of the militia. Even before he rose in the House on 25 November the writing was on the wall. However, by then he had to go ahead with his allegations against the earl. His reputation and that of his fellow generals was at stake and they all had something they did not want brought out into the open.

Chapter 9

The New Commander-in-chief

Sir Thomas Fairfax, son of Ferdinando Lord Fairfax, Parliament's lord general of the north, and lieutenant general of cavalry in Parliament's northern army for the past two years, was acclaimed as commander-in-chief of the New Model Army by a House of Commons vote on 21 January 1645 and was confirmed in post by both Houses in the New Model Army Ordinance passed on 17 February.[1]

The background to Fairfax's appointment has recently been subject to a major revision. In the past he was regarded as a man acceptable to a wide range of opinion in Parliament because he was essentially non-political. There were no doubts about the depth of his affection for Protestantism and for the reform of the church as it had been in the 1630s, but in his religious beliefs he could not be described as Presbyterian, Independent or anything more radical. His choice to replace the Earl of Essex was seen as a bit of a surprise as he was little known in London. He did, however, have the immense advantage over his predecessor of not having a track record of disobedience towards Parliament or the Committee of Both Kingdoms. Moreover, Sir Thomas was clearly eligible for promotion. He had shown an ability to inspire his men by his braveness in battle and his resilience in defeat. He had a string of victories to his credit in independent command of small armies, in which he had showed boldness and tactical flexibility, and in the case of his campaign in Cheshire he had welded a disparate and rundown mix of regiments into an effective fighting force that in January 1644 had gone on to inflict a major defeat on an army of professional soldiers from Ireland at Nantwich. There were also no doubts whatsoever about his commitment to outright victory.[2]

It is now known that politically Sir Thomas and his father had become increasingly close to the war party as they worked together to secure the trial and execution of their Yorkshire rivals, Sir John Hotham senior and junior, who had conspired with the enemy and were about to change sides.[3] A further link was with Oliver Cromwell. Cromwell and Lord Fairfax had worked together to uncover the Hothams' plot in June 1643. Cromwell had visited Hull in September when it was being besieged by Newcastle's army and he had fought alongside Sir Thomas at the battle of Winceby the following month. All three had been at the siege or York and the battle of Marston Moor where they found that they had a shared antipathy towards their Scottish allies. Sir Thomas also shared Cromwell's dislike of Lawrence Crawford, but in his case it was for military rather than religious reasons.

Furthermore, Sir Thomas was not an unknown quality in London. Although his campaigning had taken him no farther south than Lincolnshire, his deeds had been extolled in the London journals from the start of the war, and they did what they could to lessen the impact of his bad experiences by emphasising his bravery and his commitment to the cause. Finally, the application of the disenabling principle enshrined in the Self-Denying Ordinance would make Sir Thomas the most senior English officer serving in Parliament's armies.[4]

There was, however, a reverse side of the coin that is easily forgotten. First, other names must have been mentioned, and there is a hint of this in James Chaloner's letter to Lord Fairfax, written on 14 January, in which he expressed the hope that nobody who was not an Englishman would be chosen as commander-in-chief.[5] Second, Sir Thomas's extensive war wounds, though evidence that he was under divine protection, could have told against his candidature, as there was the risk that he might not be strong enough to command the army in the field on a long campaign. In addition, Sir Thomas's track record to the end of 1644 cannot be described as fault-free. Like Cromwell, his victories were nowhere near as impressive as they were to be during his time as commander-in-chief of the New Model Army. In the final month of 1642 and the first half of 1643, successes and failures alternated, culminating in the destruction of his father's army by Newcastle at Adwalton Moor on 30 June. The resilience with which the Fairfaxes bounced back once they had reached the safety of the Hull garrison a few days later has been much praised, and from then until June 1644 Sir Thomas had success after success, first at Winceby, then at Nantwich, and finally at Selby in April when, in cooperation with his father, he destroyed the corps Newcastle had left behind to keep Yorkshire secure while he faced the Scottish invasion. At Marston Moor, however, the personal courage he showed could not conceal the fact that the right wing of the allied army he commanded had been routed.[6] The Fairfaxes' infantry had fared even worse and, although father and son were named among the victorious generals, it took the northern army months to recover. As a result it was in no state to move south to take part in the autumn campaign, but given its outcome it was probably best for Sir Thomas not to have been there.

Thus I prefer to see Sir Thomas as becoming commander-in-chief by default, as there were no other serious candidates. Nevertheless, his appointment had to be choreographed, given the residual loyalty to the Earl of Essex not only in the Lords, but also in the Commons, as shown by the war party's narrow victory over the amendment to exempt him from the provisions of the Self-Denying Ordinance.[7]

Evidence of politics that promoted Sir Thomas's cause can only be dimly discerned in correspondence between members of the war party, and indeed the first sign pointed towards a different outcome. Lord Wharton, one of the leaders of the war party, dropped a heavy hint to Lord Fairfax in a letter written just after the Commons passed the Self-Denying Ordinance that Sir Thomas would succeed him as commander of the army of the north.[8] Three weeks later James Chaloner, also writing to Lord Fairfax, assumed that Sir Thomas would be lieutenant general of cavalry in the New Model Army.

If Sir Thomas was being considered as commander-in-chief, it seems a little odd that this was not mentioned in Wharton's letter. However, naming him was not something to be committed idly to paper, for fear that it would be intercepted or read before it reached York and hazard the political campaign by raising questions about his lack of experience.[9] There is, however, a gentle hint of the very high opinion Wharton had of Sir Thomas in his letter: 'I may say that I wish to God we had a successor in all places as your lordship will have'. Lord Fairfax's reply does not survive, but the wording of Wharton's next letter - 'the worst news I can send you is that there is no news' - suggests that Lord Fairfax had either suggested his son as the commander of the new army, or asked if he was in the running.[10]

* * * * *

The question of Sir Thomas Fairfax's authority has already been raised with respect to Oliver Cromwell's position in the army, but there is a bigger issue: the extent to which he was his own man rather than the mouthpiece of war party politicians. An extreme view was that taken by Denzil Holles, a leader of the peace party, writing while in exile after the first army coup of June 1647. His most damning evidence consisted of sentiments reported to him as having been expressed by Sir Arthur Haselrig, one of the leaders of the war party. Fairfax was 'fit for their turns to do whatever they would have him do without considering or being able to judge whether (an action) was honourable or honest'. In addition, he was 'hewed out of the block (of wood)' to suit their purposes. Holles, naturally, took this to mean that the new commander-in-chief was 'resolved to do whatever those his masters should bid him'.[11] At the opposite extreme are Hopper and Daxon, who agree that Fairfax followed the war party line, but through conviction. Thinking outside the box I am moving towards a third position, namely that Fairfax, though in agreement with much of the war party's programme, was also its prisoner and then the prisoner of the faction that took power after the second army coup of December 1648.[12]

One way of assessing Fairfax's independence of thought is to analyse the results of the first task he was set by Parliament on 17 February when it passed the New Model Army Ordinance: to compile a list of troop and company commanders, a task he was understood to have completed by the 25th.[13] Fairfax's best informed biographers vehemently assert or strongly imply that the officer list was entirely his handiwork, but they provide nothing in the way of evidence, and neither does Gentles, who similarly does not question the notion that the officers were selected by anybody other than Sir Thomas.[14] However, given the circumstances of Fairfax's appointment, namely that he owed it to the war party, and what is known about his character and his knowledge of the officers in Essex's and Waller's armies, I doubt very much if he had the self-assurance or the ability to compile the list single-handedly. Time may also have been a factor, but Fairfax could have been working on the list before arriving in the capital, and he would have known something about the officers in the Eastern Association cavalry because of past acquaintance with them in Lincolnshire in the autumn of 1643 and in the force covering the siege of York in 1644, but less about the infantry because they did not arrive at the siege until much later. There were also gaps in the list that look as if they may have been caused by lack of time to gather information. The biggest was the names of the company commanders in Colonel Weldon's regiment of foot, which is not surprising as it was undertaking garrison duties at Plymouth at the time. However, there is not enough internal or external evidence to show whether it was lack of knowledge on Fairfax's part, or a general lack of knowledge in London, that explains the gaps in the list.[15]

A more worrying sign that the new commander-in-chief was not the sole author, or indeed the author, is provided by the distinct lack of emphasis on Fairfax's ownership of the list as it made its way through the various stages of scrutiny before being approved by Parliament. It was not until it had passed all its stages in the Commons, and was being savaged in the House of Lords, that the former personalized it, presumably in order to make the Lords think about whether their nominations were an insult to Fairfax's honour after they had accepted his nomination as commander-in-chief a month before, whereupon the Upper House backed down and allowed Fairfax to name replacements for the officers they had rejected.[16] This raises the possibility that the list merely had Fairfax's name affixed to it, having been prepared by a group of war party MPs and peers called the Committee for the Reformation, as Holles subsequently claimed.[17]

Historians have ignored Holles's comments as irredeemably biased, but there is some supporting evidence. In a letter written in May 1645 recommending Captain Rawlins as a troop commander in the New Model to replace Colonel Sydney, Oliver Cromwell described Rawlins as having been nominated to the New Model. As he does not appear in Fairfax's list, it seems highly likely that names of officers were proposed to a vetting committee, which then may have compiled a draft list that was waiting for Fairfax when he arrived in London.[18] Here the time factor is important, as it is difficult to see how Fairfax could have had time to set up and manage a vetting process in the seven days between his arrival in London and the list being finished.

There is more to support the notion that what Parliament received was a list prepared by Fairfax, but informed by information provided by others. As a newcomer to the ways of Westminster, he had a good reason not to question openly or reject the advice of war party grandees. Powerful figures in Parliament resented his appointment and were ready to make trouble, and a split in the war party's ranks would have provided them with just such an opportunity. It was also a polite way of showing his gratitude, even if it is accepted that his later claim that he had not wanted the appointment and had only accepted it through duty was the truth.

Insofar as external evidence is concerned, there is Clarendon's allegation that Fairfax asked Cromwell to delay leaving for the West Country in late February 1645 so that he could help him with the army, which at that date can only mean the list of officers, as he had yet to receive his commission. It would be easy to dismiss this as coming from a royalist account written many years later, but Cromwell's power to nominate officers can be glimpsed in contemporary documents. John Lilburne let it be widely known through one of his publications that Cromwell offered him a position in the New Model in 1645, which he refused.[19] Second, in the letter recommending Rawlins's appointment, Cromwell's choice of words, although deferential, strongly suggested that he had the power of patronage and Fairfax was merely the rubber stamp. Much more evidence of outside influence may be revealed if the list itself is analysed, but if so this will be seen in its inconsistencies. Its consistencies may be a mark of Fairfax's single authorship, or that of a committee, but it is important for the soundness of the discussion that these are dealt with first.

First, there was a strong tendency for captains and above to be kept together, with the result that the troop and company commanders in many New Model Army regiments bear a close resemblance to those in regiments in the armies of Essex, Manchester and Waller. Second, where gaps existed they were filled not by promotion within the regiment, but by bringing in men holding the same rank in regiments that were to be disbanded. Moreover, great care was taken to choose officers who had previously served in the same army and who would have been known to their new fellow-officers, and also to the rank-and-file, who formed a nucleus of continuity and experience in most of the new regiments. Thus it was very rare for a captain formerly in Manchester's army to be inserted into a regiment that had belonged to Waller's. There were good reasons for taking a middle path. Tensions caused by promotions within the regiment would have repercussions all the way down the officer hierarchy as corporals griped over one of their number who had been raised to sergeant as a result of a vacancy caused by a promotion to ensign, with those who championed merit over longevity disputing with those who preferred Buggins's turn. By the same token, importing an officer of the same rank from one of the other two armies would potentially have been as unsettling, as it might cause animosities between the old armies to spill over into the new.[20]

Other consistencies reflected prejudice as much as principle. For example, disfavour was shown towards officers in Manchester's army who had petitioned for the earl to retain his command, and also towards those in regiments in Essex's army who had been suspected of disloyalty or cowardice in Cornwall. There had been twelve company commanders in the Earl of Essex's regiment, which Colonel Butler had commanded, but the only ones to be named in the February list had been commissioned after Lostwithiel. Lord Robartes's regiment, which was in the same brigade, suffered a similar fate, with only two of its nine company commanders being named in the February list. The third regiment in the brigade, Colonel Barclay's, escaped censure, probably because its colonel had given evidence against Butler, though Barclay may in the process have blackened the reputation of Thomas Pride, his major, who was to become famous for conducting Pride's purge of the Commons three years in the future, as Pride was the only company commander in the regiment not to be retained. Of the five other regiments that had left winter quarters with Butler's brigade in May 1644, four were incorporated in the New Model in a similar manner to the favoured regiments in Manchester's army, with eight, six, six and five of their company commanders being recommissioned.[21] Such graciousness was probably a response to the excellent performance of Essex's infantry at the Second Battle of Newbury.

On the other hand, there is not much to be said for the oft-repeated notion that there was a consistency in the list's prejudice against Scottish officers, the root of which lay in the war party's hostility against that nation's Presbyterian rulers from the autumn of 1644 onwards, which Fairfax shared for different reasons.[22] This was certainly said at the time by the Scots and their supporters, but it requires some qualification. First, in the regiments incorporated into the New Model Army from Essex's and Waller's armies, Scottish company and troop commanders were already few in number and only one was omitted from the February list. There was admittedly greater carnage in Manchester's army, with at least five Scottish company commanders belonging to Lawrence Crawford's regiment being left out, but Crawford himself was retained, despite Fairfax despising him for his behaviour during the siege of York.[23] Moreover, Scottish colonels would have commanded three out of the twelve regiments of foot and one of the twelve regiments of horse in the New Model compared with six or seven in the forty or so regiments in the field armies of Essex, Manchester and Waller in early 1645, had their government allowed them to take up commissions in the New Model. There was even a rumour that John Middleton, Waller's lieutenant general of horse, would have held that post in the new army, presumably because his regiment came second in the February list immediately after that of Sir Thomas.[24] Finally, there were probably more Scottish company commanders in the New Model Army than has been claimed from basic research in obvious places. For example, it would not have been known that Captain Melvin in Colonel Aldridge's regiment was a Scot had he not been described as such in a report of a royalist attack on Abingdon in January 1645.[25]

Thomas Juxon wrote at the time that the creation of the New Army resulted in a strengthening of the Independents and a weakening of the Presbyterians in Parliament's armies, and it has been argued that the officer list reflects this, in that the House of Lords tried unsuccessfully to remove acknowledged radicals.[26] I do not find this convincing. Much of the evidence for radical opinion in the officer corps dates from years later, and in a few cases many years later, but men's opinions change over time.[27] This is clearly seen in the case of Edward Whalley, Cromwell's cousin, and there is no reason for thinking that he was unique.[28] The most thoughtful assessment of the religious complexion of the officers named in the February list is that a cadre of Independents from the Eastern Association army were probably more firmly in place than ever, but there was little sign of this anywhere else. For example, although the officers of Haselrig's regiments of horse and foot received commissions in the New Model Army, they do not appear to have been anywhere near as radicalized as those in Cromwell's regiment, when their behaviour at the time of the First Army Coup in June 1647 is taken into account.

Kishlansky has claimed that a sign of Fairfax's handiwork in the army list is that the selection of the most senior regimental officers was such as to create a balance between moderates and radicals. The principal evidence is that in eleven of the twenty-four regiments the positions of colonel and major in the horse and colonel and lieutenant colonel in the foot were filled in such a way that one was a moderate and the other a radical. The evidence very largely relates to the officers' behaviour in the First Army Coup of June 1647, but he failed to mention that in only two of the eleven regiments were the senior officers in place in June 1647 those who had been commissioned in February 1645.[29]

Finally, although the provisions of the New Model Army Ordinance allowed Fairfax to appoint officers from outside the three southern armies, the February list contains only a single example of that practice. This may be seen as evidence of Fairfax's sensitivity towards starting off on the wrong foot. Nothing would have made his position more difficult than bringing in his own men when so many officers who had served loyally and well under Essex, Manchester and Waller could not find a place in the New Model. However, this principle need not be evidence of Fairfax's compiling the list. It was an idea that could easily have come to war party politicians alarmed at the entourage of ambitious officers who had escorted Fairfax to London and the effect that this would have on opinion in the southern armies. Thus there is no necessary causal link between Sir Thomas and the discrimination against northern officers.

So the consistencies in the February list cannot conclusively be ascribed to Fairfax, but the inconsistencies show a clear sign of the influence of two prominent members of the war party, Lieutenant General Oliver Cromwell and Sir Arthur Haselrig, who until recently had been lieutenant general of horse in Waller's army. All fourteen of Cromwell's former troop commanders were found equivalent positions in the new army, and by the time of the battle of Naseby four had been promoted. Similarly, six of the eight of the troop commanders in Sir Arthur Haselrig's regiment of horse were commissioned as captains, while his major became a colonel and his captain lieutenant a major. Moreover, one of the two infantry regiments from Waller's army incorporated into the New Model had originally been Haselrig's.

Simony also played a part insofar as Cromwell's family (but not Haselrig's) was concerned. Close relations did well because they already held posts in his regiment of horse, but cousins also benefited from the birth of the New Model. John Reynolds, for example, was the only officer to become a troop commander in the New Model in February who had not served in the armies of Essex, Manchester and Waller. Captain Richard Cromwell, a more remote cousin, was promoted from captain to major and was one of the very few examples of an officer being placed in a regiment that had previously belonged to another army, while Robert Hammond, Cromwell's cousin by marriage, became a major of horse despite the fact that his previous post had been captain of foot in the Gloucester garrison.

There were also appointments that look like rewards for recent political services. The Hon. Thomas Howard and the Hon. William Cecil became troop commanders in April or May, probably due to their fathers voting with the war party peers in vital votes in the Lords in February and March. Similarly, when James Sheffield refused to serve as a colonel of horse in the New Model, Thomas, his brother and his major, was promoted in his stead. Interestingly, it was their grandfather's proxy vote that had secured the passage of the February list through the House of Lords unchanged. However, Mulgrave was also Sir Thomas Fairfax's grandfather.

A clearer view of the general's own preferences should become visible in the appointments he made between 9 April and 13 June 1645 when it was easier for him to be his own man. This was a time when he was away from London, at first licking his new army into shape and then leading it in its first campaign, and thus to some extent protected from pressure from the war party politicians at Westminster. In addition, he was free from the influence of Lieutenant General Cromwell, who was campaigning elsewhere in England for much of April, May and early June. As a result the two men met only twice, and then very briefly, between 27 February and the day before the battle of Naseby.

However, the same guiding principles continued to be applied. No Northern Army officers were drafted into the New Model, and many of the newly commissioned officers were men of that rank from regiments formerly in Essex's, Waller's and Manchester's armies that had been disbanded. More lieutenants were promoted, but this was as likely to have been because there were no suitable captains left to appoint, rather than the result of a change in policy.

If Fairfax had disagreed with the bias towards clients of Cromwell and Haselrig in the February list, this was the time to break free, but he did nothing of the sort. Cromwell's cousin Thomas Ingoldsby and his brother Oliver joined their other brothers Richard and Henry in Richard's regiment of foot in the early summer, while Robert Hammond became a colonel and one of Haselrig's captains, who had been his groom before the war, became a major. Finally, Cromwell's protégé Henry Ireton became a full colonel. Fairfax did, however, show the first clear sign of having a will of his own in early June, though in such a way as to avoid a confrontation. Cromwell's lobbying for Captain Rawlins has been mentioned twice above, but not the outcome. The commander-in-chief did not appoint him to the post Cromwell had suggested, but he did find him an equivalent post in another regiment of horse very soon afterwards. Finally, although two more officers from outside the New Model were appointed as company or troop commanders, making a total of three, none came from the northern army. It was not until the autumn that the first such appointment was made.

The end result was an officer corps compiled in accordance with principles that were militarily adroit and politically astute, and Fairfax must receive some of the credit for this, even though it is impossible to ascertain how far he had powered and guided rather than merely headed up the process.[30] However, one example of his assertiveness must be questioned. Hopper, citing Gentles, makes much of the confident way in which Fairfax responded to changes in the February list proposed by the House of Commons, which resulted in almost all of them being reversed.[31] However, Fairfax's personal role is uncertain. The only evidence of it is his writing a letter in support of Major Harrison.[32]. In addition, the claim that in the two cases in which he failed to convince the House he subsequently got his own way is correct, but only after an interval and by accident rather than design.

In early May Fairfax was able to appoint Henry Ireton, Cromwell's future son-in-law, to succeed Sir Michael Livesey, whose regiment of horse had mutinied during April, but Livesey's removal was on Parliament's instructions. The other is less clear-cut. Algernon Sydney's replacement by Robert Rich, who had been proposed by Fairfax as colonel of a different regiment in February and rejected, may have been in accordance with a plan conceived some time before, but put on ice because it would not be politic. Sydney blamed his resignation on wounds received at Marston Moor, but that was almost a year before and would surely have been an issue when the February list was being compiled, but delaying it until late May gave sufficient time for the House of Commons not to take umbrage.[33]

Chapter 10

Sir Thomas Fairfax on Campaign 1645-46

On 30 April 1645 the New Model Army set out on its first campaign, micromanaged in such a way as to ensure that it faithfully executed a strategy devised by the Committee of Both Kingdoms. The basic problem the committee faced was to contain two royalist field armies, one besieging the town of Taunton in west Somerset, commanded by Lord Goring, the other quartered in Oxford, the Cotswolds and the counties along the border with Wales under Prince Rupert. The former was static, but the latter was capable of moving in any direction. An added level of complexity was provided by a plot privy to the war party alone, involving discontented senior royalist officers who were prepared to hand over Oxford and most of the king's cavalry to Parliament, in return for pardon and the recovery of their landed estates.[1] The only solution was to subdivide the New Model, and by the end of May there was one brigade in west Somerset and another at Alfreton in north Derbyshire, while the rest of the army, under Fairfax's command, was besieging Oxford and waiting on events. However, none of the operations had completely achieved its objectives, and worse was to follow.

Admittedly, the western brigade under Colonel Weldon, comprising a third of Fairfax's infantry and one of his regiments of horse, managed to relieve Taunton, but it was not strong enough to break out again. It therefore played no part in the decisive battle of Naseby, fought on 14 June, and had to be rescued by the rest of the New Model Army a fortnight later. The second brigade, consisting of 2,500 cavalry and dragoons under Colonel Vermuyden's command, was to make contact with the Scottish army quartered in Yorkshire so as to defend the north of England should Rupert move in that direction, but it failed in its mission through no fault of its own and was in danger of being annihilated. The Scottish army, fearful of facing the prince, had upped sticks and crossed the Pennines into Westmoreland, where it quartered in close proximity to a brigade of its own troops besieging Carlisle. There was thus no purpose in Vermuyden going farther north unless Rupert did so, but his brigade was in great danger if it remained where it was, as the royalist army, having relieved Chester, had crossed his path a few miles to the south while marching across country, apparently in the direction of Newark. He therefore kept his distance, and when the king's army stormed Leicester instead of marching north, he moved sideways into Lincolnshire so as to be able to help in the defence of East Anglia should the king's army's next move be in that direction. Picking a route that took his brigade as far to the east as Peterborough, Vermuyden reached safety in north Buckinghamshire on 8 June.[2]

An.º Dom.ºᵇⁱ 1643 · VERA EFFIGIES · ROBERTI DEVERIEUX COMITIS ESSEX ·

Robert Earle of Essex, his Excellence, Generall of y̆ Army,
Imployed for y̆ defence of the Protestant Religion, y̆ Safety of his
Ma:ᵗⁱᵉˢ Person, & of y̆ Parlıment, y̆ preseruation of y̆ Lawes, Liberties, & Peace
of y̆ Kingdome, & protection of his Ma:ᵗⁱᵉˢ Subiects from violence & oppreßion,

Lord General the Earl of Essex, c.1645.

The Right Valiant Faithfull
And Famous warriour Sᵣ Will: Waller Kᵗ
p. Stent excudit

Major General Sir William Waller, 1643.

The Effigies of the ... most Excellent & truly valliant Sr Thomas Fairfax Cap:^tin Generall of the Armies raised for the preservation of Religion, defence of King Parlia:^mt & Kinodome London Printed and sold by Peter Stent.

Lord General Thomas, Lord Fairfax, *c.*1649.

Lord Fairfax and Oliver Cromwell, the Duumvirate.

Oliver Cromwell and John Lambert, c.1654.

Lord Deputy Henry Ireton, *c.*1649.

Major General Richard Deane, *c.*1651.

Major General George Monck.

For the Committee of Both Kingdoms the dismay at the capture of Leicester, the most important loss Parliament had suffered since the fall of Bristol almost two years earlier, acted as a wake-up call, coinciding as it did with the revelation that the Oxford plot was a fiction. Fairfax was therefore to abandon the siege. At first his instructions were defensive in nature, namely to march with all the forces he could muster to the borders of East Anglia, where he could most easily meet up with Vermuyden and also with Cromwell, who had been sent to the Eastern Association to organize reinforcements. But within days his orders were changed. He was to actively seek a confrontation with the king's army, which had become easier as it had moved south from Leicester to Daventry in Northamptonshire to re-establish direct contact with its headquarters.[3] However, it was Fairfax, the new boy, and not his political masters, who came under intense scrutiny during the first days of June.

The strongest reaction to the loss of Leicester was a petition to Parliament from the Common Council of London, incensed at the inactivity of the New Model Army. The principal demand was that Fairfax should be instructed in no uncertain terms to pursue the enemy army and extract revenge for what had happened at Leicester, but the petition also asked for members of the Committee of Both Kingdom to be sent to his headquarters to issue orders on the spot. This must be seen as showing a lack of confidence in Fairfax as army leader. The only occasion of any significance when a subcommittee had been sent to the army had been in October 1644, but its purpose was to knock the three army commanders' heads together so that they were not distracted from their task by bickering and hissy fits. On this occasion, however, there was only one army and one general, and the only reason for doing so must have been concerns about Fairfax's lack of experience, but although this had been the argument of Essex's supporters opposing his appointment in January, it is significant that the petition had the backing of the war party's supporters in the city, who additionally asked for Cromwell to be given a proper military command in the Eastern Association to give teeth to his existing civilian command.[4]

To make matters worse, Fairfax was slow to leave the Oxford area, As a result he received a very reproachful letter from the committee at Cambridge, regretting that the safety of the Eastern Association had not been his first consideration, given that most of the provisions that fed his army, and much of the money to pay its officers and soldiers, came from the counties they administered. He was also criticised by the Committee of Both Kingdoms on 5 June for wasting time trying and failing to storm Boarstall House, one of Oxford's minor out-garrisons, instead of heading as fast as he could for a rendezvous with the other forces it had assigned to the defence of the Association. In a second letter sent the same day its members reminded him of his broken promise to keep them informed of his army's movements. In future he was to send them a letter every day.[5]

On 6 June the House of Commons asked the Committee of Both Kingdoms to consider responding positively to the Londoners' request that it should send a subcommittee to the army.[6] The Committee appears to have spent a lot of time debating it on the 7th, but it did not reach a decision, suggesting an even split between the sixteen members present. Further discussion was postponed until the following Monday, but an order was issued for all members to be present given the importance of the business to be considered.[7] The outcome was that the request was turned on its head. Instead of tightening their control over their general they set him free.[8]

The starting point for unravelling how granting Fairfax what amounted to operational independence came about must be the meeting on Saturday 7 June. The best guess for how the votes were cast so as to achieve a draw is that the six war party members present put solidarity with their general above respecting the wishes of their London supporters, and were against a subcommittee. Opposing them would have been the four peace party men led by Essex and the three Scots, with the others, Waller, Warwick and Manchester, dividing two to one in opposition to the subcommittee. At the meeting on the 9th the former had eight present, the latter seven and, if the two uncommitted had voted the same way as on the 7th, they would have won by a whisker. However, there is nothing to indicate that the majority on either issue was very close, as the Committee's minute book shows that there cannot have been a long and contentious discussion prior to the votes being cast. Moreover, the order in which the decisions were taken, beginning with granting Fairfax his operational independence, reads like a *fait accompli* – there was no other option given the military situation.

My view is that the majority was much larger than one, because of a letter Fairfax and his council of war had written to Parliament on the 8th asking for Cromwell to join the army as lieutenant general of horse, the circumstances of which are discussed below, but there is nothing in it that could have been read as Fairfax asking for operational independence. It did, however, make it clear that a battle was only days away. This I see as causing a change of mind on the part of former senior army officers, who had had direct or indirect experience of the problems of running a campaign by committee in the early stages of the Newbury campaign, namely Waller and Manchester, but also the Earl of Essex, Lord Robartes and Sir Phillip Stapleton, who for various reasons had not been present at Newbury, but would doubtless have reflected on what went wrong. Essex's two civilian supporters, Sir Gilbert Gerrard and the Mr Recorder, are also most likely to have followed the former lord general's lead, and possibly the Earl of Warwick had he not voted with the war party on the 7th.

In the afternoon the committee conducted a large number of pieces of business before turning again to the management of the New Model Army. They had to all intents and purposes rejected a subcommittee by their vote in the morning, but they went through the motions. They concluded that it was impossible to set one up because they could not find a member of the House of Lords who could spare the time to go to the army. It was an unlikely excuse, but suggests that all the peers present had voted in the morning in favour of the motion to loosen Fairfax's reins. It also reads like a sarcastic comment on the disenabling principle from the mouth of the Earl of Essex.

Fairfax received the Committee's new instructions on the evening of the 9th, but Gardiner went too far by claiming that military questions were at last to be answered by military men. His remit was restricted to operational decisions concerning the New Model Army. The Committee continued to have sole charge of running the war as a whole. Moreover, the minutes did not rule out a subcommittee being sent to the army in the future.[9] And there still remained the serious and very pressing problem of command on the battlefield, which Fairfax and his council of war addressed head-on in the letter of 8th June, to which a reply had not yet been sent.

In the interests of economy Parliament had only included a couple of officers higher than colonel in the New Model establishment, namely Fairfax and Skippon. The posts of lieutenant general and commissary general of horse were unfilled, and although Fairfax himself had plenty of experience of commanding cavalry at the highest level, he could not be in charge of the two wings and oversee the battle as a whole. On the 8th, with a confrontation looming, he convened a council of war to discuss the matter. The upshot was the letter concerning Cromwell's appointment.[10]

The House of Commons gave its consent on 10 June before the Lords had a chance to discuss the matter, but this should not be seen as an affront to the Upper House, as approval could be explained as being little more than a courtesy. Cromwell had not yet resigned his commission as a lieutenant general, even though the army in which he held that position had ceased to exist, and as he was leading troops from the Eastern Association towards a rendezvous with the New Model it was most unlikely that he would not soon be with the army.[11] Fairfax's problem was that Cromwell's exemption from the provisions of the Self-Denying Ordinance had been granted for forty days from 12 May. It would therefore end on 20 June, but there was no guarantee that the battle would take place before that date. Approval of an extension in advance was therefore essential to prevent a hiatus in command at what might be completely the wrong moment, with the two armies facing one another in battle array. Nothing sinister should be seen in Fairfax not mentioning an end date for Cromwell's temporary commission. To have done so might have been regarded by Parliament as presumption on his part.

The matter of overall command of the cavalry having been settled, Skippon was charged with drawing up 'the form of a battle', while Fairfax placed the regiments in brigades, which could operate as independent units if necessary. The commander-in-chief meanwhile wrote to local commanders in Warwickshire, Derbyshire, Nottinghamshire, Lincolnshire and East Anglia, asking for them to send him reinforcements as quickly as possible. Finally, the New Model set off at a measured place towards Daventry, presumably to give time for Cromwell and the rest of the reinforcements to arrive.

* * * * *

The battle that followed five days later at Naseby between Daventry and Market Harborough has been discussed at length in several recent publications. There is a very high degree of unanimity that Cromwell's cavalry tactics were masterly. The left wing, under Ireton's command, though eventually defeated, drew in Rupert's cavalry reserves apart from the king's lifeguard, and although in the end the royalists broke through, they had been held up for twenty minutes and were so shattered as to be unable to play any further part in the battle. On the other wing the royalist charge caused heavy casualties in the Parliamentary first line, forcing Cromwell to commit some of the second line, at which point the royalists fell back, the reason for which depends on which source you read. Leaving part of his wing in position to prevent the royalists returning to the battlefield, Cromwell ordered the rest of the second and the third line to wheel to the left and thus surround the royalist infantry, who surrendered en masse. The twentieth-century myth that they made a fighting retreat and were hunted down a mile away on Wadborough Hill owes its origin to the discovery of hundreds of musket balls there by metal detectorists in the 1990s. The written sources give no clue as to why the musket balls happen to be there, but there are several possibilities. They may mark the spot where the regiment guarding the royalist artillery train, which may not have been on the battlefield, was forced to surrender, but they could equally well be where the prisoners of war were told to strip themselves of all military equipment before being marched to the nearby main road that led via Northampton to London and so to prison.

The king's army had assembled at dawn on 14 June on a ridge at East Farndon, three miles to the north of Naseby, where Fairfax had ordered his rendezvous on a higher ridge that gave him a panoramic view of royalist preparations, though what lay concealed behind East Farndon ridge remained a mystery. A couple of hours later Rupert ordered the royalist regiments to turn ninety degrees to the right and march along the western continuation of East Farndon ridge towards the village of Sibbertoft. This drew the armies closer together, as the gap between the two ridges narrowed to well under half a mile to the south of that village. Rupert's reasons are clear. The enemy showed no sign of moving towards East Farndon. Indeed, they had withdrawn an advance guard of dragoons that had spent the night below the ridge line. If Fairfax's army was retreating, the king's cavalry would be in a better position to harry its rear-guard than if they remained at East Farndon, where the approach to Naseby village would entail climbing a very steep slope, where a well-placed enemy rear guard could theoretically hold up the pursuit for hours.

Fairfax's response was to order his regiments to move to the left along the ridge, to occupy a position on Closters Hill, midway between Naseby and Sibbertoft. This would give him two advantages. First, it would deny the enemy the wind gauge. Second, he would have time to deploy the army. Closters Hill was only a mile away from where the New Model had first deployed, whereas the royalists would have a march of three miles to occupy a position facing him.

The only problem with the new position was that it was cramped, with a steep slope on the east side and on the other a very substantial hedge. However, this was not necessarily a negative point. Fairfax was lacking accurate intelligence about the strength of the army facing him, and there was just a chance that the king had been recently joined by brigades of horse from Goring's army, which had managed to ride rapidly from Somerset to the outskirts of Oxford in early May, and if this had happened a second time it would give Prince Rupert a significant superiority in cavalry. The new place of deployment, however, would make it impossible for Rupert to use this superiority to deliver a flank attack on the New Model Army horse using his reserves, while Cromwell's men were pinned in a mêlée with his first line. It has recently been argued that Fairfax knew that Goring's men were still in Somerset well before the battle.[12] However, Sprigg makes it clear that this was not so. Fairfax was not aware of it until the day after the battle, when he received an intercepted letter from Goring. This would also explain why the first hurried account of the victory, written on the evening of the battle, estimated that the king's horse had outnumbered Parliament's by some 2,000. Finally, the only evidence of an earlier letter or letters comes from a royalist narrative of the First Civil War.[13]

As the New Model deployed in what looks to modern eyes like a defensive formation, Fairfax made further use of the landscape to increase his chances of winning a battle in which an infantry trap might be the key factor. The centre and right of the position on Closters Hill was some ten metres higher than the hill on which the king's army were deploying. Sir Thomas could therefore hide his strength in infantry from view, and to this end he ordered Skippon to move the first line back from the forward slope of Closters Hill to a position several hundred metres to the rear. The major general disapproved, but there was no time to argue the point as the royalists were getting ready to attack.[14]

Possibly what Fairfax had in mind was applying a lesson he had learned the hard way at Adwalton Moor two years earlier. There, though outnumbered in both horse and foot, the Northern army infantry had broken through the first line of the enemy by sheer momentum and pushed ahead of their cavalry only to be stopped and thrown into disorder by a pike charge delivered by the royalist reserves.[15] None of the accounts of the battle of Naseby mention a pike charge taking place, and the small number of casualties suffered by the Parliamentary regiments in the reserve line suggests that they had not been involved in close combat. Instead it was firepower that would do the trick. As the relatively weak regiments in the centre of the New Model Army's first line gave way, the royalists would be funnelled into a narrow corridor as they moved forward by two very strong infantry regiments positioned on the right and left flank, and then stopped in their tracks by a devastating barrage delivered by the 1,500 or so musketeers of the three regiments in the reserve line.[16] This is exactly what happened, and the strength of the barrage is indicated by the fact that the heaviest concentration of musket balls found on the battlefield by field walking and metal detecting was not on the north-facing slope of Closters Hill or on its crest, but some hundred metres farther to the rear in the direction of Naseby village.[17]

With the royalist infantry retreating as Fairfax's second line advanced, Fairfax's qualities as battlefield commander come once more into focus, but in a negative rather than a positive guise. One royalist infantry brigade refused to surrender and he took personal charge of the attack that finally overwhelmed it. However, the accounts of the action by Joshua Sprigg, Fairfax's chaplain, and Captain Doyley, who commanded his lifeguard, tell very different stories. Sprigg describes a combined infantry and cavalry operation with the general's own involvement at the head of his lifeguard in parentheses. Doyley's account is much more colourful. He states that the general, having ridden around the battlefield bare-headed, refused the offer of a helmet, and then, leading part of the lifeguard in person, he attacked the brigade in the rear while Doyley attacked it in the front with the rest. Finally, when the brigade disintegrated and they met in the middle, Fairfax killed the ensign carrying the colours. Doyley was an eyewitness describing a man who had clearly lost control and forgotten his responsibilities as army commander. And if he had been unlucky the New Model Army would have required a new commander-in-chief. Sprigg, on the other hand, may have neglected to accurately report the detail of the engagement to cover up the general's foolhardy and unnecessary act of bravery when victory had, to all intents and purposes, been achieved.[18] This raises the possibility that at Naseby, and also at Maidstone, Fairfax may have been deliberately putting his life on the line for personal reasons.

The last episode in the battle was a confrontation between the victorious Parliamentary army and the royalist horse, which had regrouped some distance to the rear of where the fighting had taken place. Instead of launching his cavalry at them, Fairfax re-formed his battle line with foot flanked by horse, which then advanced menacingly towards them. Without the firepower to resist effectively, their infantry having surrendered and their artillery having been overrun, the royalists could not make a stand but fled towards Leicester followed by Cromwell and his troopers.

* * * * *

The New Model Army's second battle was fought at Langport in Somerset less than a month later. In the interval Fairfax had been in quandary about what to do next. After securing the speedy surrender of Leicester, should he follow the king and Prince Rupert and what was left of his field army into the Welsh Borderland, or should he lead the New Model into the west of England for a confrontation with Lord Goring and the 10,000 or so enemy troops besieging Taunton?[19] He saw it as a strategic matter and waited for Parliament to give its approval to what was his preferred option: to advance on Taunton, whereupon the New Model Army headed for the West Country at full speed. Fairfax was not only concerned about his five regiments trapped there by Goring's army, but also about the safety of the new Western brigade, which had been assembling in Hampshire since

10 June under the command of Major General Edward Massey, with orders to go to the relief of Taunton in the presumption that the New Model Army's campaign in the Midlands would turn out to be a long drawn-out affair.[20]

In a letter to the Committee Fairfax informed them that he did not consider that Massey had sufficient troops to undertake the relief on its own, which was correct as a figure of less than 3,000 men was the Committee of Both Kingdom's estimate of his strength. In addition, the Western brigade was even more of a hybrid than the New Model Army, composed as it was of diverse elements of dubious quality: cavalry units formerly in Essex's army that were surplus to the requirements of the New Model; regiments of horse raised in Dorset and Wiltshire during Waller's 1644 and 1645 campaigns with little or no experience; more experienced horse from counties as far away as Gloucestershire, Middlesex and Kent; and infantry drawn from the south coast garrisons between Chichester and Lyme, some of which had in the past belonged to Waller's army.[21] Moreover, on past record of Waller and Cromwell's experience in the west earlier in the year, Goring was very capable of mounting spoiling attacks that would disperse, if not destroy, the Western brigade if it came too close.[22]

There may have been another consideration behind the haste with which the New Model marched south. The Western brigade has been seen as enjoying the favour of the peace party because it could act as a counterweight to the New Model. This was certainly the case later in the year, but the decision to create such a brigade was taken on 24 May, which makes it look like a hasty response to the importance of keeping the New Model in the Oxford area: the plot had yet to unravel; Leicester had not yet been stormed; but something needed to be done about Taunton.[23] However, if the Western brigade was indeed the peace party's darling, Massey might be tempted to relieve Taunton on his own initiative in order to gain kudos to rival that which the New Model had acquired at Naseby.

If Massey's brigade caused Fairfax any anxiety, he need not have worried. Its commander kept his distance. Instead of advancing through the ports and small towns of coastal Dorset to approach Taunton from the south, as other relief expeditions had done, he advanced inland to Blandford, where Fairfax joined him with the New Model Army on 2 July. The two forces then moved forward to Axminster and Beaminster respectively, within easy reach of Taunton, with Massey's in the lead.[24] In the meantime Goring had abandoned his siege in the hope of beating up Massey's brigade, which left the back door open for Weldon's brigade to rendezvous with Fairfax and Massey near Lyme on about 5 July.

Goring was thus heavily outnumbered, but instead of retreating into Devonshire, where the enclosed landscape would enable him to fight a prolonged defensive campaign, he was ordered to remain in Somerset. Royalist recruiting operations in South Wales after Naseby had gone well, and the king's intention was to ship his infantry into the south-west of England via Bridgwater, the port at the mouth of the River Parrett, while his cavalry took the much longer overland route. Goring was therefore to keep the enemy occupied for as long as possible, using the defensive potential of the rivers and marshland of central Somerset, where the main choke points, the bridges at Ilchester, Langport and Burrow, were guarded by royalist garrisons.

For a few days the tactics worked, but Fairfax was remorseless in his probing operations, which soon gained their reward. On 9 July some of Massey's cavalry with New Model Army support caught a brigade of Goring's horse bathing in a river at Isle Moor and put them to flight.[25] This opened up Bridgwater to a direct approach along the west bank of the River Parrett, though it would not have been plain sailing because of the extensive marshland that lay ahead. Nevertheless, if Fairfax had left Massey's men where they were with orders to make what progress they could towards the port, they would soon have blocked the Langport to Bridgwater road only four miles to the north and made the victory Fairfax achieved the following day on the opposite bank more decisive than Naseby. Goring's army would have been totally destroyed and the rest of the West Country overrun within weeks apart from a few isolated garrisons.[26]

After the setback on Isle Moor, Goring began a staged withdrawal towards Bridgwater along the east bank of the Parrett. The first stand was at Langport, where there was a bridge that would enable him to change if necessary to the west bank and, having wrong-footed the enemy, to retreat safely to Burrow. Fairfax, on encountering resistance along the Wagg Rhyne a mile short of Langport, expected a battle and therefore recalled Massey's men, but they were not needed. The defence line was merely intended to cover the royalist army's passage over the bridge, most of Goring's train of artillery having already done so before the fighting began, the royalist general having presumably learned that Massey's men were no longer a threat.

Fairfax took his time before launching an attack across the Wagg Rhyne, but his caution can be explained. The royalist musketeers in the hedges lining the slope on the far side were easily visible from his vantage point in Long Sutton parish on the other bank, but the rest of the royalist army was out of sight. He therefore did not know how many of the enemy he was facing or how they were deployed. In direct contrast to his tactics at Naseby he began the attack with a heavy bombardment of the enemy position. This knocked out two artillery pieces guarding the point where a lane that crossed the Wagg Rhyne breasted the slope and entered the open ground beyond. At the same time he ordered a body of 1,500 musketeers to clear the hedges. Once they had made good progress, Cromwell, as lieutenant general of cavalry, chose three troops of horse that had served in his own regiment in the Eastern Association army to serve as a forlorn hope to open the battle proper.

The momentum the three troops gained from the downward slope took them up the rise on the far side and into the heart of the enemy position. When they breasted the rise they charged a brigade of enemy horse, which they eventually routed with the help of a second squadron sent up the lane in support.[27] This achievement was praised to the heights by all concerned, but the Parliamentary cavalry had the advantage of surprise and also of being on the move rather than stationary.[28] Also, the six troops of New Model horse probably outnumbered the royalist brigade, which may have been only 400 strong.[29] However, what happened next was extraordinary. The entire royalist cavalry, between 3,000 and 4,000 men, apparently fled for their lives: not towards Langport bridge, their intended line of retreat, but along the east bank of the Parrett, into the marshes two miles away, where many of them were hunted down and taken prisoner or killed. The list of captives published in London a few days later gave the names of forty-nine officers of horse belonging to twenty-six regiments.[30]

The victory at Langport was highly effective in strategic terms, as once Fairfax had secured Bridgwater and Sherborne in late July and early August he controlled a string of fortresses across the narrow neck of the south-west peninsula. These were an important factor in preventing Goring's forces from leaving Devon and Cornwall and assisting the king's cause elsewhere.[31] However, it still took over a year to complete the pacification of England, and it was very largely a matter of sieges, a type of warfare in which Sir Thomas had acquired considerable experience during his campaigns in the north of England in 1644. The tactics he used in 1645 and 1646 were tailored to the particular siege he was undertaking, with storms, which frequently led to heavy casualties even when successful, being used only as a last resort unless, as at Dartmouth in January 1646, the fortifications were known to be thinly manned. Bridgwater was stormed in July 1645 immediately after the battle of Langport, but only after lengthy debates in the council of war. The deciding issue was fear that a time-consuming siege would allow Goring's army to regroup, but the low casualties incurred justified the decision. Fairfax was not so lucky at Bristol, where storming the defences was costly, but in the lives of officers rather than men. The reason was that Prince Rupert, who commanded the garrison, was deliberately drawing out negotiations for a peaceful surrender in the hope that the king or Goring would do something to cause the enemy to abandon the siege.[32]

Sir Thomas's third battle in charge of the New Model Army took place at Torrington in north Devon on 16 February 1646, and it was a classic example of how to deal with a relief expedition before it could get properly under way. The victims were regiments of the royalist army of the west marching from Cornwall to Exeter which, because of the strength of its defences, was not stormed but subjected to a prolonged siege that had begun three months earlier and would last until early May. The number of troops Fairfax had at his disposal was much smaller than at Naseby and Langport due to natural wastage and regiments being ordered back to south-central England by the Committee of Both Kingdoms, but even so his force probably outnumbered the royalists by two to one, who on this occasion were commanded by Lord Hopton, Goring having left for France for health reasons at the end of 1645.

The various accounts of the fighting add little to an all-round assessment of Fairfax's qualities as a battlefield commander. It was a classic encounter battle, which did not allow the general time to prepare a tactical plan before the fighting started. The clash occurred because of the enthusiasm of the New Model Army dragoons sent into the enemy's quarters by Cromwell to gather intelligence. The accounts of the battle do not give any sense of Fairfax controlling what was happening beyond sending in new units as required to force the royalists back through the town, but he was not in a position to see what was going on because the battle took place entirely during the hours of darkness. Nevertheless, as at Naseby he was in the thick of things. He also showed that he still led a charmed life. When the royalist magazine stored in Torrington church ignited it sent sheets of lead into the street through which he and his escort were passing, killing a man who was riding beside him.[33]

The encounter at Torrington was less decisive in the short run than either Naseby or Langport, in that in the distraction caused by the explosion, and by a short, sharp counterattack, the enemy infantry and cavalry were able to retreat into the enclosed country to the west of the town, but Hopton's army was completely demoralized. What followed over the next three weeks was the New Model Army shepherding them back across the county boundary into Cornwall, while giving them every encouragement to give up the fight. It all came to an end in a treaty finalized at Truro on 12 March. The royalist army was disbanded, the rank-and-file were allowed to return home with a little money in their pockets, and the officers were permitted to go overseas if they so desired.[34] All that now remained for the New Model Army to do was to play its part in securing the surrender of the remaining royalist garrisons scattered the length and breadth of England, from Newark in the north to Pendennis and Corfe castles on the south coast, and in North Wales from Holt Castle on the River Dee to Harlech and Caernarvon castles in the far west.

Two points need to be made about the end game. First, the New Model Army, divided for the most part into brigades, took part in sieges in the southern part of England, the furthest north being Rainborough's brigade's blockade of Worcester, which surrendered in August 1646. Second, the New Model Army concentrated on the larger garrisons – first Exeter and then Oxford – leaving the smaller ones, such as Donnington Castle, to provincial forces, the only exception being Pendennis Castle, which surrendered to Colonel Fortescue's regiment.

Chapter 11
Fairfax the Political General, February 1645–May 1646

Sir Thomas Fairfax's remit as commander of the New Model Army was to win the war as quickly as possible. This involved not only turning the mishmash he had inherited into a war-winning machine, but also gaining the confidence of those who were suspicious about his appointment without alienating those who had supported it. To this end he brought a number of personality traits which, if not apparent to his new command or to the civilian population in the spring of 1645, were to be common knowledge by the spring of the following year, via such works as *The Year of Jubilee or England's Releasement purchased by God's Immediate Assistance and Powerful Aiding of her Renowned Parliament and the Forces Raised by Them,* written by Samuel Shepherd and published in March 1646. Shepherd, who could not be classed as an out-and-out radical by the way in which he prioritized Parliament's war aims with the defence of the king's person coming first and the liberties of the subject third, depicts Sir Thomas as the veritable model of an early-modern general. He combined personal piety and bravery with wisdom, modesty and courtesy towards friend and foe alike, and above all else he had been universally successful in the field from Naseby onwards, winning three significant victories and capturing innumerable garrisons. Providence seemed to shine upon him, and the absence of setbacks meant that he was clearly the worthy instrument of God's glory.[1] Similar sentiments are to be found in a sermon delivered in April 1646 to the two Houses of Parliament and the city of London by Hugh Peter, chaplain to the army and a thoroughgoing Independent: 'The Lord hath owned you and your army and made you formidable'.

Peter also described it as 'the greatest privilege next to the crown of God in Christ in my poor soul to be a member of your army and a witness of His presence with you and it'. Later in the sermon he praised Fairfax's speed in bringing the war to an end: 'Heraldry did not miscarry that hath these words for your chief in his coat of arms – Say. Do.'[2]

All the qualities Fairfax brought to bear in exercising his new command were inherent, not invented to enhance his image and bolster his authority on becoming commander-in-chief. The unbroken string of military achievements, however, was something new compared with his patchy record in the army of the north, and served to enhance his reputation, showing in no uncertain terms that God was congratulating Parliament for choosing the right man for the job. This could have been the primrose path towards the sin of pride, which William Waller has seen as the reason for his lack of success as army commander after a very hopeful beginning. Sir Thomas, however, attributed his successes in the field not to his own abilities, but to God's grace, and by acknowledging that it was God alone to whom all glory and thanks should be given he hoped to retain God's approval. Although not as vocal as Cromwell, the central tenet of providentialism is very apparent in the letter he wrote to William Lenthall after the surrender of the king's forces in Cornwall in March 1646:

> Truly Sir this must be acknowledged as an admirable mercy from that same gracious hand of providence that hath hitherto gone along with you that so considerable a force should be so baffled at Torrington and afterwards should put themselves into a net whereby they were necessitated to the utter ruin of so great a body of cavalry.[3]

It is also interesting that he fully acknowledges his subordinate place in the chain of command when he uses the pronoun you rather than I or we.

However, personal qualities were not enough. Behind the genuine face Fairfax presented to the world lay skills that were vital in managing the army and maintaining good relations with his political masters, fellow generals and civilians. In fact in this respect he scarcely put a foot wrong between the New Model Army's setting out on campaign on 30 April 1645 and its return to the Thames valley for the siege of Oxford exactly a year and a day later. Indeed, they can be seen as being as important as the martial qualities he had displayed in command of the army: prudence and the efficient use of the resources while on campaign, being methodical and judicious in the preparation for and conduct of battles and sieges, and personal bravery in all circumstances. However, the flair he displayed in his relations with his political masters in particular from June 1645 onwards was not so sure after the war ended, which suggests that he had previously been following the advice of those members of his council of war who were more experienced than he was in political matters.

Sir Thomas's greatest political success in his first year as commander-in-chief was to successfully combine elements from the armies of Essex, Manchester and Waller into a single body that functioned as a first-rate instrument for winning the war, despite the rivalry and rancour that had characterized the relations between the generals in the campaigns of June to November 1644 and the mutinies affecting the armies of Essex and Manchester in the first three months of 1645, when regiments had refused to serve any general other than their own. Although not acknowledged by Shepherd, this achievement was recognized by Joshua Sprigg and Hugh Peter.[4]

Although he never said so, it can be inferred that when Fairfax needed to subdivide the army during the 1645–6 campaign, after gaining control of operations, he deliberately opted for brigades drawn from more than one of the former armies, and it seems likely that this was designed to promote unity in his own army. Thus the reserve line of infantry regiments at Naseby was made up of a regiment from each of the earlier armies, while Massey's surprise attack on the royalist cavalry brigade at Isle Moor on the day before the battle of Langport involved two of Fairfax's cavalry regiments, one from Essex's former army and one from Manchester's. In the battle itself the infantry assault on the royalist position along the Wagg Rhyne was carried out by musketeers from Colonel Rainborough's brigade, which included regiments from all three of the former armies.[5] At the storming of Bristol the cavalry formation designated to sweep through the gap between the city's outer and inner defences, once the former had been breached, was made up of two former Eastern Association regiments and one of Essex's, while the infantry brigade with which Cromwell captured Winchester and Basing House in October consisted of two former Eastern Association regiments and one of Waller's. In the new year, the storming of Dartmouth in January was entrusted to five regiments drawn from all three former armies.[6] However, at first, when the task ahead was uncertain and he or one of his senior officers could not oversee it, Fairfax tended to use units that had served together in the past. Thus the musketeers that were sent to aid Massey on 9 July 1645 without the protection of their pikes were from three regiments formerly in the Eastern Association army, while the fourth regiment in the brigade, formerly in Waller's army, remained at Long Sutton.[7]

Three matters of particular concern to soldiers and officers alike were that pay should arrive on a regular basis, that they were not arrested for debt or for mistreatment of members of the civilian population, and that risk was apportioned evenly between the various units. As Hopper has pointed out, the much improved administrative system for collecting money to pay Fairfax's troops, enshrined in the ordinance setting up the New Model, led to greater discipline, both within the army and in its relations with civilians. Thus in this respect he was the beneficiary, not the instigator, though he did his best to promote the smooth running of the system by being firm against offenders, pleading the cause of officers who found themselves in prison and remonstrating with Parliament if pay was delayed.[8] It is also possible to argue that his public concern about misbehaviour by Massey's troops in 1646 was caused by fear of the effect it would have on civilian opinion of soldiers in general, rather than, or as well as, the wish to support the war party's ambition to get the brigade disbanded as quickly as possible.[9]

Finally, there is no evidence that Fairfax spared some units at the expense of others through favouritism. Admittedly it looks odd that the cavalry regiments from the New Model Army quartered cosily in the centre of the country in the autumn of 1645 and the winter of 1645/6 rather than campaigning in the West Country were largely those that had formerly served in Eastern Association army, but the units concerned were chosen by the Committee of Both Kingdoms, not by the commander-in-chief.[10] Conversely, he quickly snuffed out the first sign of elitism when his own regiment of foot, following what had been the practice in

Essex's army, claimed the right to always march in the van. He shamed them by personal example, and then established a rota so that no regiment should have primacy.[11] Second, according to Hopper, he used his family's connections with the London press and its gatekeeper John Rushworth to promote the New Model Army and ensure that its successes were widely known.[12] This would surely have been appreciated by officers and soldiers alike, and presumably their families and friends. Finally, he did nothing to favour one religious opinion over another, even when this provoked a confrontation. Just before the battle of Naseby, for example, he came to the aid of two of his most radical officers when they were arrested by Sir Samuel Luke, the Presbyterian governor of Newport Pagnell, while on their way to London. Almost the last letter Luke received before giving up his post under the terms of the Self-Denying Ordinance was a dressing-down from Sir Thomas.[13]

Fairfax paid considerable attention to status where his officers were concerned. He made it a general rule for the senior colonel to be in command of a brigade, and in the area of promotions he showed sensitivity.[14] His policy towards filling vacancies in the officer corps post-Naseby was to reward both seniority and ability, as Kishlansky has noted, but these were not the only criteria and they were not necessarily of equal weighting in the selection of captains and above.[15] Religious zeal is sometimes mentioned in correspondence proposing an officer for a post that needed to be filled, but lack of evidence for the mid-1640s makes it impossible to say how important it was compared with the other two criteria. My view is that a certain level of piety and good living was a necessary precondition, but that it was never the dominant factor. Favouritism towards family members, however, seems to have ceased completely until after the first army coup in June 1647.

Analysis of regimental listings indicates that seniority was very significant with regard to field officers, with twelve out of the sixteen promoted being the senior captain in their respective regiment. Of the remainder two were officers moved in from other New Model Army regiments and two complete outsiders. As for the new captains of horse and foot, nine had been lieutenants in the same regiment against ten from other regiments or from outside the New Model, but the previous rank and regiment of fifteen of the new captains is not presently known. Even so there is enough of a contrast with the first two months of the New Model Army's existence to show that rule of prioritising experience at the rank of captain was less stringently applied. However, when it came to colonels, experience continued to be the dominant consideration. Of the four new colonels appointed between mid-June 1645 and April 1647 three had already commanded regiments as full colonels. John Hewson, the fourth, was lieutenant colonel in the regiment he subsequently commanded, but it took six months for his appointment to be confirmed and the commission issued.[16]

Fairfax did, however, use vacancies to bring officers into the New Model Army who had served in the Northern army under his father's command, but only after he had been in post for some time and established his reputation as a winner of battles. The first was John Lambert, commissioned in October 1645 as colonel of foot following the resignation of Edward Montagu, who had been elected as a Member of Parliament. He was followed by Walter Bethell, who became a captain of horse on the death of Walter Parry in January 1646 after six months' service in the New Model Army as a volunteer. Edward Salmon and Abraham Holmes filled vacancies caused by the death of a lieutenant colonel and a captain at the sieges of Exeter and Oxford respectively, while Robert Lilburne succeeded Ralph Weldon in command of one of Waller's former infantry regiments that had been raised in Kent soon after Weldon was appointed as governor of Plymouth in the spring of 1646.

The numbers were quite small, but Fairfax was wise to be cautious. The appointment of the Yorkshireman Robert Lilburne, formerly colonel of horse in the Northern army, to succeed Ralph Weldon, resulted in a petition signed by a dozen commissioned officers who would have preferred Nicholas Kempson, the lieutenant colonel, to have been promoted. Not surprisingly at least twelve of them left in May 1647 when Kempson was authorized to raise a regiment from the New Model Army volunteers to serve in Ireland.[17] Fairfax took the hint. Between June 1646 and the end of May 1647 only two Northern officers were commissioned as captains or above in the New Model Army.[18]

* * * * *

The commander-in-chief managed to achieve a similar level of harmony in his relationships with other generals and with his political masters. In this he was helped by the wording of his commission, and also by the more simplified structure of regional command that Parliament had put in place by the summer of 1645, which reduced the number of major generals in charge of regions of the country, and ensured that their commissions contained wording to the effect that they were only subject to Sir Thomas Fairfax's commands if his forces and theirs were campaigning together. Otherwise they were commanders-in-chief in their own bailiwicks.

The problems Essex had experienced with the two major generals closest to the areas in which his field army operated did not re-emerge with any force with Manchester and Waller's successors. The military affairs of the Eastern Association were managed by the committee at Cambridge and the Committee of Both Kingdoms, with military supremoes appointed only when the Association was in danger of invasion, as in late May 1645 when Oliver Cromwell was put in charge, and again the following August when what was left of the king's army plundered Huntingdon. At the time Cromwell was fully occupied as brigade commander reducing royalist garrisons in Hampshire. His replacement was the Earl of Warwick, the former lord admiral, but when the danger had passed he quietly faded away. There was no declaration of Parliament or minute of the

Committee of Both Kingdoms to the effect that his period of employment had come to an end, but they stopped sending him instructions.[19]

The officer in command of the counties of the south-west of England, on the other hand, was in continuous employment from May 1645 to October 1646 and he was an irritant, but not to the extent that Sir William Waller had been to the Earl of Essex.[20] Edward Massey and Sir Thomas Fairfax had not been in dispute previously, as Massey's war up to that point had been confined to an area within forty miles or so of Gloucester, where he was garrison commander, but he soon found cause for complaint. His letters to the Committee of Both Kingdoms in 1644 and early 1645 are full of grievances, real and imagined. Few of his letters survive for the 1645 campaign, but he was uncomplimentary about the conduct of the campaign in the Somerset marshland in July, the decision not to invade Devon and Cornwall immediately after the capture of Bridgwater, and the static role his brigade was given of defending the Somerset/Devon county line against Goring until such time as Fairfax was ready to take the offensive. As for himself, his advice on operations was ignored or disregarded and on other matters not asked for.[21] Little notice was taken of his moans if the few mentions of his brigade in the minutes of the Committee of Both Kingdoms, and the even fewer letters the Committee sent him during that period, are indicative of his importance in the great scheme of things. However, once the invasion of Devon got underway, Fairfax made use of Massey's best regiments to strengthen his own army, which was depleted by New Model Army units being ordered back east to prevent the king's cavalry, based at Oxford, raiding the towns and trade routes of the south Midlands. Nevertheless, although Colonel Birch's regiment of foot and Colonel Cooke's regiment of horse were at various times used as New Model Army auxiliaries, there is a sense in contemporary works that Massey's brigade as a whole was not quite up to standard.[22] This is most evident in Whitelock's account of its poor performance at the siege of Bridgwater. Ordered to assault the western defences of the town while the New Model attacked from the east, its response was feeble, as was the excuse that it was unprepared for the assault and therefore could do no more than scare the enemy by firing off a lot of ammunition. But Whitelock had been reading the wrong reports or the wrong journals. The guilt should have been more evenly distributed, as four of the six regiments under Massey's command at Bridgwater belonged to the New Model Army.[23]

The only political development of potential concern to Fairfax in his relationship with Massey was a later attempt to make the Western brigade into an army. On 21 January 1646 the House of Lords, in the absence of such war party stalwarts as lords Wharton and Say and Sele, supported proposals drafted by a sub-committee of the Lords and Commons committee for the defence of the west of England to expand the size of Massey's brigade to almost 9,000 men, to put it on a more substantial financial footing, and to give Massey power to issue commissions to officers under his command. It also asked Parliament to require the Committee of Both Kingdoms to issue orders to Fairfax to retain some forces in the west of England until Exeter surrendered. The Commons ignored the proposal, but it clearly showed its opinion by the actions it took in the days that followed. On 23 January praise and favours were heaped on the New Model for its capture of Dartmouth, and subsequently the committee for the west was ordered to pay expenses to Hugh Peter, the Independent chaplain to the army, who had brought news to Westminster. It also asserted that it was within Fairfax's remit to issue commissions to gentlemen wishing to raise new regiments in the west and to appoint governors for new garrisons established there.[24] Thus Massey was firmly kept in his place, in a political sense, by the House of Commons, and soon afterwards he seems to have given up the quest for an enhanced role in the running of the war. From then on he appears to have remained in London until his brigade was disbanded, when he and Fairfax worked together on a task that was easier than probably either of them had anticipated.[25]

The two other major generalships in central and southern England, those of the Earl of Denbigh in the central Midlands and Richard Browne in the counties to the west and north of London, had been feeble affairs. Denbigh was not replaced following his resignation in April 1645, but Browne remained in post.[26] He clung doggedly to his base at Abingdon, which was too close to Oxford for comfort. Short of resources at all times, he was subject to direct control by the Committee of Both Kingdoms, which drafted in forces from elsewhere to prop up his command and help him restrict royalist raiding from Oxford. This was a priority on the Committee's part, and it caused Fairfax some concern in December 1645 when he was campaigning against the royalist army of the west in Devonshire.[27]

Then there were the more remote major generalships, those in north and south Wales under command of Thomas Mitton and Rowland Laugharne respectively, but they were too far away to impinge on the operations of the New Model Army in any significant way or to require a measure of cooperation. However, Laugharne came briefly into view during the Langport campaign and it is worth mentioning because it may have been the one and only occasion when Fairfax ignored the Committee of Both Kingdoms' instructions. On 1 July 1645 it ordered him to send several hundred men to Milford Haven as soon as Taunton had been relieved, but he did nothing until two months later when he sent Laugharne some poorly armed militia and by that time the military crisis in south Wales had come to an end.[28]

The army of the north, which had been independent of the Earl of Essex's jurisdiction from late 1642 onwards, passed in June 1645 from Lord Fairfax to Colonel Sydenham Poyntz, a professional soldier who had served for many years in Protestant armies on the Continent, but with the proviso that Sir Thomas would be Poyntz's superior if the two armies ever needed to campaign together. This was always a very remote possibility until the New Model Army arrived back in the Thames valley area in April 1646 to set siege to Oxford. At that time it was thought that it might spare a brigade to support Poyntz, who was besieging Newark, but in the event this proved unnecessary as Newark surrendered on 6 May.[29]

The Scottish army clearly did not fit within Fairfax's remit, but it was politic for him to maintain a good relationship with its general Lord Leven, given that one of his masters, the Committee of Both Kingdoms, included Scottish representatives. In the week before the battle of Naseby there was a possibility that Leven and Sir Thomas Fairfax would have to combine forces to pursue the king's field army if it headed north from Daventry and managed to outrun the New Model. This all ended when what was left of it fled into south Wales, and Leven took up quarters in Herefordshire to prevent it causing trouble in Fairfax's rear as he set about conquering England south of the Thames. From then on the two armies went their separate ways but, though the Scots were suspicious of the New Model as the hotbed of Independency, and the Independents in the army and Parliament were antagonistic towards the Scots, there was still a measure of goodwill in that both saw the royalists as by far the bigger menace. This is clear from anxiety about Fairfax expressed in Robert Baillie's letters from London to his friends in Scotland between June and September 1645, and in the declaration of support and solidarity that Fairfax and twenty-seven of his chief officers sent the Scottish government after the marquis of Montrose's victory at Kilsyth in August 1645, which included the honourable comment that the Scots' troubles were the result of their generous assistance to the Parliamentary cause in England.[30]

The most important bodies with which Fairfax needed to work if he was to win the war quickly were the English Parliament and the Committee of Both Kingdoms. Gentles's narrative emphasizes the rough rather than the smooth, but by any stretch of imagination their relationship was far more amicable than that between the two bodies and the earls of Essex and Manchester in 1644.[31] In the correspondence that passed between them and Sir Thomas and between Fairfax and his father Lord Fairfax, it is extremely difficult to detect any evidence of animosity between the commander-in-chief and his political masters or vice versa. Sir Thomas's only complaint was over the instructions to besiege Oxford in late May 1645 when the king's field army was making hay in the north Midlands, but friction disappeared when he was granted operational freedom in the week before the battle of Naseby, whereas the Committee's only gripe was that for some weeks during the autumn Fairfax failed to respond to its request for troops to be sent from the army in Somerset and Devonshire to keep an eye on raiding by the Oxford garrison. This lapse he blamed on overwork, and he eventually solved it by authorising his secretary John Rushworth to act as his scribe, not only in official correspondence, but also in letters to his father.[32] Parliament was potentially more of a problem, because of the many interests and concerns of the MPs and the peers, but here again there was little friction between the general and his civilian masters, whether in comparison with what had gone on before or what would follow after.[33]

I therefore do not agree with Gentles that Fairfax's political masters were flexing their operational muscles in the winter of 1645–46 as the peace party regained confidence.[34] Instead, both sides were obeying the spirit and letter of their respective powers, as established by the New Model Army Ordinance,

Sir Thomas's commission as commander-in-chief, the ruling of the Committee of Both Kingdoms on June 9 concerning his operational independence, and the circumstances in which Fairfax's political masters could overrule him as defined in the House of Commons resolution of 21 June.[35] From that point onwards Fairfax scrupulously obeyed the rules (apart from one possible attempt to evade them noted earlier) and Parliament and the Committee did the same.

What these documents established was first that Fairfax not commander-in-chief of all Parliament's armies, but merely of the New Model Army and any other body with which it was campaigning. This gave him a much narrower, but more clearly defined, remit than that of the Earl of Essex and, as explained above, it was an important factor in avoiding clashes with other commanders-in-chief. In addition, Fairfax's independence of Parliament and its surrogate the Committee of Both Kingdoms was confined to operational matters in the theatre of war in which he was operating. It did not extend to strategy. Parliament delegated control over this to the Committee, which was therefore empowered to order units to move from one theatre of war to another as need arose, and this included regiments belonging to the New Model Army. Fairfax recognized the restrictions on his powers with regard to strategy in his insistence on a ruling from Parliament about whether he should advance into Wales or the West Country after the battle of Naseby.[36] However, the way in which tensions between strategy and his operational imperatives were resolved is best seen in relation to the campaign in the far south-west in the autumn and winter of 1645–6.

After the capture of Bristol, Fairfax convened councils of war on 13 and 25 September that hammered out the operational plan for the next stage in the campaign. There were two options: either to march into Devon to seek a confrontation with Goring, or to reduce the royalist garrisons in Wiltshire and Hampshire, which had the potential to interrupt his and others' communications with London, paralyse the trade in agricultural produce and disrupt urban markets. In the event it was decided to attempt both. As soon as pay for the army authorized by Parliament arrived, Fairfax would set out in the direction of Exeter, while a brigade under Cromwell's command would eliminate the royalist garrisons at Devizes, Winchester and Basing House. However, a letter from the Committee of Both Kingdoms written on 22 September, which probably arrived the day before the second meeting, contained orders of a strategic nature but ones that did not necessarily prejudice his own operational decisions. If Fairfax intended to march into the west to confront Goring, he was to leave behind a brigade of about 3,000 horse and dragoons to keep the king's cavalry at Oxford in check, because local forces and the London cavalry and dragoon regiments were fully committed to putting down unrest in Sussex. All of this was, of course, fully in accord with the House of Commons' declaration of 21 June, not an attempt to take any powers away from the commander-in-chief.[37]

Within a month the enemy garrisons in Hampshire and Wiltshire had surrendered or been overrun, the soldiers' pay had arrived, and Fairfax's brigades were on the outskirts of Exeter. There they were joined by Cromwell's brigade on 24 October.[38] Putting two and two together, Fairfax could see nothing in his previous order from the Committee to prevent Cromwell from joining him. He knew that the trouble in Sussex had been easily resolved, such that the cavalry and dragoons assigned to suppressing it could be employed in the Oxford area, as could the Hampshire cavalry under Colonel Norton's command given that there were no longer any enemy garrisons in that county.

In the meantime, however, the war elsewhere in England was changing shape. On 2 November the king arrived back at Oxford with a force of cavalry, and the garrison there had been strengthened by soldiers from other royalist garrisons, which had surrendered on terms. The Committee of Both Kingdoms panicked. On the 7th it sent a letter to Fairfax, which like many another written in similar circumstances, began fiercely and then backtracked. It claimed not to have received a reply to the letter of 22 September, which was probably incorrect,[39] as it knew Fairfax's intentions with regard to Cromwell's brigade. These Cromwell had made very clear in a letter to the Speaker of the House of Commons written on 14 October, in which he announced that having accomplished his mission in central southern England he was marching west on the following day. The only response had been that he should see that there were sufficient forces in Berkshire to blockade the small enemy garrison at Donnington Castle near Newbury, but that this should not impede his westwards march. The Committee of Both Kingdoms was advised of this resolution, and it duly set about putting in place a force to contain the royalist garrison at Donnington Castle that did not involve any New Model Army units. Moreover, the London brigade was to move from Sussex to Buckinghamshire, where it could keep an eye on the Oxford garrison. Finally, probably in the euphoria following Cromwell's letter describing the capture of Basing House, the Commons allowed Fairfax and Cromwell to dispose of their forces as they wished 'in relation to the affairs of the west'; in Fairfax's case a belated confirmation of the Committee of Both Kingdoms' decision of 9 June, but new powers for Cromwell.[40]

Nevertheless, Fairfax did not rise to the bait when the letter of 7 November went on to require him to send forces to the Oxford area, as instructed in the letter of 22 September. Additionally it expressed concern about the strength of the garrison at Abingdon, which was conveniently close to Oxford for it to be target for the king's forces. It did not try to make inroads into his operational independence, as it left it open to him 'to send such numbers as you can spare without prejudice to your army and the services wherein you are engaged', but it did require him to send the Committee a report on the state of his army.[41]

Fairfax duly consulted his council of war and it composed a report, which the Committee received a fortnight later. The report does not survive, but the accompanying letter does and it makes it clear that Whitelock's claim that he promised to provide 7,000 or 8,000 men for the defence of the counties around Oxford is a mistake. In fact he did not feel that the evidence he had provided showed that he was in a position to supply any. Nevertheless, he would abide by the rules. If reinforcements were absolutely necessary, he would send as many troops as the Committee thought fit, but he implied that operations in the west would suffer as a consequence.[42]

Faced by what looked like a questioning of its overall strategy for the conduct of the war, albeit indirect, the Committee appealed to the House of Commons, which forthwith ordered Fairfax to remove sufficient cavalry and dragoons from the army in Devonshire for the defence of the Midlands.[43] He responded almost immediately by despatching several cavalry regiments eastwards, Colonel Rainborough's regiment of foot which was besieging Corfe Castle in Dorset, and several troops of dragoons.[44] As a result, by mid-December there was a New Model Army brigade of horse between 2,000 and 3,000 strong operating in the Oxford area, commanded by Colonel Edward Whalley, while Rainborough's regiment was used to strengthen the Abingdon garrison, which was just as well as it was attacked by Prince Rupert a few weeks later. The cavalry in the meantime prevented the king from sending forces from Oxford to the relief of Chester. After it fell Whalley took charge of the siege of the important royalist garrison at Banbury.[45]

The Committee then required Fairfax to provide 500 or so foot to replace Rainborough's regiment at Corfe, which he obeyed.[46] In its turn it agreed to ask the committee of the west to release Skippon's regiment from garrison duty at Bristol to replace Rainborough's, but nothing happened. Four weeks later Fairfax took matters into his own hands and ordered it and the battalion at Corfe to join his army, as Hopton's army was threatening to force its way through to Exeter. There was no reprimand from Parliament or the Committee of Both Kingdoms because it was within Fairfax's rights to do so under the June 21 resolution.[47]

A final request for assistance reached the commander-in-chief before the fight at Torrington. In late January the militia horse in Wiltshire had been scattered by royalist cavalry from Oxford and the Wiltshire county committee asked for help, probably in the hope of obtaining the services of a New Model Army regiment of horse. This time the Committee left the matter to Fairfax's discretion, and he apparently ordered one of Massey's regiments quartered in Dorset to ride north, but nothing came of it, as the military situation in the latter county temporarily worsened following a sally from Corfe Castle.[48]

Fairfax's final word about the effect of the tension between reconquering the west and containing the royalist horse in the Oxford area can be read between the lines of a letter he wrote to his father, in which he expressed his appreciation of the assistance Parliament had recently given him in terms of pay and equipment for his troops. He had written to Westminster to that effect, but wondered if there was anything more he could do to show his gratitude.[49] This looks like an admission that he had been slow to obey the rules, but also that he was grateful not to have received anything more than a slight rap on the knuckles from the House of Commons and no break in his cordial relations with the New Model Army, Parliament and the Committee.

Chapter 12

Fairfax in Politics and at War, 1646–50

The political temperature in the anti-royalist coalition began to rise at the beginning of May 1646 as the New Model prepared to set siege to Oxford, and it was the action of the king that caused it to do so. Determined to keep his options open, Charles left his headquarters in disguise. For several days he was lost to sight, but on 5 May he turned up at the residence of the French ambassador, who was visiting the Scottish army besieging Newark. The war party in the Commons panicked. All their fears about secret agreements between the king and the Scots to impose a strict Presbyterian settlement on the English church with Independents being persecuted had come to fruition, and in a late-night vote Fairfax was ordered to send 4,000 cavalry and dragoons to Newark to take the king by force and to incarcerate him in Warwick Castle. Before Fairfax could take action the Lords persuaded the Lower House to think again and the order was rescinded, but the demand that the king should be handed over remained on the table.[1]

In time the crisis eased. First, the Scots' claim that they knew nothing in advance about the king's plans was accepted as truthful when it was revealed that the king's first intention when he left Oxford had been to go to London. Second, by ordering his remaining strongholds to surrender on the best terms they could, Charles made it clear that for him the war was over. Finally, the Marquis of Argyll, the nearest the Scottish Presbyterian peers had to a leader, in a speech delivered to the two Houses on 25 June, affirmed that his government was as close to the English government in its war aims as it had been when the alliance was signed in 1643.[2] Parliament was reassured, and the king remained in Scottish hands, but the debate in the English Parliament over whether or not the king should be held as a prisoner had let the cat out of the bag. In a speech opposing it no less a person than the Earl of Essex, whom most historians see by 1646 as the leader of the peace party, reminded his listeners in the House of Lords that they had gone to war to force the king to remove his evil counsellors. He had now abandoned them by leaving Oxford and seeking sanctuary with those who had fought against them. All that remained to be done was to disband the armies and conclude a peace.[3] He could also have added that disbandment would enormously reduce the burden on the nation as a whole, as taxes like the excise that helped pay for the army and its needs fell on rich and poor alike.

Disbandment, however, ushered in the third and final crisis for the anti-royalist coalition, which blew it apart. The first had occurred in the summer of 1643 when defeat was staring Parliament in the face. This was partially resolved by the Scottish alliance, and the reversal in the fortunes of Parliament's armies in the months culminating in the victory of Marston Moor in July 1644 and the conquest of the north of England. The second took place in the winter of 1644–5 following the failure of Parliament's generals to turn that victory into victory in the war as a whole. That crisis had been resolved by the remodelling of the southern armies and the realisation by coalition members, following the failed peace negotiations at Uxbridge, that the king would not agree to a negotiated peace on terms acceptable to any of them. In both the earlier crises the fact that there was still a common enemy was a powerful centripetal force. Now there was clearly no enemy. It was therefore necessary to manufacture one. For the war party it was potentially the Scots, and for the peace party potentially the New Model Army.[4]

In all previous wars the end of fighting had been followed by the disbandment of the army, but Essex's sunny words were tongue-in-cheek if not outright malicious. A force of some size would need to be kept in England and Wales to snuff out royalist uprisings, and Ireland was still to be reconquered. Conversely, there were undeniably far more men under arms in the summer of 1646 than were needed to perform these tasks. The consequence was an unnecessarily high financial charge on the state and thus on its citizens, and as time passed and the burden failed to diminish, the genuine gratitude towards to the army felt by many who had supported Parliament inexorably ebbed away. At the same time anxiety rose, with evidence that the armed forces were being politicized, as officers and private soldiers alike looked to the future beyond disbandment. Many convinced themselves that when this occurred Parliament would ignore their concerns or treat them with contempt, and in time such sentiments grew into grievances. Of these the most universal was that they would not receive all the back pay they were owed. As a result they would be unable to discharge the debts they had incurred during the war, or to achieve their dreams and ambitions for a new life as a civilian, which could well be totally dependent on the lump sum they were owed. Almost as worrying was fear that they would not be given legal protection against being sued for offences against life and property committed during their military service, when they had merely been obeying Parliament's commands. Finally they looked to Parliament to provide for those less fortunate than themselves, their comrades disabled by wounds and disease and the dependents of those who had died in the wars.[5]

Parliament's difficulties in dealing with the financial, legal and humanitarian effects of the past were compounded once the fighting had ceased by the problems of the present. When there was no pay available, soldiers were put on free quarter, which meant that the people in whose houses they were billeted were responsible for their maintenance, in return for the promise of financial compensation at a later date. Free quarter was universally unpopular with civilians and with the civilian authorities in town and countryside, as it was a potent cause of lawlessness. Soldiers took by force foodstuffs which they regarded as rightfully theirs. In addition, the disbandment of provincial forces, which began in early 1646, had been accompanied by violence as soldiers were discharged with no more than the promise that their arrears would be paid in the future. They therefore saw themselves as being cheated.[6]

Initially, the New Model Army was not affected as its pay, although many weeks in arrears, was coming through in dribs and drabs, but Massey's brigade had not been paid at all and was subsisting on free quarter in the West Country, where it was committing all kinds of misdemeanours against the inhabitants. To make matters worse, it had swollen in numbers since the beginning of the year, and rumour had it that many of the new recruits were former royalist soldiers.[7] Of more immediate concern to Parliament, however, was the need to provide troops to serve in Ireland, where most of the country was in rebel hands.

Putting down the rebellion had fallen largely to the Scots from 1643 onwards, but they had made very little progress due to lack of resources, and their only army there was badly mauled by the rebels at the battle of Benburb in June 1646. However, attempts to persuade provincial forces in England and Wales to regroup into regiments to fight in Ireland largely fell on deaf ears, other than in Cheshire, Lancashire, north Wales and the west Midlands, where, perhaps coincidentally, troops from Ireland had fought for the king in the Civil Wars. It was also thought that many of Massey's men would happily volunteer.[8]

In June Fairfax received an order from the House of Commons to proceed with the disbandment of the western brigade, but the Lords, egged on by Massey, disapproved and the disbandment did not take place.[9] In the following month MPs looked to the New Model Army to do its bit towards the conquest of Ireland. A motion for four regiments of foot and a regiment of horse to be sent there was only defeated by a single vote in the Commons, the principal argument against being that hammered home again and again by war party members in Parliament and by the more radical of the London newspapers. The Scottish army was still quartered in the north of England, with the king in its possession. It would therefore be unwise to weaken the New Model when there was a chance that the two would make common cause against it. Interestingly, one of the tellers against the motion of 31 July was Oliver Cromwell.[10]

* * * * *

The arrival of Fairfax's brigades in the Oxford area and their reunion with Whalley's cavalry and dragoons marked the start of the downturn in the relations between Parliament and its general, because it was then that Oliver Cromwell began making a list of officers serving in the New Model who were Presbyterian in sympathy, and therefore, in the eyes of the war party leadership, unreliable.[11] That he had done so only became public knowledge two years later, when it went off like a damp squib because parts of the old anti-royalist coalition were working well together in the Second Civil War. However, in the charged atmosphere of the late spring of 1646 it did make sense to think ahead and ascertain how many captains and above might change sides should a war break out with Scotland following the king's flight. But identifying who was or was not 'one of us' was the first step towards the First Army Coup of June 1647, when the army was purged of officers associated with the peace party, the Scots' allies in matters affecting the army for the past two and a half years.

Suspicions of the army rather than suspicions in the army came out into the open because of the triumphalism of William Dell, a prominent Independent chaplain, as expressed in a sermon he preached on 7 June 1646 to the forces besieging Oxford, in which his target audience was the rank-and-file. The main theme was praise for their godly behaviour, which explained their unbroken successes in the field. This sounds uncontentious, but Dell took as his text a passage from the book of Isaiah dating from a time when the prophet was berating the Judean monarchy and aristocracy for their sinfulness, and it did not take much for some civilians present to see a contemporary resonance. The nature of the audience also caused concern, as did Dell's response that he thought he was only addressing members of the army, which suggested that the sermon had a political purpose, and might even be a rallying cry. On 27 June the Lords took up the matter, but when asked to explain himself Dell was not contrite. Instead he was insolent, and to make matters worse, when the sermon appeared in print a few weeks later, he had added a preface that was partisan in the extreme, and that naturally increased the Lords' suspicions of the army and its future intentions.[12]

In late June the Upper House was also sparring with General Fairfax. When Oxford capitulated on the king's orders the general sent a copy of the articles of surrender to the House of Commons, but not to the Lords. The Upper House was angry at what it perceived as a slight, but when Fairfax sent them a suitably humble apology they did not pursue the matter.[13] However, what followed was a refusal to accede to his request to disband Massey's brigade or to allow it to be sent to Ireland. It is therefore not surprising that when Sir Thomas wrote to his father on 8 August, he referred to 'troublesome conditions', which included a provocation: the imprisonment of one of his colonels for debt.[14]

The spate of incidents that signified friction between the army and its political masters died down during the autumn, but there was one hiccup. The fate of Massey's brigade was a cause of contention between the Lords on one side and Fairfax and the Commons on the other. It ceased to exist in October, four months after the matter had been first raised in Parliament, but the disbandment went without a hitch apart from the fact that very few soldiers volunteered for service in Ireland. The Lords had opposed it to the end, but they were defeated by a procedural trick to which they were slow to react, possibly because Massey had decided to focus on a political career.[15] In fact he and Fairfax jointly supervised the operation, with two New Model Army cavalry regiments close by in case of trouble. However, six peers responded to what they regarded as Fairfax's insolence by refusing to take a visible part in welcoming the general when he returned to London.[16]

In the autumn of 1646 two events served to celebrate the end of fighting in England, though the first was a fortuitous one: the burial of the Earl of Essex in Westminster Abbey on 22 October, five weeks after he had died of a stroke. The procession to Westminster Abbey looked more like a victory parade than a funeral, as the earl was accompanied to his resting place by a cavalcade of thirteen colonels, seventy-four field officers and many more captains drawn up in regimental formations.[17] The roll call of those who did or did not attend has been seen as showing fissures in the military establishment.[18] But too much can be made of it. Many of the officers who did attend were men who had served under Essex at some time or another, but Cromwell and Ireton, who had fought at Edgehill, were not present.[19] Neither was Sir Thomas Fairfax, but that can be explained. Even though he had never served under Essex, it would have been a remarkable demonstration of his dislike of the earl if he had been in London at the time of the funeral and not attended, but in fact he was in Wiltshire supervising the disbanding of Massey's brigade, and Massey was absent for the same reason.[20]

The second event took place on 12 November when the two Houses of Parliament formally gave Sir Thomas their thanks for winning the war. The description given in Joshua Sprigg's *Anglia Rediviva* is of a magnificent occasion, with speeches heaping praise on the general to which he responded with his usual humility.[21] It is surely significant, however, that the formal declarations of gratitude from the Commons and the Corporation of London were of a personal nature. In complete contrast to William Dell's sermon of 7 June they made no mention of the army. However, Fairfax was not to get all the praise. The Speaker of the House of Commons' speech made sure that the old lord general's contribution was not forgotten:

> the honour of the late lord general was not while he lived in any way eclipsed by the succession of you to his command but rather augmented in having both rays enough to enlighten the kingdom then overset with clouds and darkness.[22]

This chimed with the reports in the London weeklies, which paid far less attention to the events of 12–14 November than they did to Essex's funeral. By the same measure Whitelock scarcely mentioned Fairfax's welcome, and Juxon did not mention it at all.[23]

At the end of January the Scottish army returned home and in the interests of economy all but 6,000 men were disbanded. Fairfax saw it off, in a manner of speaking, by providing an escort of horse and foot for the waggons carrying the first instalment of the £400,000 Parliament had agreed it owed the Scots. He also ordered Skippon's and Robert Lilburne's regiments to stay behind to garrison Newcastle and other places which had hitherto been the responsibility of the Scottish army. The horse and one regiment of foot then returned south, bringing with them King Charles, whom they left at Holdenby House in Northamptonshire under what amounted to house arrest. In the meantime, most of the rest of the New Model Army had taken up quarters in a thirty-mile circle around Nottingham. The reason given was that the east Midlands was better able to supply it with foodstuffs and fodder than other parts of south and central England that had suffered more severely during the war.[24] However, Nottingham was also conveniently placed for the army to intervene militarily should anything go wrong with the arrangements for the Scots to dis-garrison the northern counties.

The departure of the Scots and the disbanding of Massey's brigade fatally weakened the war party's argument for keeping the New Model at full strength, and even before the Scots had left the scene supporters of the peace party in London, including the lord mayor and the Corporation, were putting about a petition to Parliament, which among many other things asked for its disbandment. They cited four substantive reasons: it was too large; it was too expensive; it was a hotbed of religious extremists with mere soldiers preaching strange and erroneous doctrines, and the security of the city, and by implication of the country as a whole, could not be assured when religious radicals were 'masters of such power'.[25]

The petition was presented to Parliament and was well received, not only by the Lords, but also by the Commons, where the peace party for the first time enjoyed a majority, thanks to the change in the military situation and to the influx of new MPs elected to constituencies that had hitherto been represented by royalists. The first fruit of their discussion of the petition was a Commons resolution, passed after a division on 31 December, banning preaching by lay persons. The Lower House turned its attention to the army a month later when the committee of MPs charged with managing the affairs of Ireland was asked to say what reinforcements were needed to enable the forces there to go on the offensive.

In mid-February the Commons began to make concrete plans for remodelling the whole of the militia, not only the New Model Army, but also the units in the north and some garrisons. It was quickly agreed, against war party opposition, that the army in England was to be reduced to 5,400 cavalry and 1,000 dragoons, with no infantry other than that belonging to the few remaining garrisons.[26] At about the same time soldiers of the New Model quartered at Nottingham began discussing a petition to alert Parliament to their concerns for the future.[27] However, the exact date is uncertain. As a result, it may have been a reaction to the failure of Parliament to make satisfactory provision for the arrears owing to Massey's brigade, rather than to the London petition or the resolutions concerning remodelling.[28] Anxiety about the army's intention soon increased, when it moved its quarters into East Anglia, only two to three days' march from the capital.

The plans for the pacification of Ireland were formalized between 5 and 8 March, and they were such as to heighten the army's anxieties. The scheme for the home army was as agreed earlier, and seven regiments of foot and four of horse were to be sent to Ireland. From this it was easy to work out that just under half of the New Model Army foot and a small number of horse would be surplus to requirements, but there was no mention of how, when and where the disbanded officers' and soldiers' arrears were to be paid, or of a general pardon for those who had committed offences against the law while serving in the New Model. There was also a big devil in the detail. Nowhere did the Commons' resolutions state that the regiments to be sent to Ireland or those to be retained in England would be existing New Model Army units.

To make matters worse, as far as the officers were concerned, the Commons passed two resolutions that were blatantly political in nature, designed to massively weaken the war party influence in the army. A new self-denying ordinance was to be passed, which would present Cromwell, Fleetwood and several other colonels whose allegiance was to the war party with the dilemma of giving up their seats in Parliament or their commands in the army. To make matters worse, Independents and Baptists who chose not to swallow their principles would also have to resign, as all officers were to be forced to swear an oath of loyalty to the state church, the doctrine and government of which was to be uniformly Presbyterian.[29] Evidence that these resolutions were political in nature is shown by the fact that they only applied to the home army. Officers in the regiments sent to Ireland could be left in peace as they and the units they commanded were too far away to influence politics in England.

Finally, in a division in the Commons in which well over 200 members voted, Sir Thomas was only retained as commander-in-chief of the home army by a majority of twelve. This was not necessarily an insult, or a sign that the House had turned against him. Admittedly his association with the war party from 1643 onwards, and his involvement in the push to have Massey's brigade disbanded, would have counted against him, but at the same time it must be recognized that his undoubted qualities as a fighting general were not those required in the commander of a peacetime army. Moreover, his frequent bouts of ill-health, which were causing him to leave his duties for weeks at a time, would be a disadvantage in what was primarily an administrative job requiring day-to-day attention to masses of detailed and complex paperwork.

Despite its obvious political subtext, the plan to reduce the size of the army would have had a semblance of logic to people uncommitted to the war party or the peace party, and in the eyes of taxpayers in general it was the clearest possible sign that the country was well on the road to peacetime conditions. But for the army there were many unanswered questions, even among those who were inclined to go along with the remodelling the Commons had approved, and the majority of the officers attending a meeting held on 22 March at the army headquarters authorized the sending of a petition from the officers and the soldiers to Fairfax expressing their concerns.[30] However, the arrogant manner in which Parliament responded created the worst possible atmosphere for avoiding a clash. The first step was to instruct Fairfax to order the petitioning to stop, and then on 30 March (in response to a claim that officers and soldiers in Colonel Harley's regiment who would not sign were being threatened with being cashiered by their lieutenant colonel), the two Houses passed the so-called 'declaration of dislike', declaring that if the petitioners persisted they would be proceeded against as enemies of the state.[31]

Sir Thomas, who had chaired the meeting that had approved the petitioning and had not, as far as can be ascertained, spoken against it, refused to discipline the promoters, claiming that he had no evidence as yet that their fears for the future were anything but genuine. He also expressed his view that discussion rather than threats would be a more fruitful way of securing obedience to Parliament's commands.[32] Finally, although he kept quiet about it, Fairfax must have been surprised at the fury of the reaction to a petition that had been addressed to him on the understanding that he would only pass it on if he was satisfied that its concerns were worthy of being brought to Parliament's attention.[33] He may also have been reminded, by those of his infantry officers who had served in Essex's army, that they had been much more confrontational in the past. In December 1644 they had petitioned Parliament in person about their concerns for the future, without using the Earl of Essex as an intermediary.[34]

Nevertheless, despite its provocative nature Parliament's plan for remodelling the New Model nearly worked because it split the officer corps. From the start twenty-nine officers with the rank of captain and above agreed to serve in Ireland. Later the figure rose to over fifty, close to twenty-five percent of the total. Ranged against them by the end of April were seventy-four commissioned officers who, while expressing their loyalty to Parliament in principle, refused to serve in Ireland until their grievances had been settled. Later the caveat was extended to a refusal to disband.[35] This was an unprecedented step for the dissatisfied to take, but they had one great advantage over those who were willing to volunteer: powerful backing among the soldiers and the non-commissioned officers, who had elected their own representatives, the so-called agitators, to work for the settlement of the grievances of the lower ranks. The contents also had a second weakness: they lacked a leader among the senior officers. Fairfax and Major General Skippon were hoping for a compromise, and so, on the surface at least, was Lieutenant General Cromwell, while Commissary General Ireton and Thomas Hammond, the lieutenant general of artillery, were prominent among the dissatisfied from the start.[36]

The temperature rose in leaps and bounds between March and late May 1647, with the agitators chosen by the ordinary soldiers taking a more and more prominent role.[37] At the same time it became clear that the bare figures given for the home army in the Commons' resolutions of 5–8 March were not as favourable to the New Model Army regiments as first appeared. On 8 April the Commons decided that only five of the expected nine regiments of cavalry in the home army were to be drawn from the New Model. Three of the remainder were to be from the Parliament's northern army, while a fourth was to be made up of six troops drawn from the Midlands counties.[38]

Moreover, although it may have been Parliament's original intention for most if not all of the troops sent to Ireland to be made up of whole regiments drawn from the New Model, the declaration of dislike changed everything. On 13 April Captain Thomas Howard of Fleetwood's regiment offered his services and was granted the colonelcy of what must have been a new regiment.[39] When five commissioners drawn from the Irish committee, all peace party men, came to Saffron Walden, the army headquarters, on 15 April, they were looking for volunteers among the infantry, but they found that Fairfax would do no more than write a letter to the officer commanding each regiment asking him to encourage his men to go to Ireland and not to impede the commissioners' work in any way. He then left the army for London to undergo medical treatment, and there he remained for over a month. The nature of his illness is uncertain, but there is a strong hint that it was brought about by stress. In a letter written to his father just before he returned to the army in late May he wrote that he was feeling better, but that he 'too soon relapses with little trouble'.

After an initial burst of optimism based on the number of officers willing to volunteer, the commissioners found that many of their soldiers would not follow their example, and that those who wanted to volunteer were being put under pressure not to do so.[40] Those who persisted were eventually placed in four regiments commanded very largely by former New Model Army officers, most of whom had been promoted from lieutenant to captain, but it is doubtful if the entire body amounted to more than 1,000 foot soldiers. However, those who did not volunteer had a stark choice: disbandment or mutiny.[41]

Parliament made a number of concessions to army opinion about disbandment during late April and May, culminating on 22 May in promises that appeared to go a long way towards satisfying the discontented officers and soldiers' principal grievances, but by the time the Commons next met its temper had undergone a sea change. Perhaps, on reflection, the members thought they had gone too far. This was suggested by Sir William Constable, who had been present in the House on the 22nd, in a letter he wrote to Lord Fairfax a few days later. A final proposal to draw a veil over the declaration of dislike, which he paraphrased as 'that the Parliament and the army parted as friends and that Parliament was satisfied of the army's great affection for them', turned a fair day into a storm. When the House met again three days later and the proposal was put again to MPs they rejected it out of hand and ordered the disbandment to start on 1 June, beginning with Sir Fairfax's own regiment of foot.[42]

When Fairfax returned to the army headquarters on 23 May, he could do nothing to stem the tide of events and fell ill once more. A Council of War he convened on the 29th agreed by eighty-six votes to seven to reject the Commons' promises of 22 May as insufficient for the army to agree to disband: eight weeks' arrears on the nail was not enough, the guarantee of freedom from prosecution in the courts of law contained loopholes, and even worse, the failure to pass the resolution that would have repealed the declaration of dislike meant that they would be disbanded with a stain on their own honour and that of the army as a whole. An even larger majority then went on to agree to a general rendezvous of the army a week later, the purpose being to put pressure on Parliament.[43] All Fairfax could suggest, in a letter to the Speaker written on the following day, was that the House of Commons should step back from the brink in the interests of brotherly love – and if it would help he would resign.[44]

When Parliament's commissioners tried to disband the army on 1 June the soldiers refused. Mutinies followed, though with no loss of life, and on 4 June an ad hoc body of horse led by Cornet George Joyce, which included members of Fairfax's lifeguard, removed the king from Holdenby House. When the general learned what had happened, he ordered other regiments to take Charles back to Holdenby, but the king, sensing an opportunity to seize the political initiative, refused to go, and the escort acceded to his demand that he should continue to the army headquarters at Newmarket where the general rendezvous was to take place.[45]

Despite his surprise at the seizure of the king, Sir Thomas still felt in control, as shown by his letters written to the Speaker of the House of Commons, among others, between 7 and 11 June, but it was all an illusion.[46] The creeping democratization of the army took on concrete form in July with the first meeting, at the agitators' request, of a Council of the Army comprising two representatives of the officers and two of the rank-and-file from each regiment, at which the commander-in-chief was merely the chairman.[47] The purpose was not simply to put pressure on Parliament to redress all the army's grievances, but was also to ensure that those MPs and peers who had traduced and humiliated the army should be expelled from Parliament and brought to account. Fairfax rightly saw this as a major reduction in his power to influence events, and the process gathered momentum as time passed. During the next two months he delegated control of negotiations with the rank-and-file and with the king to a sub-committee of officers presided over by Cromwell.[48]

At first glance, however, Fairfax appeared to have gained authority following the First Army Coup. In July Parliament appointed him commander-in-chief of all its forces in England and Wales, and his official mode of address became lord general on his father's death in March 1648.[49] But these were mostly empty honours, as the First Army Coup had turned it into a sort of democracy, in which his position was similar to that of a constitutional monarch in mid-to-late nineteenth-century England. Like Queen Victoria, what Fairfax possessed was influence, and this was best maintained by keeping above the political fray until, for example, the army threatened to disintegrate through factional strife. Cromwell's role in the duumvirate was analogous to that of a prime minister of the same date, in that his powers were not autocratic, but limited by two representative bodies, the council of war otherwise known as the Council of the Officers of the Army, for the commissioned officers, and the Council of the Army for the remainder. The former was a force to be reckoned with until after the Second Army Coup had run its course, while the latter disappeared from the scene with the Leveller mutinies of the winter of 1647, but the rank and file and the non-commissioned officers continued to make their voices heard through petitioning at the regimental level.[50] Their representatives had also held discussions with a remarkably wide-ranging agenda at Putney parish church in November 1647.

There remains, however, a question mark over Fairfax's attitude towards the army's involvement in politics during his last three years as commander-in-chief, ending in June 1650. The view current for much of the twentieth century followed that of royalist writers and of Cromwell's war party colleagues who parted company with him at the king's execution or subsequently, namely that confused in his mind and laid low on occasions by physical infirmity Fairfax was swept along by the tide of events. As a result he was very largely a passive spectator, and when he did intervene to prevent strife, as for example, in trying in late 1648 to reduce pressure from the army for the king to be tried for high treason, he was ineffectual because he was too cautious to go beyond merely using words.[51]

However, this assessment of the reasons for Fairfax's passivity has been very firmly knocked on the head in the past twenty years by a number of historians, whose views are admirably summarized by Hopper in his biography of Sir Thomas.[52] Their predecessors had been naïve to take Sir Thomas at his word when he wrote in his *Short Memorials* that he was unable to influence the course of events because of his powerlessness. Instead they claim that as a man who had been closely associated with the war party from 1644 at the latest, he was not unhappy with how matters progressed until mid-January 1649, when the king's execution became a near certainty. What the revisionists failed to satisfactorily explain, however, was why Sir Thomas did not resign at that point, but continued in office for another eighteen months. There was also the curious incident during the king's trial when Lady Fairfax, in a not very effective disguise, heckled the judge, challenged the legality of the proceedings, and came close to being shot by a file of musketeers before being forcibly removed from the court.

When I began working on this chapter I thought that the lord general's sole contribution to the Putney debates might provide the answer. On the last day of the roundtable discussions Colonel Harrison identified King Charles as a man of blood whom the army had a duty to bring to trial for his dastardly deeds. Cromwell replied in words that seemed to contradict one another. First he gave examples from the Old Testament of men who had committed murder but not been put to death, but then, when Commissary General Whalley agreed but added that the process for bringing a murderer to account should be one that was clearly in accordance with the law, Cromwell saw this as boxing him into a corner. In a court of law, human machinations, human caution or human logic might serve to frustrate God's will. He therefore insisted that if this seemed likely direct action might be required on the part of the army as God's chosen instrument, evidenced by its unbroken string of victories: 'we do the work when it is disputable and the work of others to do it if it be an absolute and indisputable duty for us to do it'.

Fairfax spoke next. Firth describes him as following the same line of argument as Cromwell, but the lord general was as concerned with constitutional propriety as Edward Whalley: 'we do but secure the king in the right of another and that it becomes them to order things'. By opposing direct action he sounds less extreme than Cromwell, but in so doing he provided grounds for justifying his own conduct up to the king's execution and beyond. His take on the situation in which the army might find itself was one that would give him and his officers a clear conscience. The army's job was merely to deliver the king to its political masters and for them to decide his fate. As such it is an argument that army personnel through the centuries have used when accused of condoning or committing atrocities, namely that they were merely obeying orders.[53]

Having thus begun to nail my colours to the mast, I then turned to the *Short Memorials*, the source from which previous generations of historians had drawn evidence to support the concept of Fairfax's powerlessness, and began to have doubts. In order to smash that narrative and validate the new one the revisionists had rubbished it as evidence. The *Short Memorials* was written well after the restoration of the monarchy by an elderly man with a defective memory worried that he was about to be brought to account for his actions and/or that future generations would regard his behaviour as dishonourable. It was poorly structured and there were clear gaps and weaknesses in the argument, which showed that Sir Thomas had set himself an impossible task. Although being economical with the truth went very much against the character of the lord general as described by his biographers, concern for his reputation caused him to be so.

However, I now incline to the view that Fairfax was telling more of the truth than recent writers will acknowledge. This change of heart came from a very close reading of the *Short Memorials*, noting the gaps and inconsistencies in the narrative that might be a clue as to the audience he was addressing. In the end I came to the conclusion that it was not written in 1660s by a man with a tired mind and a deteriorating intellect, but many years earlier and not long after he resigned as lord general, when his mental powers were still good.[54] But although the new hypothesis may explain the gaps and inconsistencies in the document and the time at which it was written, it cannot add much to the debate about the reason or reasons for Sir Thomas's behaviour from the first army coup until his resignation. Was he happy with the general course of events, as Hopper and his school of thought claim, or was he politically as helpless as Gardiner described him?[55] On the other hand, did the people he described as his friends, who persuaded him on several occasions not to resign, know something about him that would destroy his reputation for good if he did resign before it was in their interest for him to do so? To go any further along that line of enquiry is to enter into the realm of pure speculation, and that is something that is best left to the final chapter.

* * * * *

If Fairfax's political role was circumscribed after May 1647, he remained commander-in-chief and this counted when war broke again in the spring of 1648 when the victors of the First Civil War were threatened by a coalition of incorrigible royalists, aided by a few aggrieved parliamentarians and a powerful faction in Scotland led by the Duke of Hamilton. There is no doubt that Sir Thomas was in his element when warfare broke out in England and Wales in the early spring of 1648, and it must have seemed like old times, with the Earl of Warwick back as lord high admiral and the Earl of Manchester and Philip Skippon serving on the Derby House Committee, the successor to the Committee of Both Kingdoms.[56]

In late April Fairfax, in collaboration with the Committee, prepared for war. Colonel Horton was sent to put down an uprising in south-west Wales led by discontented provincial officers, and when they retreated to castles on the Pembrokeshire coast the Committee sent Cromwell there with a full brigade of infantry and the promise of a powerful train of artillery. It also sent horse to assist John Lambert, who had replaced Sydenham Poyntz as commander of the army in the north during the First Army Coup, and who was facing a royalist uprising in Northumberland that probably presaged a Scottish invasion. Fairfax was close to setting out for the north with further reinforcements when he was distracted by the more immediate danger posed by an uprising in Kent.[57] Gathering together the few New Model Army units left in the London area, Fairfax marched rapidly eastwards with a balanced force of infantry and cavalry suitable for fighting a conventional battle. He found the royalists defending the line of the River Medway at Maidstone, and in customary fashion he hoodwinked them by using the landscape to conceal his line of march, such that he was able to approach the town from the enemy's side of the river and from an unexpected direction. Knowing that he faced an army of volunteers with little experience of fighting, he decided that a night attack would be sufficiently disconcerting to break their will, but the experienced royalist commanders steadied their musketeers by placing them under cover in houses, while artillery pieces were positioned so as to be able to fire down the streets. The opposition was thus fiercer than expected, but despite being in pain from gout Fairfax turned the tide with his usual inspirational bravery. Even so it took him several hours to clear the town.[58]

By that time many of the rebels had had enough and fled the scene, but Fairfax then bungled the pursuit. With his eyes firmly fixed on the Channel ports through which a foreign invasion might take place, he failed to commit sufficient forces to shadowing the best elements in the enemy army, which moved off in the opposite direction heading for London, where they had hopes of a royalist uprising. However, Skippon, who commanded London's defences, had no difficulty in keeping the peace. The rebels then crossed the Thames unopposed at Greenwich using the ferry and the few boats they could find, and shut themselves up in the town of Colchester in Essex. The ensuing siege, which Fairfax conducted personally, lasted over two months, at the end of which starvation forced the rebels to surrender, though he was unlucky not to have rushed the town on the first day before the gates had been properly closed. By late August, however, the war elsewhere in the country was almost over thanks to Cromwell's victory over Hamilton at Preston.[59]

The campaign in the south-east of England in the summer of 1648 was to be Fairfax's last, but not his best. Nevertheless he had defended the capital in a workmanlike manner and with limited resources. In the following year, however, he took the lead in the suppression of a Leveller revolt in the army, for which the spark was an expeditionary force to be sent to Ireland, but it is uncertain how far the successful plan by which the rebels were subdued without excessive violence was Cromwell's or Fairfax's, as both were involved the denouement at Burford in Oxfordshire.[60]

One year later Parliament ordered a pre-emptive strike against Scotland because the Scots were close to crowning the Prince of Wales as king, but the lord general handed in his resignation, blaming his poor state of health given the heavy physical and mental responsibility he would be taking on, but when pressed he argued that he could not in conscience command an invasion of Scotland for ethical reasons.[61] He cited an oath of fellowship he had taken in 1644 when the army from Scotland helped alter the course of the war in England, but contemporaries and historians alike have seen the root cause of his decision as pressure from his wife and the Presbyterian ministers she favoured.[62]

Seemingly, fellow generals and politicians were reluctant to see the lord general resign.[63] Conversely, it is possible that they were happy for him to go, as he had seen the army through troubled times from which it had emerged stronger and more united than ever. His services were therefore no longer needed to prevent the army turning on itself, and his departure would not cause embarrassment as it was unlikely to be followed by an avalanche of resignations among officers with similar reservations about invading Scotland. If this formed part of their thinking, they were correct. I have only come across a single case of an officer quitting the army at the same time as Fairfax for reasons of conscience.[64]

There are also signs that Fairfax's resignation was not unexpected. Some of the decisions taken by Parliament in the spring of 1650, as war with Scotland loomed, can be read as preparing the way for a smooth takeover by Oliver Cromwell. Both, for example, were to command in Scotland rather than one being left in charge of the army units remaining in England in case of a royalist uprising, and both were to be responsible for choosing officers for additional regiments of horse and foot that were being raised for the war. The fact that Fairfax's imminent resignation was seen as more than a rumour is suggested by Parliament's order for Cromwell to return from Ireland six months before the invasion of Scotland took place, and at a time when negotiations between the Scots and the future King Charles II were at a standstill. Moreover, although Cromwell had made good progress in five months he had been in Ireland, there was much to be done and his lieutenant general Michael Jones had just died.[65]

Part III

The Third Lord General

Chapter 13

Oliver Cromwell, the Army and Parliament 1646–49

In the six months following the surrender of Oxford Oliver Cromwell spent almost all his time at Westminster defending the reputation and interests of the New Model Army, as it was the strongest card in the war party hand for achieving its religion and constitutional objectives. As his personal papers do not survive, the only certain evidence of his activities is in his few surviving letters to Sir Thomas Fairfax and in the journals of the House of Commons. The rest is mainly either rumours mentioned in letters home by foreign ambassadors or their equivalent, or speculation by Cromwell's contemporaries, trying, often many years later, to construct narratives of the significant stages in his rise to power from backbench MP to lord protector of England, Scotland and Ireland, which were inevitably influenced by hindsight.[1]

As a result, all that one can say for certain about Cromwell at Westminster is that he won the battle to preserve the unity of the army on 31 July 1646 and lost the battle to allow lay persons to preach on 31 December.[2] He also failed to gain approval for Lord Fairfax to succeed the deceased Earl of Essex as lord lieutenant of Yorkshire.[3] Finally, he may have frustrated a project to send Massey's brigade to Ireland by offering the services of part of the New Model Army, which he would command while Parliament disbanded the rest, but this project seems to have come to grief in the House of Lords.

The letters he wrote to Sir Thomas Fairfax clearly show his concern for the future, but his faith in his God was so great that they almost invariably end on an optimistic note. Reading between the lines, he saw the growing authority of the leaders of the peace party in the Commons as God's will, but His purpose was to test the resolve of those whom providence had clearly shown to be His instruments. If they stuck to their guns all would be well. His will was to provide the best possible evidence of his glory, and that was best displayed not if the odds of success were not initially in the war party's favour, but firmly stacked against it.[4] In addition, Cromwell's bewailing the factional strife at Westminster in one of his letters was probably playing to Fairfax's concerns expressed in a previous letter, but it is laughable given his enthusiastic involvement in such activities in the winters of 1643–4 and 1644–5.[5]

For the first few months of 1647 the evidence of Cromwell's political activity dries up as he was seriously ill, with only the occasional letter to his general shedding light on his state of mind.[6] He therefore apparently played no part in the confrontation between the army and Parliament that gathered pace from mid-February onwards.[7] However, the rumour mill revived when he returned to full health in May, when he was one of the four army officers who were MPs chosen by the Commons as commissioners to liaise with the malcontents in the army and assure the officers and soldiers that legislation to satisfy their grievances would shortly become law. When he returned from army headquarters at Saffron Walden in Essex he was very optimistic. Although the army was full of soldiers and officers with genuine grievances, they would nevertheless obey the orders for remodelling passed by the Commons in March and early April. At the same time, however, he reminded the House that it was their duty to ensure that such grievances were satisfied in full.[8]

Two very different narratives exist of Cromwell's behaviour in the lead-up to the First Army Coup in June. The first, the view of most of his biographers over the years, is that the impassioned words he spoke in the Commons concerning the army's obeying Parliament in the last resort were genuine, and that he worked as hard as he could for a rapprochement, but when the regiments refused to disband he joined the army at Newmarket because he believed that the leaders of the peace party in the Commons were seeking armed support from Scotland or the Continent, and that he and other war party leaders were likely to be arrested. It was for these reasons alone that he gave orders for loyal troops to secure the king's person for fear that he might otherwise be carried off to London by Colonel Richard Greaves, a convinced peace party man, who was in command of the troops guarding him at Holdenby.[9]

The second narrative, popular in the writings of his contemporaries, both former associates and former enemies, was that Cromwell's protestations in the House of Commons about the amenability of the malcontents in the army both before and after he travelled to Saffron Waldon were deliberately over-optimistic, and as such intended to lull the peace party into a false sense of security.[10]

The most direct evidence for Cromwell's insincerity in the spring of 1647 comes from a denunciation of the lieutenant general presented to Parliament a year later by Robert Huntington, the major of his cavalry regiment.[11] Huntington described a meeting at army headquarters at which Cromwell and his son-in-law Henry Ireton, acting as Parliament's commissioners, addressed the soldiers' representatives. Ireton stated that 'it would then [i.e. at that time] be lawful and fit to deny disbanding till we [i.e. the officers – of which he was one – as well as the soldiers] had received equal and full satisfaction for our past services.' Cromwell followed Ireton's remarks with a comment of his own, which is obscure but seems to emphasize that he and Ireton had loyalties to the army as well as to Parliament. He did not use the opportunity to contradict what Ireton had said, but the fact that he kept silent is likely to have been understood by those listening as giving tacit approval. The continuity between the two speeches is also stressed by the words with which Huntington prefaced Cromwell's enigmatic comment: 'Lieutenant General Cromwell further adding'.[12]

It is perhaps impossible to get to the truth of the matter because of the lack of evidence, but the most generous spin I can put on Cromwell's behaviour in the months leading up to the First Army Coup was that he lived in hope that God would do something to prevent the remodelling of the army. However, if this was his Plan A, I cannot conceive of him not having a Plan B. Moreover, it would not be reliant on tentative agreements with flaky collaborators to take action in undefined circumstances, but grounded on firm commitments from senior army officers who were family and close to him both politically and religiously, like Henry Ireton, John Disbrowe, his brother-in-law, and his cousins Thomas and Robert Hammond. What would have lain behind Plan B was almost certainly not personal ambition, but rather the determination to prevent a split in the army descending into disorder and chaos. It would have been supported by the conviction that Fairfax shared his antipathy towards the leaders of the peace party, and that he would not oppose him and his allies seizing the initiative in order to prevent the army disintegrating, and the political and religious gains from the First Civil War being lost as the peace party cosied up to the royalists.[13]

For much of the period between the First Army Coup and the outbreak of the Second Civil War in the following spring, Cromwell remained with the army because his political skills were needed to prevent the political turmoil caused by the coup spilling over into civil war within the army, with regiment against regiment and officers against men and the king's supporters profiting from the ensuing anarchy. There can also be no doubt that he thoroughly approved of the first stage of the coup, in which peace party supporters were expelled from the army or left of their own accord and were replaced by loyalists, almost all of whom had been junior officers in the same regiment.[14]

The complex chain of events that followed has been explored at length in many political histories of the mid-seventeenth century,[15] and much of the detail they contain is irrelevant to the themes covered in this book. However, despite the fact that following the coup many of the soldiers' grievances were addressed by new laws, none were sent to Ireland, and the massive disbandment that Parliament had wanted did not take place, radical dissent in the ranks grew.

Some of the soldiers and the junior officers in some regiments were influenced by the democratic principles enunciated by the London Levellers and were alarmed that the Heads of Proposals, the war party's effort to reach a constitutional settlement with the king, would sell them down the river. They were then excited by expectations raised by the Putney debates, where such principles were discussed and largely rejected by the senior officers, whom they started calling grandees, and finally pushed into demonstrations of dissatisfaction by the king's escape to the Isle of Wight on the last day of the debates. Four days later, at an army rendezvous where some regiments defied their commanders' orders not to display signs of their Leveller allegiance, the army seemed on the verge of disintegration. However, the unflappability and sheer courage shown by the two generals in facing down the mutineers, with Fairfax acting as the spokesman and Cromwell as the enforcer, re-established officers' authority over their men, and during the course of the next three months the senior officers strengthened their position with the troops by forcing Parliament to promise not to negotiate with the king until he had given royal consent to bills limiting his constitutional authority.

Subsequent revelations about Charles's efforts to go to war once more, with the military assistance of members of the Scottish nobility, caused anger to replace fear for the future in what was now a united army. As the Second Civil War erupted in May 1648, with uprisings in many parts of the country led by incorrigible royalists and disgruntled former parliamentary officers, the New Model Army officers held a prayer meeting at Windsor to sharpen their resolve. The climax was the description of the king by Lieutenant Colonel Gough, who was highly respected for his religious zeal, condemning the king as 'a man of blood', a verdict about which nobody apart from Fairfax appears to have had serious reservations. The possibility of Charles being put on trial for his life, first raised by the radicals in the army at Putney in the autumn of the previous year, therefore became an item on the army's political agenda leading in due course to the final break-up of the war party.[16]

* * * * *

The first hostile acts of the Second Civil War occurred in south Wales in February 1648. A scratch force of New Model Army and provincial units under Colonel Thomas Horton was sufficient to defeat the enemy in the field at St Fagans near Cardiff in early May, but that was not the end of the fighting. The coastal castles in Pembrokeshire, which had held out successfully against the royalists in the First Civil War, were firmly in rebel hands, and before news of Horton's victory reached London Cromwell was ordered to take charge of the expanded operations in south Wales, but as soon as he had succeeded he was to join Fairfax in the north of England to face the invasion.[17] However, the failure of Fairfax to destroy the Kent royalists and neo-royalists in battle at Maidstone on the night of 1–2 June meant that it was Cromwell who was entrusted with the defence of England against the Scots.

Having secured the surrender of Pembroke Castle on 11 July Cromwell set out for Yorkshire to rendezvous with Major General Lambert, commander of Parliament's forces in the north, who had been fighting an interesting little campaign in the counties bordering Scotland for the past two months, the significance of which has probably been overestimated.[18] To outsiders it looked like a classic Fabian campaign of the mighty midget holding back the Scottish hordes until reinforcements arrived, but in fact Hamilton, hindered by substantial opposition in Scotland to the invasion of England, and the agreement with the king that had preceded it, could not make haste, and there is not the slightest scintilla of evidence that Lambert's pin-prick attacks on the northern royalists or on the Scots when they crossed the border delayed his advance in any way.[19]

On 7 or 8 August Cromwell arrived in Yorkshire, fortified by an order that he was commander-in-chief of all Parliament's forces in the north. By then he knew that the Scottish army and its English auxiliaries were on their march south. Leaving some Yorkshire regiments to maintain the sieges of Pontefract and Scarborough, he assembled some 9,000 to 10,000 men at Wetherby on 11 August, comprising five regiments of New Model infantry and five of cavalry, three regiments of Lancashire foot, some of Lambert's regiments of horse and foot and a few troops of New Model Army dragoons. Although there is some doubt about how many troops Hamilton had with him, it is clear that if they had formed a single body they would have outnumbered Cromwell's corps by about two to one.[20]

Hamilton's forces were divided when they crossed the county boundary between Westmoreland and Lancashire on 9 August. The Scottish army was close to the coast, while its English auxiliaries, raised principally in Northumberland and Durham by Sir Marmaduke Langdale, marched in parallel through the Pennines twenty miles or so to the east, protecting its flank against the English forces mustering in Yorkshire. A third brigade, comprising Hamilton's most experienced troops, a force of between 3,000 and 4,000 men shipped over from Ireland under General Monro, were ordered to wait with the artillery at Kirkby Lonsdale on the county boundary, to serve as an escort for additional military supplies arriving from Scotland, before catching up with the main body.

Cromwell knew little of the enemy's plans when he set out, but he was determined to intercept their forces while they were in Lancashire. To that end he left all his artillery behind and headed for the pinch point in their line of advance, the bridge over the River Ribble just to the south of Preston, but if they had already passed that point he could change his line of march at Whalley, ten miles short of Preston, so as to intercept them at the bridge over the Mersey at Warrington. However, when he reached the halfway point his scouts informed him that Langdale's brigade was ahead of him on the road and was presumably also marching towards Preston.[21]

Skirmishing between the royalist rear-guard and the Parliamentary advance guard began at Longridge, four miles short of Preston, and continued for another two miles until Langdale decided to make a stand at Ribbleton, where the road passed from open moorland into enclosures. Cromwell's advance guard tried to rush the hedges, but they were not strong enough to break through. While they waited for the rest of the army to catch up, the royalist general completed his deployment. He placed his pike in the roadway, protected by musketeers in the hedges ready to fire into the front or the flank of the enemy as they tried to move forward, but probably because of lack of numbers he did not extend his defensive line as far south as the escarpment, which followed the north bank of the Ribble between Ribbleton and Preston. He then informed Hamilton that he was facing the entire enemy army and needed reinforcements, but this would not be easy as most of the Scottish infantry and one wing of the cavalry were already on the far side of the Ribble, while the remainder of the Scottish cavalry were arriving on Preston Moor to the north of the town in penny numbers. Moreover, Hamilton did not believe him for quite some time. What Langdale was facing, he surmised, was a feint. Most of Cromwell's army were already in central Lancashire, having crossed the Ribble at Whalley.[22]

When Cromwell's main body arrived in front of the royalist position Cromwell drew up his army, with two regiments of New Model horse in the centre, to charge up the lane towards Preston. They were flanked by infantry regiments drawn up in formations on either side of the lane, whose task it was to clear the hedges. In the reserve line were the Lancashire regiments of foot and a single regiment of cavalry to provide support if necessary for the two that were in the van. The rest of the cavalry were placed on the wings.[23]

The upshot was the clearest possible sign of God's will rather than Cromwell's skill or his men's courage. What the lieutenant general probably had in mind when he deployed his regiments was a second Langport, as the topography of the battlefield and the way in which the enemy general had deployed his forces were very similar.[24] However, the tactics that had worked at Langport did not do so at Preston. The enemy musketeers could not be cleared from the enclosures and a premature cavalry charge was frustrated by the enemy pikes, supported by a regiment of Scottish lancers.[25] Moreover, the determination of the enemy defence suggested that they were not a flank guard that would fall back in easy stages to the bridge over the Ribble if allowed to do so, but an usually large forlorn hope charged by Hamilton with defending the position where he wished to fight a battle until such time as the rest of his army arrived. Given that the Scots were stronger in infantry than cavalry this made perfect sense, as at Ribbleton there would be little chance of Cromwell making much use of their horse.

What Cromwell did next is uncertain, and it is necessary to have recourse to Lieutenant Colonel Burne's concept of inherent military probability for a possible answer. This would suggest that he went on the lookout for signs of a Scottish counterattack. As the way in which Langdale had deployed his brigade in the enclosures would make it difficult for Hamilton to push large formations of infantry through the centre of the position, the counterattack was most likely to come from the direction of Preston Moor to the right, and he therefore probably rode off with his lifeguard to reconnoitre. As such, his was probably the small number of parliamentary horse sighted by Hamilton, who was waiting on Preston Moor for the last of his troops of horse to arrive. Cromwell, however, would have seen no sign of Scottish infantry formations massing there before beginning the push towards Ribbleton. His not being at Ribbleton when the breakthrough occurred may explain why, in his report of the battle, he spent some time defending the inactivity of two New Model Army infantry regiments he had placed at the right of the battle line, which had no enemy in front of them but had remained where they were rather than moving towards the centre of the battlefield where renewed action was taking place. Although he did not say so, they were probably under his orders to stay put in order to provide covering fire in case he and his lifeguard returned hurriedly from Preston Moor pursued by hordes of Scottish cavalry, and also to create time for the rest of the army on Ribbleton to deploy to face an attack coming from a different direction.[26]

According to Hodgson, Cromwell did nothing to investigate a possible Scottish advance through the gap between the enclosures to the left of the road and the Ribble escarpment, but this is understandable. It was narrow and it did not have an open flank to the left. It would therefore be easy for Cromwell's own regiment of foot to plug it until such time as the Lancashire regiments came to its support. Like the two New Model regiments on the other side of the road, it was not currently engaged in the fighting as it had no enemy units to its front. According to Lieutenant Hodgson, it was his warning that the Scottish advance might come from that direction that induced John Lambert, the only senior commander on the spot, to order the uncommitted infantry regiments and the horse on the left wing to prepare for such an eventuality by moving forward into the mouth of the corridor. However, once they were there they discovered not a Scots' advance guard moving towards them, but a void. Seeing an opportunity for outflanking Langdale's men in the enclosures, the officer in charge launched an attack down the corridor. However, not only did this make Langdale's position untenable, it also cut the north/south road, the present-day A6, between Preston town and the bridge over the Ribble, which split Hamilton's army in two by preventing it from being reinforced by an infantry brigade that Hamilton had finally ordered to go to Langdale's support, Monro's brigade at Kirkby Lonsdale and the last of his own cavalry. It also meant that Langdale's men were at the mercy of Cromwell's army, but this was only halfway through the battle, as the bridge over the Ribble remained in Scottish hands.[27]

When Langdale realized that the enemy had achieved the vital tactical breakthrough, it made no sense for him to continue defending the position at Ribbleton, but an orderly withdrawal into Preston was soon disrupted by the cavalry regiments on the parliamentary right wing, probably led by Cromwell in person. They chased the English royalists and the Scots supporting them into the town, where attempts by Hamilton to organize a defence were frustrated by lack of time and confused counsels. As a result the infantry stranded on the north bank of the Ribble were cut down in large numbers, though most of the cavalry escaped northwards following Hamilton's orders to join Monro at Kirkby Lonsdale.

The second and last phase of the battle began very soon afterwards, and here it was soldierly skill rather than a lucky break that clinched the victory. The regiments of Cromwell's left wing were in a precarious position. Even though the prospect of a counterattack from the town was receding by the minute as Langdale's command disintegrated, one from the opposite direction across the Ribble bridge was a real possibility given that most of the Scottish army was to the south of the river. It was therefore necessary to drive the enemy from the bridge. Artillery would have been useful at this juncture, but Cromwell had left his behind in Yorkshire and none had been captured. Instead he, or whoever was in charge, lined the hedges that ran parallel to the escarpment with musketeers and presumably drew up his pikes in the roadway. The musketeers were then ordered to make the Scots' infantry brigade posted at the bridge uncomfortable by firing barrage after barrage in that direction. This also served to prevent the Scottish generals from sending in reinforcements from their position on the rising ground on the other side of the valley, as the flood plain was devoid of cover. Finally, once the enemy had been sufficiently cowed, the Lancashire regiments carried out a pike charge, which overran the bridge's defences. This was followed up by a troop of Lambert's regiment, which also carried the bridge over the Darwen less than half a mile to the south.[28]

Cromwell ended the day by rushing forces to guard all the bridges and fords from Whalley to the mouth of the Ribble to the west of Preston. Thus the Scottish army had no chance of returning the way it had come, and as its provisions had been captured at Preston, it could not remain where it was or else it would quickly be starved into surrender. Hamilton therefore ordered it to carry on moving south in the hope of linking up with the royalist uprising in north Wales, but the organized invasion of England came to a halt at Warrington four days later. The infantry, unable to cross the bridge over the Mersey because it was guarded, surrendered en masse, the musketeers having expended the last of their ammunition in a hopeless engagement at Winwick, just to the north of the town, the previous day. The cavalry did manage to cross the river, but were quickly rounded up in Cheshire and the north Midlands by local forces assisted by the cavalry regiments that had fought at Preston. Wisely Cromwell had not sought to destroy the enemy on their march south in a textbook battle. He had merely used his army to shepherd them into a trap from which they had no chance of escaping.

The high degree of competence Cromwell displayed throughout the campaign is seen at its best not on the battlefield, but in the execution of an operational plan that began very well with the surprise of the enemy army, and ended without the need to fight a second major battle with all the additional lives that would have been lost as a result. His exact role in the fighting at Preston is impossible to ascertain. He had nothing to do with the initial breakthrough, and he may or may not have given the orders for the capture of the bridge over the Ribble, but to give the credit to Lambert is misplaced, as it relies on reading between the lines of John Hodgson's account and jumping from knowledge that it was a troop belonging to Lambert's regiment that captured the bridge over the Darwen, to an assertion that Lambert masterminded the whole of the second phase of the battle. The fact that Cromwell did not mention Lambert's name in either of his accounts of the battle is neither here nor there. It was his practice to attribute his army's success to God alone, and not to himself as God's instrument, for fear of being punished for the sin of pride, and he applied this rule to others as well as to himself.[29]

* * * * *

The regiments which had not been trapped to the south of the Ribble or been caught up in the sack of Preston made their way back to Scotland unscathed under Monro's leadership, but a coup by the party that had opposed the invasion of England soon made them militarily inconsequential. When Cromwell's army marched north in late August part entered Scotland, but their sole purpose was to ensure that those who had carried out the coup were firmly in control of the country. He used his undoubted charm and his army's excellent behaviour to win friends, but the relationships were not strong enough to withstand the trauma caused by the execution of the Scottish king in the second army coup three months later.

Leaving Scotland in the second week in October Cromwell took charge of the sieges of the remaining royalist strongholds in Yorkshire, a responsibility that should have been Lambert's, but Lambert was ordered to remain in Scotland with a body of about 1,200 horse to provide protection for the new government until it had raised a force for its own defence. In the meantime, momentous events were taking place 400 miles to the south, in which Cromwell was apparently no more than a watcher from afar, but in the complete absence of his incoming correspondence it is impossible to ascertain for certain whether or not he had been consulted in advance about the first moves in the Second Army Coup, namely the abduction of the king from the Isle of Wight by army officers on 1 December and the stationing of troops close to the Parliament building on the following day. Summoned south by Fairfax in late November, after the general collapsed mentally having failed to prevent a resolution to put the king on trial being passed by the Council of Officers, or to convince the king to agree to a new set of demands reducing his constitutional powers, Cromwell arrived in London on 7 December. This was the day after Colonel Pride had expelled from the Commons those members who had supported an accommodation with the king. The lieutenant general claimed to have had no foreknowledge of what is usually described as Pride's Purge, and this was not a lie, as the decision to go for a purge rather than an outright dissolution had only been agreed as a result of discussions between some of the leading army officers and some of the war party MPs the night before it happened.[30]

More problematic is Cromwell's attitude to what followed – the trial and execution of the king – but even so, there is one piece of evidence that shows Cromwell's mind-set long before he left Yorkshire. On 20 November he sent several petitions from regiments and garrisons in his part of the north of England to Fairfax. With them was a covering letter that shows a clarity of thought that is not at all apparent in the much more widely known letter written some days later to his cousin Robert Hammond, the governor of the Isle of Wight, who was having doubts about handing the king over to the army. The petitions urged Fairfax to put pressure on Parliament to begin legal proceedings against Charles as the enemy of the kingdom and a self-confessed man of blood. All incendiaries, of whom the king was the greatest, should be subject to impartial justice without exemption of birth, but this should not be before the conventional judges, who were corrupt and could not be trusted. And finally, most ominous of all, incendiaries should suffer the death penalty, as God required their lives to appease his wrath. In his covering letter Cromwell thoroughly endorsed their sentiments. He was convinced that their sentiments came from God.

Cromwell wavered in the weeks that followed. Assuming that the wavering was not for public consumption to test what the reaction would be if he came out in his true colours, it was a struggle between earthly sentiments and heavenly directives. In the end Charles's rejections of attempts to save his life by making last-minute concessions were further examples of providence, but this time taking the form of an enemy of God bringing about his own destruction. In the end he followed his religious instincts and the sheer pleasure that these had won is shown in his joy and relief during the play-fight with Henry Marten when they were signing the king's death sentence issued by the court that had tried him.

In his move towards the heavenly solution Cromwell would also have been fortified by his knowledge of the Old Testament, in which kings who had clearly lost God's favour also lost their lives, either in battle like Saul, or at the hands of their subjects like Amon. It is also inconceivable that Cromwell did not travel down the providential way of reasoning hinted at in Lucy Hutchinson's biography of her husband John, who attended the king's trial and signed the document condemning him to death. God had given his verdict on the king in the First Civil War. This should have been enough for the victors to punish him in an appropriate manner, but instead they had entered into negotiations with him and a second war had followed. All the lives lost in that war were a warning to Parliament, and indeed to the army. If they ignored God's clear instructions to take action a second time, His wrath would be unimaginable.[31]

But why had Cromwell declared what he felt so early in his letter to the general? Possibly he hoped that his words, which are couched in the most personal and direct terms, might win over Fairfax. However, he hedged his bets. If the earthly influences won in the end and the king was spared, he could claim that he had not read the petitions as carefully as he should have done before endorsing their contents.

Chapter 14

Army Commander and Lord General, 1649–51

The Second Army Coup caused a change in the political and constitutional relationship between the army and Parliament. For the first time ever Parliament's relationship with its army commanders was not vitiated by struggles within a coalition, whose groupings had different war aims and often pulled in different directions, dragging the military men with them. All that was left in February 1649 was a single House of Parliament (the House of Lords having been abolished along with the monarchy) comprising members acceptable to the army, most of whom had previously been war party supporters. Moreover, tensions in the war party in Parliament over negotiations with the king had caused it to fragment over the issue of the king's trial and execution. Of its leading supporters in the Commons from the start only Sir Arthur Haselrig went along with the whole process. Vane and St John refused to take part, but were reconciled very soon afterwards and played a prominent part in government from February and August 1649 respectively. However, the leading war party peers, lords Say and Wharton, ceased to attend Parliament from the day after Pride's Purge, and played no part in the government of the Commonwealth.[1]

In March 1649 Parliament established a new executive, the Council of State, which in time of war fulfilled the same role as its predecessor, the Derby House Committee. It acted as an intermediary between the commanders in Ireland and Scotland and the House of Commons, passing requests in one direction and pushing resources in the other. It left operational matters to the generals, which is unsurprising given the distances involved, but it also retained control over home security matters, which on occasions resulted in New Model Army units the army commanders intended for use in Scotland or Ireland being moved elsewhere, and it had the authority to quickly assemble a reserve army in August 1651 at the time of another Scottish invasion.[2] However, Parliament no longer determined strategy. Once the decision had been taken to attack Scotland in 1650 the MPs were content merely to accept reports from the Council on decisions made concerning the overall management of the various fronts.

Woolrych saw potential conflict between Parliament and the army arising because the latter was under-represented on the Council of State, seemingly as a deliberate policy by Parliament to create a distance between the government of England and its senior officers, with two being rejected as potential members in February 1649. However, there was only the occasional spat between the Council and the army as, for example, when Cromwell left reinforcements he had urgently requested quartered on the English side of the border at a cost to the state, because he did not want them to march through the territory of the Western Association, a party of Scottish Presbyterians critical of the agreement made by the Scottish government with the Prince of Wales. The Council of State was also critical of Cromwell's subordinates, Harrison and Lambert, for what it saw as their inactivity in the face of the Scottish invasion in August 1651. However, if we accept that Woolrych's comment is a valid one, and not an example of hindsight based on what was going to happen in 1653, the differences between the army and Parliament were clearly papered over for the time being because of the security situation.[3]

* * * * *

Cromwell prepared to take the field again in March 1649 when he was appointed lord lieutenant of Ireland, with a mandate to bring the whole of the country under the control of the Commonwealth. Not only had the war there been a drain on resources and a reproach to good Protestants for the past seven years, but Ireland was also a base from which the Prince of Wales could launch an invasion of England. Such a possibility had been on the cards for some weeks before the king's execution, as he had sent the Marquis of Ormond there to try and construct a grand coalition to oppose Parliament, but the execution acted as the catalyst drawing together Catholics, Anglicans and Presbyterians in a rainbow coalition to restore the monarchy, and the new republican government needed to act fast as the coalition began overrunning those parts of the country it did not already control. First, however, came a mutiny in the army. Cromwell was to take with him *inter alia* a corps of the New Model Army comprising five infantry and four cavalry regiments, chosen by lot. Leveller theorists had consistently written against trying to impose English forms of religion on the Irish, and in the rank and file there was residual resentment against compulsory service there. The grievances that had caused trouble in 1647 rose once more to the surface

If Cromwell and Fairfax had not acted promptly, the anarchy that both had feared could have been the consequence, as the number involved in the unrest was in the low thousands, with others threatening to join.[4] Moreover, putting down the mutiny would not be a matter of browbeating the miscreants at a rendezvous, as they were on the move in the Thames valley and the Cotswolds trying to draw in other units. However, the brief and almost bloodless campaign against the main body only resulted in the disbandment of one cavalry regiment and part of another, the cashiering of several hundred officers and men, and the execution of three of the leaders.[5] Nevertheless, the expeditionary force did not set sail for Ireland until early August, though this was in part due to Cromwell's determination that it should be well equipped and fully paid.[6]

Cromwell only spent nine months in Ireland and did not fight a single battle, but the political and military strategy he pursued was sufficiently adroit to ensure that when he left final victory was much closer. The storming of Drogheda and Wexford showed how merciless he was prepared to be, but such tactics yielded dividends during the autumn in terms of enemy garrisons voluntarily surrendering. However, alongside the succession of sieges that followed Cromwell pursued policies designed to divide and weaken the enemy. Using his political skills to win military advantage while on campaign can first be seen in his wooing of the Scots, who had opposed Hamilton's invasion of England in 1648, but this had been like pushing at an open door given the extent of the opposition to the war north of the border. Ireland was a more difficult case. His promise to Irish Catholics that they would be treated with clemency if they would only give up their religion fell on deaf ears, but he won over most of the forces in Munster commanded by Protestant officers, who returned to their original allegiance during the winter of 1649–50 and were forgiven for going over to the enemy. They were then reincorporated into what was now an army in Ireland, which also included English regiments that had arrived there after the First Civil War and others commanded by Protestant loyalists, as well as the forces Cromwell had brought with him. The leader of the Munster brigade, Lord Broghill, then went on to pursue a most successful political career during the 1650s, with Cromwell's blessing.

By the time he left Ireland in May 1650 to prepare for a war against Scotland, Cromwell and his deputies had extended the Commonwealth's control from Dublin and its immediate environs and a few square miles around Londonderry to a huge swathe of territory stretching across south and central Ireland. A month later Ulster was secured by the Protestant settler commander in the north, Sir Charles Coote, aided by English troops under Colonel Venables, who destroyed the last and best of the coalition's armies at the battle of Scarrifhollis. All that remained for Cromwell's successor to do was to secure the surrender of the major enemy garrisons at Athlone, Galway, Limerick, Waterford and a host of minor garrisons mainly in the west; and to conquer the province of Connaught on the far side of the River Shannon.[7]

It has been claimed that the chink in Cromwell's armour as army commander was his maladroitness in siege warfare, caused by lack of professional training in the art of war and his natural impatience, the evidence for which was to be found in his failure to capture Waterford in December 1649 and in the huge losses he incurred in the storming of Kilkenny and Clonmel in the spring of 1650.[8] This is not an argument that is easy to defend, as much of the evidence points the other way. First Cromwell had extensive experience of siege warfare in the last year of the First Civil War at Bridgwater, Bristol, Winchester and Basing House, and at Pembroke in the Second. He would also have known that, unless the besiegers were very fortunate, storming a town almost invariably resulted in heavy casualties. Third, it was winter weather, not the military skills of his opponents, that forced him to abandon the attack on Waterford, while the number of officers and men killed in storming Kilkenny was probably closer to Cromwell's estimate of a single company commander and about thirty other ranks, than to Irish claims of massive casualties, even though two assaults through the breach opened up by cannon fire were driven back using tactics that later were to be used very successfully at Clonmel.[9] Moreover, if Cromwell was so keen to return to England by the time he set siege to Clonmel, why did it take him ten days besieging the town before storming it?

Finally, although according to Ireton the losses at Clonmel were larger than those suffered at Naseby,[10] they have almost certainly been over-exaggerated by later commentators, and were probably in the region of 500 or less, rather than 1,000, 2,000 or even 2,500. I have given my reasons elsewhere, but my more recent research into the New Model Army commissioned officers provides additional, though admittedly indirect evidence, in support of the lowest figure, in that the number of company and troop commanders killed or mortally wounded at Clonmel was smaller than those killed or mortally wounded at Drogheda or Bristol.[11]

* * * * *

After Fairfax's resignation, Cromwell was in sole charge of the army being put together to invade Scotland and rather surprisingly, in view of his dread of the sin of pride, he was happy to be referred to as lord general from the start, even though he did not possess a peerage. Only eight of the original New Model Army regiments were involved, as there were six and a half in Ireland with the rest kept in England to guard against a royalist uprising. However, he also had the services of three regiments of foot and two of horse from Parliament's northern brigade, which had fought under Lambert's command in the 1648 campaign, and he was soon joined by some newly raised regiments of foot, many of which contained a nucleus of experienced soldiers from existing regiments.[12]

Like the commanders of earlier English armies invading Scotland, Cromwell chose the east coast route along the line of the present A1. Progress was good because the landscape through which it passed was largely flat all the way to Edinburgh, with only a single choke point at Cockburnspath between Berwick and Dunbar where the southern uplands reach the sea. Hugging the coast also enabled the army to be supplied by sea and contact to be maintained with London and with Newcastle, Cromwell's army base. Hoping for a quick victory, he was not interested in occupying territory. Instead he headed straight for the Scottish capital, but when he arrived there he faced an enemy army of some 15,000 men deployed in a tight cordon around the city.[13] Storming was obviously out of the question, as initial success, if success was achieved, would be contained and driven back by the enemy using interior lines, so as to concentrate overwhelming force against the assailants. A naval blockade to prevent food and fodder being shipped across the Firth of Forth would eventually force the Scots to surrender, but that would take time to take effect. A much quicker result would be obtained if the enemy could be tempted into fighting a conventional battle. This was tried on several occasions, but David Leslie, the Scottish general in charge, refused to be tempted, and success was not guaranteed. The few small-scale encounters that did occur outside the lines showed that the Scots were in good fighting form and well led.

After a few weeks the English army withdrew, weakened by the effects of bad weather and disease. On 1 September it took up a position at Dunbar, but marching any further would be risky, as Cockburnspath was in enemy hands. The Scottish army followed in the New Model's wake, taking up a position in the hills to the east and south-east of Dunbar that came within two miles of the town, thus penning the enemy in in the same way as the royalists had penned the first lord general in the Fowey peninsula in 1644. The L word was used at the time, but there was a difference. Fowey was unusable because the royalist artillery dominated the mouth to the estuary of the River Fowey, whereas Dunbar was out of reach of the Scottish artillery and, being a deep water port, could be used to supply the English army with large quantities of food from Newcastle or to evacuate it by sea. Cromwell could therefore bide his time in the hope that the enemy would make a mistake, which they did on the following day when the sight of ships leaving harbour with soldiers on board looked like the beginning of an evacuation. So as to be able to disrupt the proceedings, and to prevent a possible cavalry breakout along the road towards Berwick, Leslie ordered his forces to leave the hills and deploy along a small stream known today as the Spott Burn, which made its way around the west side of Dunbar, reaching the sea about two miles south of the town. This gave Cromwell the chance to fight the set-piece battle that had so far eluded him, but given his army's inferiority in numbers the battle plan had to contain an element of surprise.[14]

A council of war convened late on the afternoon of 2 September decided on an attack on the Scottish position before dawn, with the aim of achieving a break-out along the road leading towards England, the principal reason being that the left of the Scottish army would be unable to intervene as it was squashed between the valley of the Spott Burn and the slopes of the hill from which it had descended.[15] Cromwell committed six of his eight regiments of horse and two of his three brigades of foot, but the direction, if not the timing, had been what the Scots were expecting, and Leslie sent in what units he could to block the advance.

The assault on the Scottish line, led by generals John Lambert, Charles Fleetwood and George Monck, did not do well at first, as the Scots fought back with vigour, but then the whole course of the battle changed, due to what was probably a battlefield inspiration on Cromwell's part rather than a move planned in advance. As the sun rose he led the reserve brigade of foot and possibly his two remaining cavalry regiments across the burn close to where it entered the sea, and wheeled them to the right so that they struck the enemy army in the flank. This move would have been impossible at the start of the battle because Lesley had placed the right wing of the Scottish cavalry facing the burn at that point.[16] However, it had been sucked into the fight along the Berwick road, which Leslie would have seen as the sharp end of the break-out. But what it turned out to be, by accident or design, was the pin of a classic pin and flank battlefield tactic.

As Cromwell's attack gathered strength, the regiment on the far right of Leslie's infantry line fought doggedly to block it, but it was eventually overrun by sheer force of numbers. The centre of the Scottish army then came under extreme pressure from the right flank as well as the front and collapsed into confusion. By mid-morning the infantry had surrendered while the mounted troops fled over the hills towards the central lowlands, pursued for some distance by English cavalry. Cromwell's battlefield tactics had thus worked like clockwork, in part due to the impotence of Leslie's left wing, caused by the initial deployment, but also because the enemy assault in the centre had created a void on the right wing.[17]

What happened next was the biggest mistake of Cromwell's entire military career. The scale of the victory at Dunbar seemed to presage the war coming to an end in weeks rather than months, but it took an entire year for the Scottish military machine to be smashed beyond repair. Leslie's only hope of prolonging Scottish resistance was to deny the English army access to Fife and the lowlands of north-east Scotland, and the physical geography of the country gave him the chance of doing so, provided he was allowed the time to put his house in order. The key to success was retaining control of the crossing over the River Forth at Stirling in the narrow gap between the Scottish mountains and the Firth of Forth, which for centuries had been guarded by a formidable castle. Cromwell was well aware of the strategic importance of the pass at Stirling,[18] but instead of sending cavalry and dragoons to seize it straight after the battle, when the Scots were in a state of shock, he sent his mounted troops supported by infantry to Edinburgh dazzled, it seems, by the prestige of capturing the Scottish capital. He duly captured the town, but not the castle, seemingly without a fight, but when the New Model Army arrived outside Stirling ten days later the Scots had recovered their nerve and Cromwell withdrew, blaming his lack of scaling ladders and the fact that his cavalry would not be able to operate in the marshy ground of the Forth valley. What followed was nine months of stalemate. Leslie would not come out and fight and Cromwell could neither force nor trick him into doing so, while head-on assault on Stirling's defences became less feasible day by day as the Scottish army grew in size, thanks to the arrival of new levies from northeast Scotland and the Highlands.

In the closing months of the year Cromwell explained his failure to engage with the main body of the enemy by saying that he was busy consolidating English control over southern Scotland. Some important strongholds along the south side of the Firth of Forth were captured; Edinburgh castle surrendered in December, and Leith, Edinburgh's port, was fortified and replaced Newcastle as the gateway into Scotland for supplies and newly raised regiments. However, there was one political failure. The Western Association of Presbyterian ministers and laity refused in the end to listen to his blandishments. However, when its tiny army set out to join Leslie it was destroyed by Lambert, in Cromwell's temporary absence, at the battle of Hamilton on 1 December, due to the rashness of the Scottish commander.

In the new year the stalemate continued unabated. It has been customary to blame it on the serious bouts of ill-health Cromwell experienced in February and March, and between April and June, but these, though real and not an excuse for his inactivity, are irrelevant. The fact of the matter was that Cromwell had only one way of forcing Leslie to fight and that was to outflank the pass at Stirling by landing troops in Fife, but without the right resources this would be impossible. He had the necessary shipping, but did not control a harbour on the north side of the Firth of Forth. Capturing one by seaborne assault was an option, but a trial run or two during the winter showed the immense difficulties involved. The other was to land troops on the open shore, but this required specialist vessels, the seventeenth-century equivalent of modern-day landing craft. The technology was not a problem, but there were none immediately available. Some could be manufactured from boats with a shallow draught, like barges operating in the Thames estuary, but others would have to be built from scratch, and they would also have to be seaworthy enough to sail to Scotland. Contracts were duly issued to English shipwrights in London and Newcastle in December 1650, but the full complement of fifty boats did not arrive in the Firth of Forth until seven months later. Even so, the risk of failure was high. Just over twenty years earlier an English army had attempted a similar amphibious operation in France, preparatory to relieving the besieged Protestants of La Rochelle. The disastrous failure would have been remembered by Cromwell and his more senior officers, while Monck had actually been present. However, if the plan for the landing in Fife did not work, the English army faced another debilitating winter in Scotland at enormous expense to the English taxpayer. The note of relief in the letter Cromwell wrote to Speaker Lenthall after the landings had taken place sounds completely genuine.[19]

The successful landing at North Queensferry on 17 July and the minor battle at Inverkeithing that followed three days later was the work of Cromwell's understudies, but the operational plan put in place once it was clear that Leslie still refused to fight a set-piece battle was all his own. First he ordered the capture of Burntisland, some miles to the east, where the harbour was deep enough to accommodate sea-going vessels, whereupon he flooded Fife with troops, but instead of attacking Stirling from the rear he marched them north to Perth and the only bridge over the River Tay between the mountains and the sea strong enough to be used by his train of artillery. After a two-day siege the city surrendered, thus cutting Leslie off from the rest of the north-east lowlands and the resources needed by the Scottish army, most particularly food and reinforcements.

It has as often been argued that in avoiding a direct attack on Stirling, Cromwell deliberately left England vulnerable to yet another Scottish invasion,[20] but this was almost certainly not his original intention. As he assembled his army in Fife prior to marching on Perth he was convinced, possibly due to lack of accurate intelligence, that he had left sufficient troops on the south side of the Firth of Forth to deter Leslie from making such a move.[21] There were also other options available to the Scottish commander, the best being to break his army up into smaller units and place them in garrisons throughout the north of Scotland, from which they could wage a guerrilla campaign against the English. The outcome would be a long and messy war, like that taking place in Ireland at the same time, which would gobble up military resources and lives until the English government threw in the towel.[22] On the other hand, Leslie's army, if it remained where it was, might disintegrate because of tensions in the Scottish camp between three different factions: strict Presbyterians who had been wary of the new king and his advisers, the former supporters of the Duke of Hamilton, and the Scottish and English royalists who had flocked to young Charles's standard.

However, once it became clear that Leslie was on the march south with his army almost intact, Cromwell changed tack, claiming that he knew from the start that he did not have sufficient troops in Scotland to keep a large army on both sides of the Firth of Forth, but that it had always been his plan to close down operations in Scotland and set off in pursuit if the enemy showed any sign of moving towards the English border. Nevertheless, he urged Parliament to mobilize the county militia regiments and assemble them in a position covering London, but there was a reassuring note. He did not doubt that the 5,000 New Model horse in south Scotland and the Borders under generals Lambert and Harrison would be able to delay the Scottish army. This would give him time to catch it up and force it to fight well before it reached the London area, but he did warn the English government that this Scottish army was different from the one which had invaded England three years earlier – it was experienced militarily and it was desperate. Finally, he informed the Speaker that he had left Scotland in charge of George Monck, with sufficient troops under his command to be able to hold his own until such time as he could send him reinforcements.[23]

Cromwell's prognosis was slightly on the optimistic side. As in 1648 the Scottish army chose the west coast route into England, but with Stirling Castle still garrisoned he could not follow in its footsteps. Instead he faced the difficult task of shipping his army back across the Firth of Forth, followed by the prospect of the more circuitous route out of Scotland following the coast. To make matters worse, Lambert and Harrison were unable to slow down the Scottish army, which brushed them aside in a brief engagement at Warrington bridge, where Hamilton's infantry had surrendered three years earlier. It then threatened to swing eastwards into Staffordshire and so on to Watling Street, the fastest road to London, but by the time it reached Nantwich its commanders knew Cromwell was gaining ground and was thus highly likely to catch them up before they reached London.[24] They therefore changed the direction of their army's march and headed instead for the Severn valley and the walled city of Worcester, hoping for support from local royalists. This looked like the Scottish army, exhausted by its long march, going to ground and waiting for the end be it battle or siege.[25] However, having rested for a day or so it could continue marching south into the former strongly royalist areas of Herefordshire and south Wales in the hope of picking up more recruits before having to fight the New Model Army.[26]

In the event the Scottish generals decided to remain where they were, giving Cromwell plenty of time to prepare his operational plan. First, having reached Warwick and met up with Lambert and Harrison, he required county militia regiments that had been mobilized to counter the Scottish menace to join him and his regulars at Evesham, twenty miles to the south-east of Worcester, in the unlikely event of the Scots deciding to resume their march towards London. Next he ordered the capture of the bridge over the Severn at Upton. Once it was in his hands he could completely encircle Worcester and thus prevent the Scots from retreating into the Welsh borderland, where the heavily enclosed landscape would favour an army strong in infantry that had been forced onto the defensive. Finally, in order to catch as many Scots as possible in his net, he stationed regular units at bridges and fords to the north of Worcester and gave orders for militia units to guard similar choke points in Lancashire and Cheshire.[27]

Apart from a feeble attempt to defend Upton Bridge, the Scottish army remained inactive, which gave Cromwell plenty of time to prepare for the attack on Worcester, and it was the most ambitious yet. He had a big advantage in that his forces outnumbered the enemy by between two and three to one, but control over the bridge over the Severn at Worcester gave the enemy an important advantage. If he tried to storm the city from the east or from the west and looked likely to succeed, all the Scottish generals had to do was inflict as many casualties as possible on the attackers and then withdraw to the other bank, breaking down the bridge behind them. If, on the other hand, he decided to attack the city from both directions, they could use interior lines to move resources to one side or the other in response to the tempo and timing of the assaults.[28]

On September 1 the net tightened. Cromwell placed most of his infantry and cavalry regiments on rising ground to the east of the city. On the day of the battle they were to remain where they were, ready to defend their positions if the enemy tried to stage a breakout along the roads leading to the north or the east. Meanwhile, a strong corps of regular and militia regiments was to push north from Upton along the west bank of the Severn under Charles Fleetwood's command. Their orders were to break through the defensive line the Scots had established along the valley of the River Teme, which joined the Severn two miles to the south of Worcester. They were then to seize control of the west end of Worcester bridge. The weakness of the plan was that the forces on the east bank could do nothing to help their comrades should the enemy throw his entire strength against them. However, Cromwell had devised a stratagem which would allow him to reinforce them should it prove necessary.

Pontoon bridges carrying roadways were to be built across the Teme and the Severn on the day of the battle close to their confluence, and with their bridgeheads on the west bank of the Severn and the north bank of the Teme no more than a pistol shot apart. The pontoons were to be provided by large boats that sailed the Severn as cargo carriers. Assembled at Upton, they were to be dragged upriver using the towpath, and as soon as they were seen to be nearing the confluence a convoy of waggons carrying bridge-building materials and sappers escorted by infantry and several pieces of artillery would leave the high ground to the east of Worcester and proceed to the bridging point on the east bank of the Severn. Then, probably using boats that normally formed part of the artillery train, some of the bridge builders and some of the infantry would cross the river just before the larger boats arrived and establish a foothold on the far bank. The construction of both bridges could then proceed as Fleetwood's soldiers would already be in control of the south bank of the Teme at the point at which it joined the Severn. If the Scots then tried to stop the bridge building, there would be sufficient musket and cannon fire from Cromwell's forces on the east bank of the Severn to force them to back off.

All went well with the convoy of boats being dragged upriver from Upton, but observers stationed on the tower of Worcester Cathedral spotted the waggons containing bridge-building materials and their escort leaving the high ground to the east of the city and correctly guessed Cromwell's intentions. The Scottish forces along the Teme, which had hitherto been preoccupied in stopping Fleetwood's attempt to capture the bridge at Powick two miles upriver, were probably not alerted for some time, as they could not see what was going on to their left. In due course they attacked the enemy foothold on the west bank of the Severn in force, but they were too late to prevent the Severn bridge being finished. The bridge over the Teme, however, may not yet have been operative, as there is no evidence of units belonging to Fleetwood's corps fighting in the pocket until much later. However, Cromwell in person came to the rescue, leading his lifeguard, two regiments of foot and one and a half regiments of horse across the bridge over the Severn. They forced back the Scots, thus increasing the size of the pocket, and when the bridge over the Teme was completed they were joined by six additional infantry regiments from Fleetwood's corps.[29] The force thus assembled in the pocket was now large enough to take the offensive. It outflanked the key Scottish defence point at Powick bridge, forcing it to be abandoned and allowing the rest of the corps to cross the Teme. The Scots were then pushed back towards Worcester bridge, helped by a cavalry breakthrough on the west flank led by Fleetwood in person.

The Scottish generals responded to the crisis on the west bank of the Severn by launching a sortie from Worcester against the enemy forces on the east bank. Initially it went well, and Cromwell was sufficiently alarmed to move troops back across the Severn via the pontoon bridge, but the crisis was over by the time they arrived, and the Scots were falling back towards the city. Fighting could have stopped there and then, with the endgame being a conventional siege, but the overwhelming numerical superiority of the parliamentarians ensured that the momentum created by the repulse of the sortie was quickly followed by the capture of Fort Royal, a First Civil War redoubt overlooking the city, and the storming of a gate on the south side of the city walls. The Scottish infantry continued the fight in the streets, but surrendered well before midnight. The Scottish cavalry, which like Cromwell's had played little part in the battle, fled northwards, taking their king with them, but the exhaustion of their horses meant that nearly all were taken prisoner well before they reached Scotland.[30]

Thus ended Cromwell's last campaign. It would have been logical for him to have returned to Scotland or Ireland, but he did not, presumably on health grounds. There were also other considerations. In Ireland it was only fair to give Ireton the chance to show that he had military qualities to supplement his undoubted political ones, while in Scotland Monck had taken great strides towards the pacification of the country before the victory at Worcester.

Chapter 15

The Lord General and his Understudies: Ireton and Lambert

From the king's execution onwards, grand strategy dictated that there should be a strong military presence in England and Ireland, and in Scotland too from the summer of 1650, causing the New Model Army to be divided. This necessitated an increase in the number of senior officers, but it ran up against Parliament's tradition of parsimony in this respect.[1] Thus, when Philip Skippon, who as major general of foot was third in command of the New Model Army, resigned he was not replaced.[2] Nevertheless, the army managed. Cromwell in Ireland had Henry Ireton and Michael Jones, who had been lieutenant general in the army in Ireland, as his deputies.[3] Fairfax had a larger force to manage, but it was not expected to have to go to war and there was little sign of civil or military unrest. He had his various units quartered all over England and Wales as a deterrent, and if rebels did manage to seize control of a castle or a fortified town he could call on the experience of Thomas Hammond, the New Model's lieutenant general of artillery, who had not gone to Ireland.

Early the following summer, however, a crisis threatened similar to that which Fairfax had faced just before the battle of Naseby in 1645. In Ireland Michael Jones had died during the winter and not been replaced, while Cromwell had been recalled to England in May, leaving the inexperienced Ireton on his own. To make matters worse, Fairfax's resignation was followed a few months later by that of Lieutenant General Hammond. Parliament's response was to promote Cromwell to lord general, to give the religious radical and cavalry colonel Thomas Harrison command of the home army as major general, while Cromwell rather than Parliament appointed Charles Fleetwood, the senior colonel of horse, as his successor as lieutenant general of horse in the New Model. The posts of major general of foot and lieutenant general of artillery remained unfilled, but Cromwell was to have the support of the former commander of the northern brigade, John Lambert. Invariably addressed by his former rank of major general, he does not seem to have held an official position in the New Model higher than that of colonel of horse and foot, but he was Cromwell's deputy in all but name. Cromwell could also draw on the services of senior colonels to command the infantry and the artillery on an ad hoc basis. Ireton in Ireland, like Cromwell in Scotland, also made use of senior colonels like John Hewson to supply the gaps in the highest levels of command.

These arrangements seem to have worked well until the spring of 1651, but Ireton probably took on too much responsibility, and in the future this was to affect his health, but not his army's level of activity. However, health became a major issue in Scotland when Cromwell was twice taken seriously ill in the early months of 1651. This raised the strong possibility that he might die or become unable to command his army in person before the Scots had been defeated,[4] but the choice of a successor was more problematic than it had been in either 1645 or 1650. The major general probably saw himself as the next lord general, but Cromwell did nothing to improve Lambert's chances until after his victory at Inverkeithing in July, by which time he had fully recovered, and it was safe for him to give credit to an ambitious underling.[5]

In the year following Fairfax's resignation other officers had the chance to show qualities that would fit them for supreme command - first Harrison and Fleetwood, and then Richard Deane and George Monck, who were commissioned as major general of foot and lieutenant general of artillery in late May 1651, just as the war in Scotland was beginning to hot up. Interestingly, Lambert was not promoted to lieutenant general at the same time as was rumoured in the London press.[6] The four months of active campaigning that followed would give all of them the chance to strengthen their case, but the most senior general in terms of rank and experience in commanding a large body of men was Henry Ireton, whose army in Ireland had increased to at least twenty-five regiments of foot and thirteen of horse by September 1651.[7]

* * * * *

Ireton was well known as a politician of conviction who happened to be an army officer, and moreover one whose pre-war experience as a lawyer gave him the ability to argue the war party case convincingly on paper and in open debate, and it was he rather than Cromwell who took the lead in the first stages of both the army coups. His religious views were also very close to Cromwell's. In the army, however, Ireton's elitist attitude to the ramblings of the representatives of the non-commissioned officers and the rank-and-file in the Putney debates made him an object of distrust in the army. He also lacked Cromwell's bonhomie and his military achievements were limited despite his military career beginning at the very start of the First Civil War.

At the battle of Edgehill Ireton was captain of a troop of horse raised in his native Nottinghamshire, but nothing is known about the part it played in the battle, other than that it did not form part of the cavalry reserve that performed so well under Sir William Balfour's command.[8] As several troopers were wounded, it was probably chased from the battlefield by Prince Rupert's charge.[9] Ireton then returned to Nottinghamshire and was promoted to major. In the summer of 1643 he took up a commission in Oliver Cromwell's regiment of horse in the Eastern Association army, but too late to have fought under him at Grantham or Gainsborough, and he may not have been at Winceby as he was acting as Cromwell's deputy governor of the Isle of Ely from August 1643 onwards. For the same reason he was not at the battle of Marston Moor, as a letter was addressed to Major Ireton at Ely on 26 June, but he was at York a month later.[10] By the autumn of 1644 he was quartermaster general in Manchester's army, and he does seem to have been at the Second Battle of Newbury, but with Cromwell's under-performing cavalry not with the earl, as the evidence he subsequently gave against Manchester's conduct during the Newbury campaign does not begin until the day after the battle.[11]

With his star firmly fixed to Cromwell's bandwagon, Ireton climbed quickly up the ranks of the New Model Army. Although only a captain of horse in Fairfax's list of February 1645, he succeeded Sir Michael Livesey two months later as colonel of a regiment that had served in Waller's army. This was not unprecedented, as there is another example in the New Model at that date of a former staff officer with the substantive rank of captain becoming a colonel of horse, but what happened next was.[12] On the day of the battle of Naseby, despite being the junior cavalry colonel present, Ireton was promoted to commissary general of horse and given charge of the left wing, while Cromwell took charge of the right. Initially the regiments under his command did well. They withstood Rupert's charge for a vital ten minutes or so, forcing the prince to draw in his reserves. During the pause, what appears to have been over-confidence on Ireton's part caused him to try to go to the assistance of Skippon's regiment of foot to his right, which was taking a tremendous punishment from the royalist infantry. As a result the left wing of the New Model became disordered and then gave way when Rupert's cavalry charged again. Ireton was captured, but as Rupert's cavalry passed to the rear of the New Model position troopers in Ireton's command not hustled to the rear by the enemy regrouped and played a significant role in the final stages of the battle.[13] How far it was Ireton who masterminded the recovery it is impossible to say, but he certainly managed to escape from his captors, which shows that the seven wounds he suffered during the course of the battle were not incapacitating and were possibly hyped-up in narratives of the battle in pro-Independent journals in London.

In the western campaign that followed Ireton's regiment seems to have done nothing of significance. It is not mentioned in the accounts of the battle of Langport, while at the storming of Bristol, where cavalry were engaged in the final storming of the royalist defences, it was operating on the north side of the city in a supportive role. Soon afterwards it returned to the east to protect London's environs from the depredations of royalist horse operating out of Oxford, but Ireton remained with the New Model Army and participated in the complex negotiations for the surrender of Hopton's army at Truro, probably on account of his legal expertise.[14] He then went on to play a major role in the run-up to the First Army Coup.

Ireton's military record in the Second Civil War was even lower key. His regiment did not accompany Cromwell into Wales and the north of England.

Instead it remained in the London area and, although it left for Kent with Sir Thomas Fairfax, the lord general seems to have sent it to assist the defenders of Dover Castle. It thus missed the battle of Maidstone. Moreover, Ireton did not join the regiment until the siege of Colchester as his major was in charge during the campaign in Kent.

After Colchester surrendered Ireton was even more heavily involved with army politics both prior to and during the Second Army Coup than he had been in the First. As a result he can have spent little time with his regiment from April 1648 onwards, and it was probably no accident that a year later, when it was selected for service in Ireland, four of its six troops joined the Leveller mutiny. As a result it was extensively remodelled, but probably through Ireton's influence it escaped being disbanded, the fate of the other cavalry regiment most heavily involved, and it duly accompanied Ireton to Ireland in August.[15]

Once in Ireland with the rank of major general, Ireton's name appears only occasionally in correspondence or in reports in the weekly journals until he took over operational command as Cromwell's deputy in May 1650. Soon afterwards the momentum of the campaign lessened, but this owed nothing to Cromwell's departure or to Ireton's lack of experience or drive. The destruction of the last enemy field army at Scarrifholles in June 1650 meant that Ireton lost the chance of establishing a reputation as a battlefield commander, but his subdivision of the army into brigades, each under a senior colonel and each charged with a specific task, achieved considerable success.[16] In June, July and August a number of important garrisons surrendered including Waterford, which had eluded Cromwell in the winter of 1649, but like Cromwell at Waterford a year before, Ireton arrived too late in the season to capture Limerick, the largest fortified town still in enemy hands. The siege recommenced in June 1651 and Ireton was yet again denied a victory in the field when a scratch relief force was intercepted by Lord Broghill at Knocknaclashy and destroyed. Ireton's tactical plan followed that of Fairfax's at the siege of Colchester, rather than Cromwell's at Clonmel which Ireton had implicitly criticized in the aftermath. After an attempt to secure the outer suburbs of Limerick had resulted in the loss of almost a hundred officers and men, Ireton set about starving the city into surrender by sweeping the surrounding countryside of supplies and instituting a naval blockade, and it duly surrendered on terms in October.[17]

The prospect of Ireton succeeding his patron as lord general ended when he succumbed to disease a few weeks after the fall of Limerick. It is generally agreed that Ludlow's testimony that Ireton worked himself to death is largely correct. One sign of his level of anxiety was his minute attention to administrative detail and process, as evidenced by the huge quantities of documents relating to his soldiers' pay that he sent to England during his time as Cromwell's deputy, which is in stark contrast to the practice of his predecessor Cromwell and his eventual successor Charles Fleetwood.[18] However, all in all Ireton conducted the war in Ireland after Scarrifholles with a high degree of competence. The charge of incompetence made by Gardiner and accepted uncritically by many subsequent writers (including me in 2010) does not stand up to close scrutiny.[19] For example, Gardiner's claim that Ireton wasted six weeks of the 1650 campaigning season subduing enemy forces in King's County and Tipperary, thus delaying his attack on Limerick until too late in the year, is easily contradicted by looking at a map of Ireland. It was essential for both areas to be in parliamentary hands before the siege began. This was because they stood astride the overland route between Limerick and Dublin and Limerick and Cork respectively, the ports through which supplies from England arrived in the country. These could not be shipped direct to the west coast of Ireland, as the only major port there in Commonwealth hands was Sligo, and that was sixty miles to the north-west of Limerick and on the far side of Connaught, which was entirely under enemy control.

*****

John Lambert's early military career was as meteoric as Oliver Cromwell's. The younger son of a middling Yorkshire landed gentry family, he joined the Fairfax rather than the Hotham faction of the Yorkshire parliamentarians and was commissioned as cornet in Sir Thomas Fairfax's troop of horse. This was more significant than might be thought. For the first nine months of the war in the north, when fighting was very largely confined to the cloth-making towns of the West Riding of Yorkshire, the Fairfaxes were only able to raise a few hundred cavalry[20]

Lambert almost certainly fought at Adwalton Moor, and like his troop commander he escaped to Hull, where he was promoted to colonel and praised for his bravery in commanding a body of 500 musketeers in the sally against the royalists which broke the siege in October 1643. He cannot therefore have been at Winceby, but at the battle of Nantwich in January 1644 he was a full colonel, mentioned along with several other officers as achieving the vital breakthrough in the centre of the enemy line.[21] In early March he gained his first independent command, but at the same time he displayed the first sign of the impatience and self-belief verging on arrogance that was to become more and more apparent the nearer he came to supreme command. Put in charge of the vanguard of Fairfax's force as it left the north-west of England to re-establish a Parliamentary presence in the West Riding of Yorkshire lost after Adwalton Moor, he chafed at the slowness with which Sir Thomas moved across the Pennines to reinforce him. The tone of a letter he sent to his general a fortnight or so later after he had secured Bradford says it all:

> (We) here exceedingly long for and desire your appearance here, which, I am informed, were enough to clear these parts if the opportunity is not to be slipped.

The plea for assistance is acceptable. Like many another commander in such circumstances, Lambert found himself outnumbered and thrown onto the defensive, for Halifax and Leeds were still in royalist hands, but the final words of the sentence suggest that if Fairfax did not stir himself the chance of regaining the other principal cloth-working towns would be lost. Reading between the lines, Lambert was criticising his general for being distracted from following up the advantage that he had gained at Nantwich by laying siege to Lathom House, a minor garrison in Lancashire in terms of its size. In the event the garrison refused to surrender and Fairfax duly joined Lambert in Yorkshire, but if it had succeeded Fairfax would have captured the Countess of Derby, the wife of the king's commander in Lancashire and the north-west.[22]

Lambert and Sir Thomas Fairfax joined forces at Leeds in mid-April, by which time Sir Thomas and his father had decided to destroy Lord Bellasis's corps of the Marquis of Newcastle's army quartered at Selby. This was a most successful venture in that it brought about the collapse of royalist resistance to the north of the Trent, but the tactical move that broke the back of the royalist defence was Sir Thomas Fairfax's, not John Lambert's.[23]

At the battle of Marston Moor that followed Rupert's relief of the besieged garrison of York, Lambert and his regiment were deployed in the second line of the right wing of the allied horse, directly behind the regiment of Sir Thomas Fairfax, who was in command of that wing. His orders were to follow in the wake of Fairfax's regiment when it broke through the enemy formation. According to a Scottish eyewitness, Lambert and his men charged through the enemy and, when they discovered that the rest of their wing had been chased off the battlefield by the enemy horse, they joined the Eastern Association horse on the other wing, which was gradually rolling up the royalist battle line. This is not confirmed by Sir Thomas Fairfax in his narrative of fighting in the north in 1642–44. Instead he delivered what looks like a backhanded compliment, or a rebuke, depending on how you read it: 'Colonel Lambert (who should have seconded me but could not get up to me) charged in another place.' However, this was not the only sign of lack of warmth on Sir Thomas's part. Throughout his narrative of the northern campaigns of 1642–44 there is scarcely a mention of Lambert, a complete contrast to the coverage Lambert received in the London press,[24] and this was not because he and Lambert were rarely engaged in the same military operation.

Writing Lambert out of the narrative may have been deliberate. By the time Fairfax wrote his *Short Memorial of the Northern Actions* Lambert, a highly ambitious man, had tied his flag firmly to Cromwell's mast, and he may have resented it. Conversely, the comment on Marston Moor may have been designed to cover embarrassment on Fairfax's part. In Captain Stewart's account of the battle Fairfax and Lambert were described as joining Cromwell on the victorious left wing with six or seven troops of horse. Fairfax's narrative shows that his regiment had been scattered and that he made a solitary journey through the royalist army to reach his destination. Therefore the troops of cavalry must been belonged to Lambert's regiment which, having fought its way through the royalist army or, more likely, found a gap in their line of battle, had arrived substantially intact.[25]

The year and a half following the victory of Marston Moor was the low point in Lambert's career. There was little fighting in the north involving the cavalry in the following six months. The Fairfaxes were busy rebuilding their army after its experience on the battlefield, and they used what forces they had available to set siege to the remaining royalist garrisons in Yorkshire, which was infantry work, but more responsibility may have been placed on Lambert's shoulders when Sir Thomas Fairfax was badly wounded in the siege of Helmsby Castle in August.[26]

Sir Thomas's appointment as commander of the newly modelled armies in the south opened up new opportunities, as immediately after the House of Commons vote Lambert was named as Sir Thomas's replacement as lieutenant general of cavalry in the army of the north, whereupon he became involved the siege of Pontefract Castle, the only stronghold there capable of serving as a royalist army base, What followed was the most serious setback in his entire military career.[27]

On 20 February the cavalry of Newcastle's army of the north, which had escaped after the battle of Marston Moor, rode from their quarters in Wiltshire under their commander Sir Marmaduke Langdale to disrupt the siege operations. After brushing off attempts by local forces to stop their passage they arrived at Newark six days later, where they were reinforced by 400 horse and 400 foot, which probably increased the size of the flying army to just short of 3,000 men. Crossing the River Don at Doncaster they arrived on a ridge facing Pontefract soon after midday on 1 March. Below them they found Lambert's force, which was probably twice their size, deployed along a hedge line. The narrative of the engagement that followed based on contemporary sources rather than subsequent surmise is that Langdale found it exceedingly difficult to break through, but by managing his forces carefully he ensured that his casualties were few. Nevertheless, after three hours had passed he only had a small number of mounted troops who had not been in action. In a final move of desperation he threw these against the front and his foot against the flank of the Parliamentary line at the same time as 200 musketeers sallied out of the castle and attacked the enemy in the rear. At this point the parliamentarians broke and ran, but as darkness was falling Langdale failed to capture more than a single artillery piece and two carriages loaded with barrels of gunpowder. Nevertheless, the defending force lost several hundred men killed or taken prisoner and a large number of hand weapons. More importantly, the biggest component of the Parliamentary army of the north had been badly beaten up.[28]

What Lambert's role was in all of this is unclear, as there is no detailed account of the battle from the parliamentary side, while the reports in the London journals are confused and read like a cover-up.[29] What is obvious is that the actual siege operations were the responsibility of a Colonel Forbes, and that Lambert's cavalry suffered a defeat some miles from Pontefract, but whether Lambert was in charge of the actual battle, or whether his troopers were worsted earlier and fled the area, leaving the besiegers to their fate, is uncertain. However, the royalist account claims that the enemy battle line contained more horse and dragoons than infantry, which makes it more than likely that Lambert fell back on the siege works, and then as the senior officer took over from Forbes when the enemy attacked.

If the battle of Pontefract had gone the other way, there is little doubt that Lambert would have been in serious contention for the post of commander-in-chief of the northern army when Lord Fairfax resigned in accordance with the terms of the Self-Denying Ordinance. However, what had happened at Pontefract did a lot to blot out the kudos he had gained by his performance earlier in the war. As a result it was not Lambert, but the English professional soldier Sydenham Poyntz, with years of experience fighting in Germany, whom Parliament appointed colonel general of the forces in the north in Lord Fairfax's stead.

Lambert presumably continued to enjoy the title of lieutenant general of cavalry in the Northern army under Poyntz, but he seems to have played little or no part in the fighting in the north during the summer and autumn of 1645. He was not with his general at the battle of Rowton Moor in September 1645, or with the Yorkshire horse in the leaguer around Chester either before or after the battle. He was not at the siege of Scarborough or at the renewed siege of Pontefract.[30] However, an opportunity arose in the New Model Army in October with the resignation of Edward Montagu, one of the colonels of Fairfax's infantry regiments, who had been elected to parliament as member for Huntingdonshire. Although not commissioned as colonel until December, Lambert quickly involved himself in the fighting in Devonshire. He began by commanding the reserves in the storming of Dartmouth in January 1646 and then took an openly political role for the first time in the negotiations that ended in the surrender of the royalist army in the west at Truro two months later.[31]

Active in the politicisation of the army in the spring of 1647, Lambert received his reward following the First Army Coup when, having given up his infantry regiment to a fellow Yorkshireman, Sir William Constable, he replaced Poyntz as commander of the forces in the north with the rank of major general.[32] After instituting some important reforms and a major slimming-down operation, he was extremely active in the first months of the Second Civil War in the counties along the Scottish border. However, his harrying of royalist recruiting efforts in Northumberland failed to prevent Sir Marmaduke Langdale assembling a brigade of some 3–4,000 men, and his subsequent antics in Westmoreland had no real impact on the southward march of the Scottish army, even if it appeared so to the readers of the reports in London journals. However, if Hodgson was not exaggerating, Lambert was at the very least the instigator of the move that caused Langdale's defence of the eastern approach to Preston to collapse and the Scottish army's retreat to be cut off.[33]

Using his undeniable charm to prevent the Scots being alienated by the invasion of their country that followed the Preston campaign, Lambert ably seconded Cromwell's efforts to secure a friendly government there. He then spent the next few months conducting a second siege of Pontefract Castle, which ended in its surrender in March 1649. As a result he took no part in Pride's Purge, the trial and execution of the king, or the institution of the Commonwealth.[34] In the short term, however, he was the loser, as his brigade was dissolved with regiments either being disbanded or incorporated into the New Model Army. By July 1650 he was a major general without a command, though as was the custom in the mid-seventeenth century with officers in such circumstances, he retained the title. In addition his cavalry regiment was taken into the New Model establishment, and just before the invasion of Scotland in July 1650 he became colonel of an infantry regiment that had been part of his brigade.[35]

While in Scotland in 1650–51 Cromwell used Lambert as de facto second-in-command and this gave him a good opportunity to improve his image as a dashing and effective commander of cavalry.[36] In the ineffective operations probing the lines of Edinburgh in August 1650 he was wounded and briefly captured. Then, according to Hodgson, it was he who proposed the tactics that won the battle of Dunbar. However, comparing Hodgson's narrative with those of George Monck's contemporary biographer and Oliver Cromwell, it looks as if the plan was compiled by the three of them prior to a meeting of the council of war, which Lambert then addressed and by his eloquence won over those who doubted that a frontal assault on the Scottish lines at night would be effective. Moreover, the initial battle plan depended on overwhelming pressure being imposed on the Scots infantry by a frontal assault. The flank attack that won the day appears to have been a spontaneous move on Cromwell's part when he saw the void in front of him that the Scottish right-wing cavalry had previously occupied. Conversely, if the cavalry attack in the centre had not been so courageously conducted by Lambert and Fleetwood, there would not have been a void on the Scottish right and Cromwell could not have carried out the manoeuvre that decided the outcome of the battle.

Chapter 16
Cromwell's Other Understudies

A third contender for Cromwell's position is less famous than Ireton or Lambert. His rise in the military hierarchy had been almost as rapid as Lambert's, but nowhere near as spectacular. Richard Deane, unlike the other five possible contenders for the lord generalship, was an artillery man first and foremost until new opportunities arose following the First Army Coup. Having possibly served in the navy before the war under a Captain Button and/or been involved in trading in naval supplies with northern Europe, Deane took part in securing the fort at Gravesend, which guarded the seaward approach to London, in June or July 1642, seemingly as a volunteer.[1] He then disappears from view in previous biographies or biographical sketches until August 1644, by which time he had risen to the position of controller of the artillery in the Earl of Essex's army, in effect second-in command to the general of artillery Sir John Merrick.

A recent edition of the accounts of Sir Edward Petoe, lieutenant general of the train of artillery, however, enables the gap to be filled. These show Deane as one of the dozen or so gentlemen of the artillery in mid-November 1642, and then as controller in succession to a Mr Forbois in June 1643, but the fact that he was paid considerably more than the other gentlemen suggests that he was already Forbois's deputy. As controller Deane was head administrator in the artillery, responsible for the acquisition and distribution of equipment and pay and also for keeping Petoe's accounts, which were highly complex due to the vast range of equipment required by the train. He may also have acquired greater responsibility as time passed. Petoe died in September 1643 and was not replaced.[2] Yet the fact that he was with the Earl of Essex's army when it surrendered at Lostwithiel in September shows that his was not just a desk job.[3] However, although he owed his position to the lord general, Deane saw the way the wind was blowing and ingratiated himself with his opponents by giving evidence against Colonel Butler, who had come under suspicion because of his behaviour during the fighting in Cornwall.[4] He may also have been full of righteous indignation at the way in which the campaign had been managed, ending in all the artillery pieces, barrels of gunpowder and technical equipment, for which he must have felt a fair degree of ownership, being handed over to the enemy.

Deane remained controller of artillery in Essex's army until the end, and was then transferred to the New Model in the same capacity with the rank of captain. His new superior officer was Thomas Hammond, who had been Manchester's general of artillery in the Eastern Association army.[5] The first chance of promotion came in May 1647 when the House of Commons proposed Deane as officer in charge of the artillery train to be sent to Ireland, but it did not come about due to the First Army Coup. He was then commissioned as adjutant general of foot, his first actual command outside the artillery, but one that required administrative skills.[6]

If, however, Deane had suffered a demotion, the experience was a brief one. When Thomas Rainborough was moved from an army command into the navy in September 1647 Deane took over as colonel of his regiment of foot, which fought in Wales and at Preston in the Second Civil War, but he relinquished command when appointed as one of the three generals at sea in February 1649, following the dismissal of the lord high admiral and the admiralty being put into commission. In the meantime, despite his previous command in Essex's army, Deane had clearly become Cromwell's man, and like Cromwell he took part in the king's trial and signed his death warrant.[7]

After an extremely active year and a half pursuing royalists and privateers in the seas around Great Britain, and protecting the flank of Cromwell's army as it advanced into Scotland, Deane was brought back into the army in December 1650 after the death of Colonel Maleverer, who had commanded one of the three infantry regiments added to the New Model establishment after the disbandment of the Northern army.[8] Six months later he was promoted to major general of foot.[9]

What distinguished George Monck from the rest of the senior officers in the New Model Army in 1651 was the length and variety of his military experience, which had begun in 1625 with the expedition to Cadiz. By the end of the Duke of Buckingham's wars four years later he had risen to captain lieutenant in command of the colonel's company in the Earl of Lindsey's regiment of foot. Reverting to his original rank of ensign, he enrolled in the Dutch army in 1630 and served in the Netherlands for nine years, ending up as major of his regiment with a reputation for bravery. Having resigned for what seem to have been personal reasons, he found employment as lieutenant colonel in the armies sent by King Charles I to fight the Scots in the First and Second Bishops' Wars, where he distinguished himself in the only serious encounter between the two sides at the crossing of the River Tyne in August 1640. Monck's final employment before the outbreak of the First Civil War was again at the rank of lieutenant colonel in a regiment raised to combat the Catholic uprising in Ireland. As in the Bishops' Wars his colonel had other duties and in combat situations Monck was effectively the regiment's commanding officer.

Immediately after the king negotiated a truce with the Irish insurgents in September 1643 Monck returned to England, and in a private interview with Charles he gave him advice on how to discipline his troops, but his career as a royalist ended when he was captured at the battle of Nantwich in January 1644. He then spent almost three years as a prisoner in the Tower of London, where he wrote a very competent treatise entitled *Observations on Military and*

Political Affairs. In November 1646 he was released through the influence of the Sydney family. Robert Sydney, Earl of Leicester, who was his cousin, had been his patron from the start of his career, and Monck was now to serve under Leicester's heir, Lord Lisle, whom Parliament had just appointed as lord lieutenant of Ireland. Stationed in Ulster first as a colonel of foot and then as commander-in-chief of the English forces in the province after Lisle returned to England, he achieved some success in capturing enemy-held towns and in campaigning against the Irish field armies with Michael Jones, the governor of Dublin.[10]

From the start of the war in Ireland the dominant force in the north of Ireland had been a Scottish army commanded by Sir Robert Monro. Militarily, however, the Scottish presence weakened over time. Regiments were withdrawn to strengthen the army in England in 1644 and to help put down the Marquis of Montrose's uprising in 1645, while those that remained were severely mauled by the Catholic army of Ulster under Owen Roe O'Neill at the battle of Benburb in 1646. As a result English troops became more prominent in the defence of the north-east of Ireland as time passed, while Sir Charles Coote, Lord President of Connaught, who had been active in the Protestant cause from 1645 with regiments raised from English and Scottish settlers, maintained a parliamentary presence in other parts of Ulster.[11]

The Scottish commanders in Ulster, however, became uneasy neighbours as relations between England and Scotland deteriorated, culminating in their support for Hamilton's invasion of England in the summer of 1648. This gave Monck his first chance to draw Parliament's attention to his skills of generalship beyond those of active campaigning, and also to demonstrate his commitment to the parliamentary cause. Had he been a secret royalist all along, as seems highly unlikely, the outbreak of the Second Civil War would have given him a good opportunity to serve his king, but instead he intrigued with anti-Hamiltonian Scottish officers in Ireland and with their help seized Belfast, Coleraine and Carrickfergus by a coup and also Sir Robert Monro, whom he sent to London as a prisoner.[12] Carrickfergus then became Monck's headquarters. A few months later he provided further evidence of his loyalty when, together with Jones and Coote, he refused point blank to join Ormond's rainbow coalition in support of the Stuart monarchy.[13]

There followed soon afterwards an episode that could easily have ended Monck's military career for good, and also laid him open to a charge of high treason, namely his truce with General O'Neill, who as a proto-Irish nationalist, had also refused to join Ormond's coalition. It was the clearest possible case of 'my enemy's enemy is my friend', but the circumstances surrounding it were obscured by propaganda from the royalist side and a smokescreen put up by Cromwell and his associates to hide their intrigues with foreign Catholics.[14] First, primary sources show that it was O'Neill who made the first move in early March, and that Monck immediately informed Michael Jones, his superior officer. Second, the truce coincided with tripartite negotiations between Cromwell's closest ex-war party associates, the abbot of Newry, O'Neill's agent in London, and the king of Spain's ambassador, at a time when the king's execution threatened to unite all the countries in western Europe against the Commonwealth, and when Cromwell was acting chairman of the Council of State prior to being appointed as the new lord lieutenant of Ireland.[15]

It is clear that the Commonwealth commanders in Ireland were permitted by the Council of State to talk to O'Neill, but not how far they were allowed to go before crossing the red line of collaboration. Michael Jones kept his contacts at an informal level and nothing resulted, while Coote made a truce with O'Neill, but kept it quiet until much later. In May Monck also negotiated a truce to last three months, but kept his superiors informed in such a way as hopefully to secure their protection if the news leaked out. Within a fortnight at the latest he had sent all the documentation to Oliver Cromwell, who on becoming lord lieutenant had replaced Jones as his superior officer. In his covering letter Monck stressed that it was the precariousness of his position that caused him to act as he did. He could not collect provisions or money from east Ulster without O'Neill's connivance, and without such protection he would be forced to capitulate to Ormond's supporters, as his troops were beginning to waver in their loyalty. If that happened the ensuing domino effect might result in the Commonwealth not having a single foothold left in Ireland by the time Cromwell's expeditionary force was ready to set sail. Cromwell may or may not have replied, but he did forward all the papers Monck sent him to the Council of State.[16]

The truce became public knowledge in June when it was revealed in a piece of propaganda printed by the royalist press in Ireland. The public reaction in London should have been devastating, as O'Neill's officers and soldiers were widely believed to have been those most directly involved in the massacre of Protestants during the first few months of the rebellion. However, the Council of State ignored the publication and so did Parliament, while most of the London journals merely printed the cessation document without comment.[17]

A month later, however, the Commonwealth government was forced to react when the war in Ulster turned first into farce and then into abject humiliation for Colonel Monck. O'Neill's army was short of gunpowder and Monck agreed to supply a limited amount. Such a level of cooperation was not covered by the terms of the truce, but otherwise O'Neill would be unable to assist Coote, whose garrison at Derry was under extreme pressure from forces belonging to Ormond's coalition and likely to surrender. But it all went wrong. The escort O'Neill sent to Carrickfergus drank themselves silly and blurted out the nature of their mission in the hearing of the coalition's spies, who gave Ormond's officers details of the convoy's return route. They attacked it the following day, took its escort prisoner, and made sure that the Carrickfergus garrison knew the circumstances, whereupon the garrison mutinied and joined the coalition army.[18]

Monck surrendered Carrickfergus to the enemy, having no men left with which to defend it, and immediately left for England, arriving at Chester on

23 July, the day before news of the mutiny arrived in London. Reasoning that he would be summoned to Westminster to explain why he had agreed to give O'Neill gunpowder, he went in search of his commanding officer, which in the circumstances is just the sort of behaviour to be expected of a professional soldier. He met Cromwell at Bristol on the 27th or at Milford Haven a few days later, just before his expedition set sail for Ireland, and probably received a better reception than he expected. Cromwell also had anxieties about what would be revealed by a Parliamentary investigation of the O'Neill affair. First, he had probably not replied to Monck's letter explaining the reasons why he had concluded a truce with O'Neill, and this was something Monck could use in his defence.[19] Second, although he had presented Monck's letter and papers to the Council of State, explaining the terms of the truce, they had not been presented to Parliament as Monck had requested. Instead the Council did nothing, while swearing all its members to keep the business secret, probably because negotiations had resumed with O'Neill's representative in London.[20] Third, information about the negotiations with the king of Spain's ambassador and with the abbot of Newry was likely emerge during Monck's cross-examination, and this would cause a storm involving Cromwell's closest associates and, insofar as the February round of discussions was concerned, the lord lieutenant of Ireland himself.

Cromwell therefore proposed a deal. Monck would take full responsibility for the truce with O'Neill and everything that followed, thus absolving Cromwell and the Council of State from blame, while Cromwell's friends in the Council and in Parliament would ensure that he received no more than a rap over the knuckles for his actions. Monck made encouraging noises, but did not agree to go through with the deal until he had talked to Cromwell's friends, which he clearly did on arriving in London on 7 August or soon afterwards, and the deal was struck. On the 10th a carefully stage-managed event in the House of Commons concluded that Monck had gone too far in his negotiations with O'Neill, but that the end had justified the means. Monck had thus nailed his colours firmly to Cromwell's mast and shown Cromwell that he could be trusted. He was nevertheless out of a job, but for less than a year.[21]

By June 1650 at the latest Monck was chosen to serve in Ireland once more, but in the event he did not do so.[22] Instead Cromwell wanted him as a colonel of a regiment of infantry in the army that was about to invade Scotland. Thus began the close professional relationship between the two that would last until Cromwell's death. Although the Sydney family were members of the war party through Lord Lisle, and Monck was one of their clients, the meeting in south Wales was the first time they are known to have met face to face. Each must, however, have made a favourable impression on the other, and the fact that both kept to their side of the bargain created a firm basis for future relations. Mutual regard must surely have been significant. Monck as a professional soldier had found a superior officer who possessed leadership qualities he respected, while Cromwell had found a subordinate who was highly competent, loyal and capable of exercising independent command. However, it should also be recognized that each had a hold on the other. Cromwell could ruin Monck by portraying him as untrustworthy because of his royalist past, while Monck could embarrass Cromwell by revealing his involvement in secret diplomacy with European Catholics.[23]

Cromwell's other understudies, Charles Fleetwood and Thomas Harrison, can be quickly dealt with as their military careers prior to the invasion of Scotland were unspectacular. What gave them their promotions to lieutenant general of horse and commander of the homeland forces respectively were their loyalty to Cromwell and their religious zeal. Fleetwood, like Lambert and Monck, was the younger son of a gentry family. A lawyer by training, he had acquired considerable military experience in the British wars, but had not served on the Continent prior to that. A volunteer in Essex's lifeguard in 1642, he was captain of horse in the Eastern Association by mid-1643 and colonel of horse by March 1644, but Cromwell gave Ireton rather than Fleetwood overall charge of the left wing at Naseby, despite Ireton being much the junior colonel.[24] Fleetwood duly commanded his regiment under Fairfax in 1645 and in 1648, but at no time did it or its colonel do anything to distinguish themselves. Fleetwood, however, had staying power and it is probably this that finally brought promotion in the summer of 1650.[25]

Harrison, the son of a provincial master butcher but a lawyer by profession, took much longer to come into contention for high command. Like Fleetwood he was a volunteer in the Earl of Essex's lifeguard in 1642, and then successively captain and major in Fleetwood's regiment of horse in the Eastern Association army. He first came into the public limelight when he rode rapidly from York to London the day after Marston Moor to let the press know that Cromwell and his cavalry had won the victory. When Fleetwood's regiment passed into the New Model Army Harrison continued as major. His religious zeal was already known, but it had burst forth at Langport in 1645 when he broke into loud and spontaneous prayer as the royalists fled the field of battle. He then took up the officers' and soldiers' cause in the lead-up to the First Army Coup and his reward was to be commissioned as colonel of what had been Thomas Sheffield's regiment of horse. Harrison then fought in the campaign in the north in 1648 under Lambert and Cromwell, but neither he nor his regiment distinguished themselves at the battle of Preston. He was recuperating from wounds sustained earlier in the campaign, while his regiment failed in its attempt to rush Langdale's position at the start of the battle. Harrison continued to play a prominent political role from the Putney debates of November 1647 until the Second Army Coup had run its course in March 1649, but some of his troopers mutinied in May. Perhaps, like Ireton, he had recently spent too much time away from his regiment, which had not been chosen for the Irish expedition, unlike the other two cavalry regiments principally involved.[26]

* * * * *

The British Wars of 1649 to 1651 gave Cromwell's understudies the chance to show how they would perform in independent command. The first to benefit was Ireton, who had charge of the war in Ireland as Cromwell's deputy from June 1650 onwards.[27] The next was Harrison, who took charge of the home army a few days later, but for the rest the opportunities were limited as the army in Scotland campaigned as a unitary body on a single front under a single commander until July of the following year. Their activities could therefore be closely observed by the lord general, who seems to have deliberately set them tasks to test their potential. However, sometimes it was a matter of luck that they caught his eye. As stated earlier, Lambert only gained credit for the victory over the Western Association at Hamilton because Cromwell was inadvertently absent.

The first example of Cromwell's delegation of responsibility was at Dunbar, where Lambert and Fleetwood commanded the horse and Monck the foot in the head-on assault on the Scottish position on the road south. Given the importance of the cavalry, Fleetwood's role is understandable as lieutenant general of horse, but Monck was the most junior of the New Model Army's colonels of foot. Possibly Lambert was included because that aspect of the battle was what he had recommended at the planning meeting the day before, while Monck's is understandable if he had backed him up. Cromwell may also have wanted Monck to gain some authority, as his first experience of the New Model was to be rejected as colonel of what had been Colonel Bright's regiment because of his royalist past. If he failed at Dunbar he could then have been quietly dropped, but if the account of the battle in Gumble's biography is correct, he played a very significant role in preventing the enemy infantry playing a greater part in the battle.[28]

Harrison, in the meantime, was busy organising the raising of militia troops of horse and dragoons. With the New Model Army units still in England located hundreds of miles apart, the Council of State was naturally keen on getting the militia organised to suppress any royalist uprisings, or at least contain them until such time as regular troops arrived. The militia forces could also be combined to form a large home army should anything go seriously wrong in Scotland. In March 1651, unsatisfied with the progress in the north of England, where there was the clearest intelligence of royalist plotting, Harrison was ordered to attend to the matter in person. The explanation was that he was better known there because he and his regiment had fought in the north in the 1648 campaign. However, it provided an excuse for bringing Fleetwood in over his head to command the home army. By July Harrison had been relegated to the command of what Cromwell estimated as at least 4,000 horse and dragoons, most of which were militia stationed in the Scottish Borders.[29]

Fleetwood was back in London by early 1651, well before Harrison's competence was called into question. This may have been because the cavalry had little to do so long as there was a stalemate, but possibly there was some difficulty over who was in overall charge of the horse, him or Lambert. Alternatively, managing the horse was a way of distracting Lambert from putting pressure on a sick Cromwell to formally appoint him as his deputy. However, the fact that Cromwell did not do so may be significant. He may have shared the concern of the Committee of Derby House in 1648 that Lambert was too impulsive, and later he clearly played to Lambert's strengths. He was very happy for him to command a brigade for a specific operation in which quick thinking was necessary, as for example at Inverkeithing and at Upton during the Worcester campaign, but if he relinquished overall command of the army in Scotland, Lambert was quite of carrying out a surprise attack on the lines of Stirling without adequate preparation in the hope that bravado would carry the day.[30] It may also explain why he was not prepared to give Lambert his best regiments when he put him in charge of defending the pocket at North Queensferry prior to Inverkeithing.

Cromwell also allowed his understudies to carry out experiments to test their hypotheses as to how the stalemate could be broken. Monck was of the opinion that a port suitable for accommodating sea-going vessels on the north side of the Firth of Forth could be captured by assault from the sea, but his attempt to do so at Burntisland failed twice during the winter. On neither occasion did the attacking flotilla get anywhere near effecting a landing, and as a result no lives were lost, but they did show the extreme difficulty of such a task. On the other hand, Deane probably won kudos first by pointing out the difficulties of landing in Fife in early October 1650, when Cromwell managed to collect a large number of seagoing vessels at Leith, and the efficiency he showed in escorting the first consignment of landing craft to the Firth of Forth in late March. These, together with his range of experience at sea in 1649 and 1650, probably explain why in May 1651 it was Deane rather than Monck who was promoted to major general of foot, as by that time it was clear that only an amphibious operation could bring a quick end to the stalemate.[31] Monck, having lost the contest, took command of the artillery, for which Deane seemed to be a natural.

Another experiment involved Colonel Overton who, like Lambert, was an experienced officer whose martial qualities Cromwell would have noted when he was campaigning in Yorkshire in the autumn of 1648. He commanded the second infantry brigade at Dunbar when Monck commanded the first and Cromwell the third, and had presumably supported Monck in the push down the road to England. Overton had long been concerned with the defence of Hull, and his acquaintance with matters affecting the sea may explain why it was he who was ordered to land a force a few companies strong on the open shore in Fife as a trial run for the major landing on 17 July. This he did successfully. He also commanded the initial landing at North Queensferry, but was then superseded by Lambert, who went on to defeat the Scottish counterattack on the pocket at Inverkeithing. This seems unfair, but it was logical for Cromwell to have appointed Lambert, given his experience in commanding mixed brigades in the early weeks of the 1648 campaign.[32]

Monck's chance to build up his reputation came in August when he was left behind in Fife with about 6,000 men, drawn mainly from the newer regiments, while Cromwell led the rest of the army into England in pursuit of the Scottish army. Before the Scottish army was destroyed at Worcester Monck had taken steps to ensure that if part of it managed to return, it would not be able to act as the nucleus for armed resistance. Stirling Castle was forced to surrender by well-directed mortar fire and the Scottish government was taken prisoner in a surprise raid on the obscure town of Alyth where it was hiding. He then stormed and sacked the city of Dundee as evidence of his determination to crush any opposition.[33] These taken together were an impressive display of military professionalism that removed any opprobrium sticking to him after the failure of the seaborne attacks on Burntisland. They also lessened the likelihood of the war in the north carrying on indefinitely, something that was still probably a matter of concern to Cromwell.

Deane had also done well. He commanded the naval operations which removed the threat to amphibious operations in the Firth of Forth from artillery located in castles along the south shore and ships moored in the estuary. He also probably supervised the procession of flat bottomed boats as they moved to and fro across the Firth. The operation having been successfully completed, he joined Cromwell in Fife and then marched with him to Worcester. It is most likely, given his wealth of experience in managing the artillery train with its bridging equipment, that he oversaw the construction of the pontoon bridges over the rivers Severn and Teme that were so crucial to the smooth-running of Cromwell's battle plan for 3 September.

The other general who may have gained kudos in the closing stages of the 1651 campaign was Charles Fleetwood. He worked well with the Council of State in assembling a reserve army when the Scottish army broke loose from Stirling. Quite a number of militia regiments fought at Worcester and the Cheshire regiments in particular excelled themselves. But he was not in command of them as they were split between the two parts of the army. However, he was given a role appropriate for his rank, namely command of the army corps that approached Worcester from the south along the far bank of the Severn while Cromwell was in charge of the corps on the high ground to the east of the city. Although it was held up at the bridge over the Teme at Powick, the impasse was resolved by reserves led across the Severn by Cromwell. Fleetwood then used his cavalry regiments to move steadily around the Scots' right flank, thus cutting off all possible escape routes to the west. He had thus performed the role expected of him. However, he was several miles away from the Severn when the infantry broke out of the bridgehead, while Cromwell had returned to the east bank with the reserves. It is therefore almost certain that Deane, as senior officer present, masterminded this and the pursuit of the Scottish infantry to the west end of Worcester bridge.[34]

Thomas Harrison and John Lambert's experience of the Worcester campaign was very different. They failed to delay the Scottish army's march south as they had been ordered. Cromwell's intention had been for them to defend the bridge over the Mersey at Warrington, where Hamilton's army had been stopped in 1648.[35]

This caused alarm to the Council of State, which wrote to them repeatedly about the need for them to be more proactive.[36] Lambert had then showed his tactical skills with small units by his capture of Upton bridge. Neither, however, played a leading part in the battle of Worcester. Harrison was given the undemanding task of intercepting fugitives fleeing north once the battle had been won, while Lambert may have deputized for Cromwell on the east bank of the Severn while the lord general was paying his brief visit to the west bank with the reserves. It is interesting that it was Fleetwood and Deane and not Lambert who Cromwell put in command of the corps operating on the far side of the Severn, despite the fact that it was Lambert who had made such a deployment possible by his success at Upton bridge.[37] This probably represents cautious thinking on Cromwell's part. To place an officer with Lambert's impulsive temperament in command of some 10,000 men facing an enemy defending a previously prepared position might be dangerous. What was needed was a calm head and the composure to wait for the best opportunity before mounting an assault. If Lambert was in charge, any delay in constructing the bridges might cause him to devise a tactical plan on the hoof with uncertain consequences.

* * * * *

It was exactly eight years between the victory at Worcester and the lord generalship becoming vacant on Cromwell's death. In the interval most of his understudies had disappeared from the scene. Ireton died in Ireland, while Deane was killed by a cannon ball in a sea battle against the Dutch in June 1653. Harrison and Lambert had been dismissed from their commands for opposing Cromwell after he became lord protector and king in all but name in the mid-1650s, while Fleetwood, though still an army general, was no longer lord deputy in Ireland because of the favouritism he showed towards radical officers unhappy with the protectorate. Only George Monck remained, to all intents and purposes Cromwell's viceroy in Scotland. He had shown all the military professionalism and political nous Cromwell had seen in him in 1649 and subsequently, but his royalist past told against him even if it took the form of jests.

The army's candidate for lord general on Cromwell's death was Fleetwood, but Cromwell's successor as lord general as well as lord protector was his son Richard, who did not have the respect of the army, and who soon showed that he lacked the political skills and the bonhomie that might have compensated for it. Monck did what he could to help Richard by giving him advice on dealing with opposition in the army, but the task of governing England was too much for Richard and he resigned in May 1659. Almost exactly a year later Monck welcomed back the king at the head of an army purged of radicals.

The process by which Monck became a royalist has been the subject of much debate over the years, and it is highly doubtful that any new source will bring it to an end. However, his entire career in the army pointed to his being most comfortable with government by a single person, and there is no evidence whatsoever that he saw himself as that person. He may therefore have favoured the restoration of the Stuarts immediately after the fall of the House of Cromwell, but it would have been impossible for him to have done anything other than deny it before mid-February 1660, when he was appointed lord general with complete authority over the army by a restored House of Commons in which he had allowed MPs expelled by Colonel Pride in 1648 to take their seats. Even then there was a risk of trouble from republican officers still in post, and it was only after a feeble fightback led by John Lambert had been defeated, and dissident officers removed, that he could finally reveal his and the remodelled army's preference for King Charles II.

Monck's career as lord general with plenary powers only lasted four months. With the monarchy restored, the commissioning of officers reverted to the Crown, and by the end of January 1661 almost all the New Model Army regiments stationed in England had been disbanded, with those in Scotland following a year later. Monck did what he could to soften the blow for the officers who had given him the greatest assistance. His foot regiment was reconstituted as the Coldstream Guards, with the company commanders almost all remaining in place. Other favoured officers found positions in the army in Ireland, while a few more were re-employed later in Charles II's reign as the army expanded in size.[38] Monck, now Duke of Albemarle, continued to be addressed as lord general until the end of his life, but that form of words was not revived even for John Churchill, Duke of Marlborough, who became captain general of Queen Anne's armies in 1702. It carried with it too many reminders of the republican past.

Chapter 17

An Afterthought

It is customary to use the last chapter of a book to briefly summarise its contributions to knowledge, but it is not necessary in this case as it is a new account of the military/political careers of the lords general, their rivals and their understudies, not an analysis, a comparative study or a compendium of biographical information. Instead I want to speculate about an aspect of Cromwell's man-management techniques that is impossible to fit into the tale of his generalship, as its effects can only be glimpsed fitfully during his military career. What his contemporaries marvelled at was the mix of good and bad qualities that explained his rise to supreme authority from a comparatively lowly baseline, while speculating about what had been the crucial factor.

Those who came nearest were probably Sir William Waller and Lord Clarendon. Waller had the opportunity to observe Cromwell at close quarters during the campaign they fought in the West Country in March and April 1645.

His verdict was as follows:

> while he was cautious of his own words not putting forth too many lest they should betray his thoughts, he made others talk until he had, as it were, sifted them, and known their innermost designs.[1]

Clarendon had very little direct experience of Cromwell, but he had distilled a similar draught from listening to other people:

> He must have had a wonderful understanding of the natures and humours of men and as great a dexterity in applying them... that contributed to his designs and to their own destruction.[2]

Cromwell thus had a gift for uncovering men's secrets and therefore their weaknesses. And it can be inferred from Clarendon in particular that he used such information as occasion arose, either to dissuade individuals from taking action, or to ensure that supporters remained loyal, and doubtless a political biography which pursued that line of enquiry would uncover a succession of examples.

Much has been made, in this book and elsewhere, of Cromwell's attack on the Earl of Manchester in the winter of 1644–5, and I have hinted that Philip Skippon's failure to speak up in to Manchester's defence may have been partly because of what the war party had uncovered about his own behaviour in Cornwall. Cromwell may have tried to silence Manchester in the same way in mid-November, but the earl's respect for the truth made him impervious to blackmail, and this might easily lead to his own downfall.[3] This forced him into the dangerous procedure of resorting to the big lie, which succeeded because it was just the sort of conspiracy theory that the MPs and the citizens of London wanted to hear at that time. Manchester's innocence or guilt was not, however, put to the test in 1645, but the fact that it was not may explain the earl's curious behaviour two years later.

After resigning his commission in April 1645, Manchester resumed his earlier position as speaker of the House of Lords *pro tem,* at first intermittently and then almost continuously from the beginning of 1646 until the purged House of Commons decided to put the king on trial in December 1648. With his well-known Presbyterian sympathies, the leaders of the peace party regarded him as one of their inner circle.[4] However, at the time of the First Army Coup in June 1647 he was not one of the peers and MPs identified by the army as its enemies. Moreover, when anti-army unrest broke out in the capital two months later encouraged by the peace party leaders, Manchester fled to the army for protection and was seen as having common cause with Cromwell for the next year. Such a volte face was untypical of Manchester's conduct in his long and eventful political life from out-and-out radical in 1641 to lord chamberlain to Charles II in the 1660s, but there is a logical explanation if he had been threatened with the charges Cromwell made against him in 1644 being revived. Indeed the pot had been kept bubbling for some time. In 1646 John Lilburne, at that time close to Cromwell, published a pamphlet reminding Parliament and the people of unfinished business concerning the campaign of the autumn of 1644, which hinted at a traitor's death for the earl.[5] And blackmail was in the air at the time. William Lenthall, the speaker of the House of Commons, like Manchester, sought the army's protection against the mob in August 1647, but only after receiving a letter signed from Cromwell and Fairfax threatening him with prosecution on charges of peculation and treasonable correspondence with the king.[6]

It is also not inconceivable that this was why Waller gave evidence accusing Manchester of persuading the council of war not to fight a third battle at Newbury, rather than just for not coming to his help in the West Country.[7] Cromwell's hold on that occasion would have been what he knew about decision-making during the night following the second battle.[8] Finally, if it is agreed that Fairfax's claim that he was unhappy with the army's proceedings from the first army coup to the king's trial, then he might have been kept dangling on a similar type of string, but of a different nature, and my hunch is that it was something affecting Sir Thomas's honour. His defence of his conduct in the *Short Memorials* looks weak, but if the person or persons to whom it was addressed already knew his secret, it would have been immeasurably stronger.

The ins and outs of Cromwell's political behaviour beyond the confines of the army are for others to explore, and there are signs that this process is at last underway with regard to his rule as lord protector and his conduct in the run-up to the king's trial and execution.[9] However, his modus operandi in the military/political sphere is sufficiently clear for me to state in no uncertain terms that the way in which he sought to entrap the Earl of Manchester in 1644 comprehensively destroys the traditional stereotype of him as a man of towering integrity, as stated in the conclusion of the entry in the *Oxford Dictionary of National Biography*. The best I can say about him is that for Cromwell the ends justified the means, and that his guiding principle was probably the passage in Matthew 10, verse 16, which enjoins followers of Christ to be as wise as serpents when placed in a hostile political environment. They should also be as innocent as doves, but presumably for Cromwell innocence was conditional, a moveable feast determined by providence, with the proof of the pudding being in the eating. If his endeavours were crowned with success whatever the human cost, it was a clear sign of his innocence in the eyes of God.

Appendix

The Dating of Thomas Lord Fairfax's
Short Memorials

The *Short Memorials* has been slated by historians as a source for the momentous events of the late 1640s and Fairfax's role in them. Sir Clement Markham's verdict in the first full-length biography of the general was that it was written twenty years later by an elderly man recently widowed and relying on his memory. As a result it contained errors and inconsistencies. As for its purpose, Markham argued that Sir Thomas's cousin Brian Fairfax, who published a bowdlerised version in the 1690s, was correct when he stated that it was to assist his family in defending his honour after his death, but this has recently been rejected. Daxon and Hopper, while accepting Markham's dating, have suggested that the principal audience was Fairfax trying to explain his conduct to himself; that he found it impossible without including palpable falsehoods; and that it was indeed the work of a tired and troubled mind. Gardiner went even further a century ago. Fairfax's account of his involvement in the momentous events of 1647–50 was 'not as it had actually been, but as he fancied it ought to have been.'[1]

All of this is dependent on accepting Markham's date for the *Short Memorials*, but in my opinion the first draft cannot be firmly ascribed to the 1660s. Although the earliest extant version may have been the product of some tinkering towards the end of Fairfax's life, there is every possibility that it was preceded by a document written at about the time of his resignation as lord general in June 1650. The first give-away is that he uses the phrase 'during this war' at one point, which clearly shows that parts of it cannot have been written any later than 1651. Another pointer is the non-deferential way in which he refers to Charles I. Throughout he is referred to merely as the king. If the purpose of the *Short Memorials* was to engage the sympathy of a post-Restoration audience, he would surely have referred to the monarch as His Majesty or His Late Majesty of blessed memory. In addition it was tactless not to have missed the opportunity to distance himself from Oliver Cromwell by naming him as one of the 'cunning and deceitful men' who had subverted the parliamentary cause for their selfish purposes. Instead Cromwell is mentioned only twice, and on both occasions Fairfax describes him as lieutenant general, the rank he held in 1650.

Historians have not worried too much about the gaps in the *Short Memorials*, as Fairfax had explained at the start that he was not writing a narrative of the 1640s, but a defence of aspects of his conduct that the world might judge to be dishonourable.[2] However, if that was the whole story, it does not explain why some contentious issues are not addressed head-on, while others are avoided. Hopper has interpreted his weak account of his conduct in the run-up to the king's execution, which went no farther than words spoken in the Army Councils, and of his failure to resign as lord general until well over a year later, as indicative of the impossibility of giving an honourable explanation of his actions. I, however, wonder if the reason was that the audience he was addressing was already very well informed about his behaviour between December 1648 and June 1650, had agreed to accept his reasons for it, and therefore did not to require any further explanation.

I am also not as convinced as Hopper about the falsehoods in the *Short Memorials*. In the first place it seems totally out of character for Fairfax to have lied, especially in a document in which he expressed the hope that 'God (by his grace and assistance) would ensure that he would truly set down the grounds for his actions'. Second, the alleged falsehoods may be nothing of the sort. Hopper singles out Fairfax's claim that officers were removed and replaced by the agitators without his approval.[3] This clearly came to an end with the eclipse of the agitators' power after Cromwell and Fairfax suppressed the Leveller revolt in late November 1647, but between August and November Fairfax does seem to have lost some control over the commissioning of officers. There is a gap covering those months in the commissions' book kept by his secretary from June 1647 to June 1650, and there is a volume in the Clarke Papers recording the discussions of a committee which was responsible for commissioning between August and November 1647, and which might have included representatives of the rank-and-file.[4] I would also not dismiss out of hand Fairfax's claim that he was instrumental in preventing the king being put on trial after the Windsor prayer meeting in early May 1648, preceded, as it would need to have been, by the dissolution of Parliament. By delaying signing the warrant for the march on London, he created time for the war with Scotland to become inevitable. In such circumstances a move against the king would have been more than stupid, both militarily and politically.

Who then was the audience for the *Short Memorials*? All I can suggest, very tentatively, is that it began as a confessional, which formed part of the reconciliation between the lord general and the Presbyterian clergy favoured by his wife, an event Gardiner believed to have taken place just before he resigned.[5] What points me in that direction is Fairfax's description of the Earl of Essex as a 'very noble and gallant person'. I cannot see that epithet being applied after the First Army Coup other than by somebody wishing to make his peace with former members of the peace party. Moreover, if my argument is correct, it weakens the strongest pointer to the 1660s as the date for the composition of the *Short Memorials*.

In the first paragraph Fairfax reflects on God's behaviour: 'Now when the Lord is visiting the nation for the transgression of their way as formerly it did to one set of men, so now doth he it to another'. It is easy to see this as coming from the same stable as General Fleetwood's despairing comment about the army in 1660 that 'God hath spat in their faces'. However, Fairfax's statement could as easily apply to 1650 when men who fought against the king in order to limit the royal prerogative and increase the power of the Two Houses (which Fairfax stated were his own reasons for doing so) discovered that God had turned his face against them by allowing the 'cunning and deceitful men' to seize power.

Notes

Prologue

1. M. Wanklyn and F. Jones, *A Military History of the English Civil Wars* (2004); Wanklyn, *Decisive Battles of the English Civil Wars* (2006); Wanklyn, *The Warrior Generals: Winning the British Civil Wars* (2010).
2. 'The Earl of Manchester as army commander in the Second Newbury Campaign', *War in History* 14 (2007), 133-156; 'Oliver Cromwell and the performance of Parliament's armies in the Newbury campaign 20 October to 21 November 1644', *History* 96 (2011), 3-25; 'Choosing officers for the New Model Army, February to April 1645', *J. Society for Army Historical Research* 92 (2014), 109-25.

Chapter 1

1. J. Adamson, *The Noble Revolt*, 511-12.
2. Firth and Rait, *Acts and Ordinances* i, 14; JHC ii, 673; JHL v, 212.
3. *ODNB* 15, 960-5.
4. *Old Parliamentary History* 11, 364; JHC ii, 760, 778; JHL v, 367-9, 429, 431-2.
5. BL, Thomason Tracts, E 202 (24-27).
6. Ibid, E 112 (7); JHC ii, 724.
7. See, for example, BL, Thomason Tracts, E 117 (11) and (26).
8. Wanklyn, *Warrior Generals*, 32-3.
9. Codrington, *Life and Death*, 29.
10. Smith, *De Republica Anglorum*, 51-2.
11. BL, Harleian Ms 163, 324. A London journal tells a different story. Essex had rapidly left the Parliament building for his house on the Strand preparatory to leaving the capital that afternoon. Learning of this the MPs decided not to follow him, but to wish him well as a group at his departure. This sounds plausible, but it does not rule out the possibility that it was a cover-up for what had really happened: BL, Thomason Tracts, E 202 (44).
12. CSPV 1641-2, 154.
13. JHL v, 327. The earlier order was probably issued on 13 August: BL, Thomason Tracts, E 202 (33). There is no mention of it in the journals of either House, but the wording of the later order suggests that it may have been issued by the Committee of Safety. For this committee and its powers see below 13, 41.

14. *ODNB* 15, 965-6.
15. BL, Thomason Tracts, E 116 (25). The mention of the king and Essex in a single phrase would have been particularly gratifying to the earl if he had aspirations to be lord high constable. The words were taken from the Coronation service at the point when the king's subjects greet the newly crowned monarch immediately after he has made his solemn vow to God to exercise his office in a conscientious and Christian way.
16. Wanklyn, *Warrior Generals*, 16-21.
17. *ODNB* 15, 966.
18. Wanklyn, *Warrior Generals*, 42.
19. See below 17-18, 33-4.

Chapter 2

1. *Cromwell*, 121; *The English Civil War*, 335.
2. Snow, *Essex the Rebel*, 498-9.
3. Braddick, *God's Fury, England's Fire*, 285, 336, 353; Gentles, *English Revolution*, 153-8, 190, 212, 225, 229-30.
4. Woolrych, *Battles of the English Civil War*, 60, 81; Burne and Young, *Great Civil War*, 227.
5. See, for example, my publications from *A Military History* (with F. Jones) onwards and Scott and Turton, *Hey for Old Robin*, 42-48, 182-4.
6. *ODNB* 15, 966.
7. Firth and Rait, *Acts and Ordinances* i, 14-15. Snow, his biographer, noted that Essex had no authority over strategy, but did not develop the point: *Essex the Rebel*, 498.
8. To make matters worse Essex has suffered from criticism by historians keen to display the virtues of their favoured generals and to absolve them from blame. See, for example, the account of Sir William Waller's conduct during the Roundway Down campaign in the second edition of Adair's *Roundhead General*.
9. CSPD 1644 and 1644-5; NAS, PA11/1-4, 16. The minutes begin with the committee's first meeting in mid-February 1644, but its incoming correspondence is not recorded until May. For the rest of Essex's time as lord general copies of most of its correspondence appear in its letter books, but some of the missing items can be found in Lord Wharton's papers and in the parliamentary diary of Sir Simons D'Ewes: Bodleian Library, Carte Ms 80; BL, Harleian Ms 165-6.
10. Firth, *Cromwell*, 79.
11. Whitelock, *Memorials*, 62-3; Adair, *Roundhead General*, 32-4; BL, Thomason Tracts, E 112 (15).
12. Rushworth, *Historical Collections* v, 27; JHC ii, 775; JHL v, 390, 412; HMC, Bouverie Mss, 88.
13. BL, Thomason Tracts, E124 (26); Ludlow, *Memoirs* i, 45-6.
14. For a full discussion of this see Wanklyn, *Warrior Generals*, 32-3.

15. This is what his officers meant when they wrote about refreshing the army at Warwick: BL, Thomason Tracts, E 126 (38).
16. Whitelock, *Memorials,* 65-6; Rushworth, *Historical Collections* v, 59-60.
17. For Warwick's successful recruiting operations see below 35.
18. Woolrych, *Battles,* 19. If the flank attack had been allowed to continue, Essex may have been left with as few as four battle-hardened regiments at Turnham Green. Of the fifteen he had available after Edgehill, five were the detritus of those that had fled the battlefield, two had been subsequently shattered, two were approaching Acton, and another two probably on the march from Kingston. I do not accept that the Kingston brigade were not part of his army, as argued by Porter and Marsh in *Battle for London,* 89. They were described as regulars at the time, and they were commanded by one of Essex's officers: Rushworth, *Historical Collections* v, 59; Whitelock, *Memorials,* 65.
19. Ibid, 66; Gaunt, *English Civil War,* 82.
20. JHC ii, 894; BL, Thomason Tracts, E 242 (14), (27).
21. JHL v, 456.
22. JHC ii, 860; Vicars, *Jehovah-Jireh,* 234-5.
23. BL, Thomason Tracts, E 242 (34); Scott and Turton, *Hey for Old Robin,* 68.
24. Snow, *Essex the Rebel,* 393; JHL v, 614.
25. BL, Harleian Ms 164, 243, 318.
26. JHL v, 603, 610, 614, 619, 624-5; JHC ii, 970, 978, 982.
27. HMC, Portland Mss i, 707; JHL vi, 43.
28. Green, *Letters of Henrietta Maria,* 193, 197.
29. BL, Thomason Tracts, E 71 (9). See also below 68-9.
30. For an appraisal of the campaign and the clash of personalities see below 29-32.
31. Luke, Journals ii, 116-18.
32. Essex received another letter asking him to make a diversion on the evening before the battle, but by then it was far too late to do anything.
33. JHL vi, 127; JHC iii, 161-3.
34. Adair, *Roundhead General,* 128-9; BL, Thomason Tracts, E 74 (1), (4), (19).
35. Snow, *Essex the Rebel,* 420; CSPD 1644, 27-8, 49.
36. Codrington, *Life and Death,* 32-5; BL, Thomason Tracts, E 70 (10).
37. The number of musket balls discovered is too small and too dispersed to support the new hypothesis that the battle lines were at a 45 degree angle to Edgehill.
38. BL, Thomason Tracts, E 126 (13).
39. BL, Harleian Ms 3783, 50
40. BL, Thomason Tracts, E 126 (38); Rushworth. *Historical Collections* v, 33-6.
41. See, for example, Young and Holmes, *English Civil War,* 77.
42. BL, Thomason Tracts, E 124 (26); ibid 669 f6 (88); Wanklyn, *Decisive Battles,* 44-5 developing a hypothesis in Kitson, *Prince Rupert,* 97-8.
43. This is an updating of the description of the deployment given in *Decisive Battles* informed by BL, Thomason Tracts, E 128 (20).

44. See, for example, Gardiner, *Great Civil War* i, 45; Young, *Edgehill*, 38; Reid, *All the King's Armies*, 22-3; Scott and Turton, *Hey for Old Robin*, 45.

45. BL, Thomason Tracts, E 128 (20).

46. This is not a mere flight of fancy. There was a spy among Prince Rupert's staff who could well have picked up some loose talk among the prince's officers about their intentions. For this see Wanklyn, *Warrior Generals*, 238.

47. Rushworth, *Historical Collections* v, 32-3; BL, Thomason Tracts, E 124 (32); ibid, E 126 (38).

48. Ludlow, *Memoirs* i, 42-3.

49. Wanklyn, *Decisive Battles*, 51-2.

Chapter 3

1. Snow, *Essex the Rebel*, 370-1; JHL vi, 246-7, 505-6.

2. See above 18.

3. JHL v, 493.

4. Ibid v, 454

5. Ibid v, 593.

6. Hopper, *Black Tom*, 46

7. Carpenter, *Military Leadership*, 166.

8. Gaunt, *English Civil War*, 128; Hopper, *Black Tom*, 48.

9. JHL v, 520; Hughes, *Warwickshire*, 152-4. His successor Basil Feilding, Earl of Denbigh, got into trouble through no fault of his own. A letter from his mother intercepted in May 1643 urging him to change sides aroused suspicion of a man who had been a courtier before the war, and whose father had been killed fighting for the king at Birmingham in April 1643. To make matters worse his mother was a sister of Charles I's assassinated favourite the Duke of Buckingham and a Roman Catholic. Denbigh was not in contention for Essex's command as he was unable to assemble an army until the spring of 1644: ibid, 224-5; Warburton, *Memoirs* ii, 157-8.

10. JHC ii, 886; *ODNB* 23, 850-1; Hopton, *Bellum Civile*, 86-7.

11. Thomas, Lord Grey of Groby, eldest son of the Earl of Stamford, commanded in the east Midlands. He relied exclusively on the regiments his county commanders could raise, but he proved totally incapable of managing forceful personalities like Sir John Gell in Derbyshire and Oliver Cromwell in the Isle of Ely. Apart from assisting Essex in the relief of Gloucester, little is heard of his command after the summer of 1643: Beats, 'East Midlands Association', 160-74; BL, Thomason Tracts, E 70 (10).

12. Holmes, *Eastern Association*, 69-70.

13. JHL v, 505; BL, Thomason Tracts, E 124 (32); JHL vi, 134-5.

14. Terry, *Life of Leven*, 282.

15. Wanklyn, 'General much maligned', 140-7.

16. Firth and Rait, *Acts and Ordinances* i, 79.
17. An ancestor had captured the Duc d'Orleans at Agincourt.
18. Adair, *Roundhead General,* 17-22; *ODNB* 56, 986.
19. See Wikipedia entry.
20. *Roundhead General,* 29.
21. JHC ii, 726.
22. Ibid ii, 870; Firth and Rait, *Acts and Ordinances* i, 79.
23. Warburton, *Memoirs* ii, 141.
24. Washbourne, *Bibliographica Gloucestrensis,* 35.

Chapter 4

1. HMC, Portland Mss i, 703, 710-11; BL, Thomason Tracts, 70 (1).
2. BL, Thomason Tracts, E 103 (10); ibid, E 71 (7), 5-6; Warburton, *Memoirs* ii, 195-6.
3. HMC, Portland Mss i, 709-11; Atkin, *Worcestershire under Arms,* 65.
4. Warburton, *Memoirs* ii, 141, 195-6; BL, Thomason Tracts, E 100 (19); HMC, Portland Mss i, 709-10. A letter from the lord general to the governor of Bristol written on 27 May assumed that Waller was already making a move against Prince Maurice and the Marquis of Hertford.
5. Ibid i, 710-11.
6. Ibid i, 709-11; Hopton, *Bellum Civile,* 46-9.
7. HMC, Portland Mss i, 708-9; Atkyns, *Vindication,* 12.
8. BL, Thomason Tracts, E 60 (8), (12); HMC, Portland Mss iii, 112; Hopton, *Bellum Civile,* 49-56, 96.
9. BL, Thomason Tracts, E 60 (12); Bodleian, Tanner Ms 62, 164; Wadham College Library, Manuscript Collection, A18.14, 63. See below 37 for Waller's subsequent caution.
10. The western army infantry did not appear on the battlefield until the fighting was almost over. Despite Hopton's pleas their officers refused to leave Devizes for fear that the noise of battle on the downs might be a ruse to tempt them out into the open: *Bellum Civile,* 57.
11. Young, Royalist army, 131; BL, Thomason Tracts, E 61 (1).
12. Atkyns, *Vindication,* 23.
13. BL, Thomason Tracts, E 60 (12); Bodleian, Tanner Ms 62, 164; HMC, Portland Mss iii, 112-13.
14. Atkyns, *Vindication,* 22-3. According to Sir John Byron they were very tired after their long marches: Young, 'Royalist army', 130.
15. BL, Thomason Tracts E 61 (9).
16. Ibid, Thomason Tracts, E 63 (11); ibid, E 71 (7); Adair, *Roundhead General,* 98.
17. Ibid, E 61 (13), E 63 (13). Lady Waller blamed the lord general in a more direct way: CSPV 1642-3, 304-5.

18. BL, Thomason Tracts, E 61 (9), (11), (13), (15), (16).
19. JHC iii, 176.
20. BL, Thomason Tracts, E 63 (8), (10). The final comment was a Parthian shot at the Earl of Essex and his army. The lord general's leisurely way of fighting the war was seen as having severely impoverished the capital and its inhabitants.
21. JHC vi, 188-218.
22. JHL vi, 144, 188-9.; JHC iii, 188-9.
23. Wanklyn, *Warrior Generals.* 57-8.
24. JHC iii, 237, 249-50.
25. These calculations are based on the regimental listings in Spring's, *Waller's Army,* and the passage in Elias Archer's *A True Relation* in which he described the army as it was about to set out from Farnham on 31 October 1643.
26. JHL vi, 175, 175-6, 182; Firth and Rait, *Acts and Ordinances* i, 51, 242; HMC, Portland Mss iii, 119. The confusion between Waller's and Manchester's jurisdiction was caused by an ordinance concerning impressment: JHL vi, 177.
27. CSPV 1643-4, 5, 19.
28. For Waller's appointments see Adair, *Roundhead General,* 116-117, 122.
29. Hopton, *Bellum Civile,* 101-2; Roe, *Military Memoir of Colonel Birch,* 12; Walker, *Historical Discourses,* 30-33.
30. CSPD 1644, 95, 101-2, 109, 116; ibid 1644-5, 36.
31. For an assessment of the size and composition of the parliamentary army at Newbury see Wanklyn, *Decisive Battles,* 145-6.
32. Wanklyn, *Warrior Generals,* 132-6.

Chapter 5

1. Snow, *Essex the Rebel,* 402-3.
2. *ODNB* 47, 637; Woolrych, *England in Revolution,* 275, 298-300.
3. The development of the two parties during 1644 and 1645 can be glimpsed through the distorted spectacles of Thomas Juxon, a London merchant, who kept a detailed but idiosyncratic diary of political events.
4. Stevenson, *Revolution and Counter Revolution,* 2, 3.
5. *Acts of the Parliaments of Scotland* v, 285; ibid vi, 448, 460; NAS, PA 11/1, 71,87; Meikle, Correspondence, 44-5.
6. Woolrych, *Britain in Revolution,* 270-2; Baillie, *Letters,* addition to vol. 1, xliv.
7. JHC iii, 429, 442; JHL vi, 476-7, 481, 492-4; Firth and Rait, *Acts and Ordinances* i, 417.
8. Ibid i, 369. Essex seems to have resented the independence and favours granted to his major generals more keenly than anything else: CSPD 1644, 234.
9. Firth and Rait, *Acts and Ordinances* i. 398; Scott and Turton, *Hey for Old Robin,* 125-6.
10. JHC iii, 415-27, 443: Wanklyn, Choosing officers, 114-15.

11. It was customary for votes in the Lords to be unanimous, but from 1642 onwards those who disagreed with a measure had their dissents entered in the Lords Journals: JHL v, 4.

12. JHC iii, 452-4; JHL vi, 504; BL, Thomason Tracts, E 42 (18).

13. *ODNB* 15, 967; Firth and Rait, *Acts and Ordinances* i, 381-2.

14. JHC iii, 392. The original wording appears in ibid iii, 504.

15. JHL vi, 405, 427-8.

16. BL, Additional Ms 11692, 25, 27; *Old Parliamentary History* xii, 466, 475.

17. Baillie, *Letters* ii 141-2.

18. It is just possible that Essex created a rumpus in order to increase his authority over the army. There is a hint of this in Snow, *Essex the Rebel,* 419 citing a Scottish source I have been unable to locate.

19. CSPD 1644, 153.

20. Ibid 1644, 181-2.

21. Ibid 1644, 198.

22. Wanklyn and Jones, *Military History,* 161-6.

23. See CSPD 1644, 224, 237 for anxieties about the north.

24. CSPD 1644, 124; JHC iii, 525; JHL vi, 588.

25. JHC iii, 526; CSPD 1644, 223, 228; BL, Harleian Ms 166, 72; ibid, Additional Ms 31117, 146-7.

26. CSPD 1644, 232-4.

27. Ibid 1644, 288, 433; JHL vi, 602-3, 607-8.

28. Ibid vi, 599, 602-3, 615-19; CSPD 1644, 262, JHC iii, 540, 542, 544; BL, Harleian Ms 166, 86. The first draft of Parliament's letter to Essex is printed in Rushworth, *Historical Collections* v, 683-4.

29. The king had sent Henrietta Maria to Exeter in April as Oxford was deemed unsafe for a woman whom Parliament would put on trial if captured.

30. CSPD 1644, 351, 358.

31. Ibid 1644, 456; JHL vi, 602; Walker, *Historical Discourses,* 37-47.

32. Rushworth, *Historical Collections* v, 703.

33. It has been alleged that two-thirds of Essex's infantry disappeared in the march back to parliamentary quarters: Gentles, *English Revolution,* 229. This is probably an overestimate. He fielded 3,000 infantry in October as opposed to 6,000 in August, but the 6,000 had included two London trained bands regiments and a Plymouth regiment that had since returned home.

34. Scott and Turton, *Hey for Old Robin,* 154-5.

35. Maseres, *Tracts* i, 204. Several historians, including myself, have had doubts about this comment made after Essex and Waller had been reconciled, but it need not have been mentioned by Sir William in his very thorough confession of his sins compiled towards the end of his life because he had only been obeying orders.

36. CSPD 1644, 399.

37. Ibid 1644, 352, 353.358-9.

38. The Commons approved a letter to him on 22 July in reply to his of the 15th, but it was not copied into the Committee's letter book and may have related to affairs in Ireland: JHC iii, 566; CSPD 1644, 350. A second letter written on the same day did not require a reply.
39. Cotton, *Barnstaple*, 293-4.
40. BL, Harleian Ms 166, 96.
41. CSPD 1644, 413, 420.
42. JHC iii, 576; CSPD 1644, 434-6,439-40,446.
43. HMC, Appendix to the 4th report, 308.

Chapter 6

1. Snow, *Essex the Rebel*, 428, 454-79, 498.
2. Adamson, 'Triumph of oligarchy', 116-19.
3. Gardiner, *Great Civil War* ii, 5,79.
4. Gentles, *New Model Army*, 10, 23-4.
5. Snow, *Essex the Rebel*, 363-6, 377, 421-5.
6. CSPD 1644, 301.
7. Ibid 1644, 301. For the city's control over its militia see, for example, JHC iii, 624-8, 640.
8. Ibid iii, 648; JHL vii, 4,6.
9. CSPD 1644, 491-2.
10. JHL vi, 430, 565.
11. CSPD 1644-5, 39-40; Baillie, *Letters* ii, 237-8; NAS, PA11/1, 71, 87; Meikle, Correspondence, 44-5.
12. Adamson is incorrect in his claim that it was still in operation in late November, see 'Triumph of oligarchy', 117-18.
13. JHC iv, 163,166; CSPD 1644-5, 437-46. An attempt by the Commons to revive it after the royalists' storming of Leicester came to nothing, see ibid, 565.
14. Ibid 1644, 33-4, 49; ibid 1644-5, 341-5, 353.
15. Ibid 1644-5, 12-13 (Waller to the Committee, 4 October). The other two hypotheses concerning Essex and the birth of the New Model Army, those of Snow and Gentles, are to a greater or lesser extent tied up with happenings after the Newbury campaign had come to a messy and unsatisfactory end. They are therefore discussed in Chapter 7.
16. Ibid 1644, 493, 530.
17. Ibid 1644, 520; ibid 1644-5, 36, 44-5, 56-7.
18. Ibid 1644-5, 15, 21. In this campaign the mantle of caution had passed from Essex to Waller, and the Committee may have worried that the new Essex would exert his authority over Sir William and lead them both into the mire.
19. CSPD 1644-5, 13, 29, 46, 57; Adair, *Roundhead General*, 211.
20. Waller had either converted his foot into dragoons, or used them to reinforce the south coast garrisons: CSPD 1644, 501-2.

21. Ibid 1644-5, 62; HMC, Appendix to the 10th Report vi, 155.

22. It has been alleged that the lord general's illness was feigned: Wedgwood, *The King's War*, 374; Adair, *Roundhead General*, 211. This seems highly unlikely given the wealth of evidence stretching over several weeks that he was seriously ill. Admittedly Whitelock reported a rumour that Essex had been instructed 'by private intimation to forbear engaging himself in that service', but the language he used suggests strongly that he was unconvinced: *Memorials*, 108. It is possible that the rumour stemmed from the Committee of Both Kingdoms' instruction mentioned above issued on 7 October that Essex should not join his cavalry.

23. CSPD 1644-5, 75-7; BL, Harleian Ms 166, 136; BL, Thomason Tracts, E 14 (16).

24. Rushworth, *Historical Collections* v, 722-3.

25. Wanklyn, *Warrior Generals*, 135-6.

26. CSPD 1644-5, 77-90; Luke, *Letter Books*, 372.

27. CSPD 1644-5, 84, 89.

28. Ibid, 1644-5, 90.

29. Walker, *Historical Discourses*, 119. Although Essex's reply is undated, the form of words is such that he cannot have been referring to the manoeuvring around Donnington Castle on 8-10 November.

30. CSPD 1644-5, 94.

31. JHC iii, 685-7; JHL vii, 46: *ODNB* 27, 211; Snow, *Essex the Rebel*, 464.

32. CSPD 1644-5, 94, 96.

33. See above 75.

34. CSPD 1644-5, 110.

35. Ibid, 117-18; House of Lords Record Office, Nalson Papers, microfilm roll iii, 148.

36. CSPD 1644-5, 118.

37. JHC iii, 695; CSPD 1644-5, 116; BL, Thomason Tracts, E 18(4).

38. CSPD 1644-5, 116,117; Rushworth, *Historical Collections* v, 731.

39. Holmes, *Eastern Association*, 207-10.

40. CSPD 1644-5, 128,145,161-2.

41. Ibid, 130,133,137.

42. Ibid, 138-9,144,161,164.

43. Ibid, 108; NAS, PA13/6, 89.

44. Snow, *Essex the Rebel*, 418-37; Baillie, *Letters* ii, 235-6.

Chapter 7

1. JHC iii, 699-700. The matter of quartering was raised by the Committee with the generals two days later: CSPD 1644-5, 138.

2. *Great Civil War* ii, 78.

3. JHC iii, 648, 652.

4. Ibid iii, 721.

5. Ibid iii, 702-4; CSPD 1644-5, 130-6; Walker, *Historical Discourses*, 120.

6. JHC iii, 704.

7. CSPD 1644-5,138-9.

8. JHC iii, 703, 704. What Stapleton also brought to the Commons was a resolution of the council of war concerning Basing House, which incriminated both Oliver Cromwell and Philip Skippon, see BL, Harleian MS. 166, 143.

9. Haselrig and Waller were long-standing opponents of the lord general. For this see above, 43, 29-31. Cromwell and Haselrig were closely associated with Sir Henry Vane and Oliver St John in the war party.

10. Adamson, 'Triumph of the oligarchy', 121-2; JHC iii, 707; CSPD 1644-5, 404,411, 414, 417. The order for Buller to be cashiered if the allegation turned out to be true was not put into effect. In fact Buller's career flourished. In 1645 he was promoted to major in Major General Massey's Western Brigade: CSPD 1644-5, 414, 603.

11. JHL vi, 61, 77.

12. Whitelock, *Memorials,* 116-17. This was at a secret meeting held at Essex House on 6 December, or thereabouts, over which Essex presided. Writers from Gardiner onwards have described it as taking place before 4 December. However, the order of the paragraphs in Whitelock's manuscript diary shows that the meeting followed some days later: Gardiner, *Great Civil War* ii, 87; Spalding, *Whitelock's Diary,* 160-1.

13. This was at the end of a long debate in which Cromwell had pleaded passionately for the reform of the army for fear that if the war lasted any longer Parliament's civilian supporters would be alienated. Woolrych, who gives the best account, believes that Tate and Cromwell were in collusion, with the latter preparing the ground for the proposal, which was made at the end of the debate by the chairman: *Britain in Revolution,* 301-2.

14. JHL vi, 77.

15. Whitelock, *Memorials,* 116. At first glance the very short report seems to relate to the speech of 25 November, but this cannot be so as it is immediately followed by the Commons deeming the Lords' intervention a breach of privilege, which occurred on the 4th. Whitelock did not mention the earlier speech as he was at Oxford preparing the way for a new round of peace negotiations. A secure dating for the report is given in *Whitelock's Diary.* For this see Spalding's edition, 160-1.

16. JHC iii,.713-14; BL, Harleian Ms 483,120; BL, Additional Ms 31116,178.

17. His informant was probably Bulstrode Whitelock who, though generally a peace party supporter, kept a foot in both camps. However, this may have come later after Whitelock had escaped a charge of high treason for his conduct in discussions about peace at Oxford: *Memorials,* 159-61.

18. Abbott, *Writings and Speeches* i, 314.

19. *Cromwell,* 117. For contemporaries see Baillie, *Letters and Journals* ii, 247; Juxon, Journal, 69-70.

20. Rushworth, *Historical Collections* vi, 5; CSPD 1644-5, 151.

21. Ibid 1644-5, 30,126,161. Disappointment that the quarrel had not ended appeared as early as 19 December: BL, Thomason Tracts, E 21 (17).
22. JHC iv, 26; JHL vii, 335; CSPD 1644-5, 461.
23. Luke, *Letter Books*, 741.
24. Whitelock, *Memorials*, 116; Spalding, Whitelock's Diary, 160-1. This may be the line Cromwell took in his speech of 4 December. It appears to be confirmed by a passage in D'Ewes's diary that is heavily crossed out and only legible in parts.
25. House of Lords Records Office, Main Papers 177, 102. A slightly different version containing one additional signature can be found in D'Ewes's diary: BL, Harleian Ms 166, 174.
26. JHL vii, 110; JHC iv, 13, 14; Whitelock, *Memorials,* 123.
27. Wanklyn, *Reconstructing* i, passim. Of the remaining twenty at least one was too decrepit to serve, another had died, two were offered commissions but refused to serve, and at least one was a staff officer.
28. JHC iii, 726; ibid iv, 31, 94; JHL vii, 136, 202, 301.
29. Gentles, *New Model Army,* 10.
30. CSPD 1644-5, 204, 231; JHL vii, 205-7.
31. CSPD 1644-5, 205, 232-3.
32. Gardiner, *Great Civil War* ii, 91-2,116-29, 185-96; Gentles, *New Model Army,* 10-25.
33. CSPD 1644-5, 204-5; JHL vii, 175-6, 191-201.
34. JHC iv, 26.
35. Stoyle, *Soldiers and Strangers,* 129-31.
36. Juxon, Journal, 75; Luke, *Letter Books,* 479; BL, Harleian Ms. 2224, 89.
37. Wanklyn, Choosing officers, 115-16.
38. JHL vii, 277.
39. JHC vii,726.
40. Gardiner, *Great Civil War* ii, 116.
41. JHL vii,128-9.
42. Ibid vii, 117,123,133.
43. JHC iv, 15-16.
44. JHL vii, 136; JHC iv, 61-2, 94.
45. JHL vii, 195.
46. Ibid vii, 128-9.
47. JHC iv, 27. The only colonel who had probably not commanded a regiment on campaign was Colonel Ayloffe of the Abingdon garrison, and he was rejected by the Commons in March when the House discussed Fairfax's list of officers: Wanklyn, *Reconstructing* i, 46-7.
48. Gentles, *New Model Army,* 24.
49. JHL vii, 136, 277, 296-303; BL, Additional Ms. 31117, 203.
50. JHC iv, 96-101.

51. JHL vii, 300.
52. Bodleian Library, Fairfax Ms. 36, 15.
53. Wanklyn, Choosing officers, 55-64.
54. This first occurred in late September 1645 when the Earl of Warwick, the former lord high admiral, was appointed military commander of the Eastern Association when East Anglia was threatened by a royalist invasion: JHL vii, 296-302; BL, Additional Ms. 31116,.203; Bodleian Library, Tanner Ms. 60, 244.

Chapter 8

1. CSPD 1644-5, 578-81; Carlyle, *Letters* i, 204-5, 212-18; ibid iii, 245-7; JHC iv, 309, 323.
2. Carlyle, *Letters* i, 204-5.
3. Gardiner, *Great Civil War* ii, 252-3.
4. Carlyle, *Letters* i, 11; Gardiner, *Cromwel* l, 209, 210; Firth, op.cit., 486.
5. *ODNB*. 14, 351, 352.
6. This is the message of the conclusion of a speech delivered on the 350th anniversary of Cromwell's death and printed in Gaunt, *Cromwell Four Centuries On*, 133-4.
7. See, for example, the essays by Sadler and MacKenzie in P. Little ed., *Oliver Cromwell: New Perspectives*.
8. See, for example, Marshall, *Oliver Cromwell Soldier*.
9. Carlyle, *Letters* i, 117. He was still a civilian on 20 August: JHL v, 307.
10. Ibid i, 113.
11. JHC ii, 726; Carlyle, *Letters* i, 112-14 (a transcription of Sir Simon D'Ewes's account of proceedings in the House of Commons).
12. BL, Thomason Tracts, E 104 (34).
13. See above 16.
14. HMC, Portland Mss i, 706-8. Carlyle, *Letters* i, 131; BL, Thomason Tracts, E 101 (10).
15. Carlyle, *Letters* i, 134-5; BL, Thomason Tracts, E 102 (8), E 104 (12).
16. Carlyle, *Letters* i, 140-3; Bodleian Library, Tanner Ms lxii, 194.
17. Estimates of the numbers involved on each side vary between 2,000 and 3,000: www. Battlefield Trust and Historic England ex English Heritage websites.
18. BL, Thomason Tracts, E 71 (5), (18).
19. Firth and Rait, *Acts and Ordinances* i, 368; Holmes, *Eastern Association*, 107-9, 114; Carlyle, *Letters* i, 168.
20. Wanklyn, Choosing officers, 123.
21. JHC iii, 626.
22. Maseres, *Tracts* i, 199-200.
23. Holmes, *Eastern Association*, 194, 204-5, 225.
24. BL, Thomason Tracts, E567 (1), p. 30; ibid, E400 (5), p. 9.

25. Wanklyn, 'General much maligned', 134-56; Rushworth, *Historical Collections* v, 734; CSPD 1644-5, 150, 151; Bruce and Masson, Manchester's quarrel, 78-95.
26. Wanklyn, 'General much maligned', 137-8.
27. CSPD 1644, 526-46; ibid, 1644-5, 9-43, 157-8.
28. For a fuller account of Manchester's behaviour from 10 September 1644 to 10 November 1644, and Cromwell's misinformation about it, see Wanklyn, 'General much maligned', 139-56.
29. Abbott, *Writings and Speeches* i, 305-6; CSPD 1644-5, 152, 154.
30. Ibid, 1644, 533-4, 536.
31. Ibid, 1644, 539-42; ibid 1644-5, 2, 58. The letter's contents can be inferred from entries in the Committee's minute book and from the Committee's letters to other commanders.
32. Luke, *Letter Books*, 23; Parsons, *Diary of Sir Henry Slingsby*, 128-30.
33. They cannot have arrived there much before 22 September, having fought an engagement at Ferrybridge in Yorkshire on the 20th. They did not leave for Oxford until December, see ibid, 130-6.
34. CSPD 1644, 539-42; Luke, *Letter Books*, 29, 340, 345, 348.
35. It was Manchester who had apparently convinced the Committee of this: CSPD 1644-5, 2.
36. Ibid 1644-5, 8, 21. The number of horse needed was taken on the advice of Essex's most senior officers, Skippon and Balfour, see NAS, PA 13/6, 73.
37. CSPD 1644-5, 32, 33, 41; Luke, Letter Books, 25.
38. CSPD 1644-5, 41.
39. Ibid 1644-5, 50.
40. Ibid, 1644, 516-45 passim; ibid, 1644-5, 2-44 passim; JHC iii, 635, 641, 658.
41. Wanklyn, 'Oliver Cromwell', 15-16.
42. Ibid, 16.
43. Hopton, *Bellum Civile*, 38-9.
44. Bruce and Masson, Manchester's quarrel, 65; HMC, Portland Mss iii, 112-13; Bodleian Library, Tanner Ms 62, 164-5.
45. CSPD 1644-5, 83-4.
46. Rushworth, *Historical Collections* v, 730; BL, Harleian Ms 166, 143. Documents written at the same time signed by Balfour and others were also copied down by D'Ewes, but they are mentioned in the Commons Journals: JHC iii, 703.

Chapter 9

1. JHC iv, 26; JHL vii, 204-9.
2. Gardiner, *Great Civil War* ii, 119-20; Firth, *Cromwell*, 122; Wedgwood, *King's War*, 420.
3. The discovery of the links between the Fairfaxes and the war party is admirably summed up in Hopper, *Black Tom*, 57-63

4. Ibid, 56. The four army commanders – Essex, Waller, Manchester and Lord Fairfax – and also Oliver Cromwell were peers or MPs, while the three other lieutenant generals were Scots.
5. Bell, *Memorial* s i, 155.
6. Carpenter, *Military Leadership*, 75; Gibb, *The Lord General*, 54-9; Hopper, *Black Tom*, 46-7.
7. See above 60.
8. Lord Fairfax was a Scottish peer and therefore eligible to sit in the English House of Commons where he was one of the MPs for Yorkshire.
9. An attempt to debar him on these grounds was debar by thirty-two votes in a House of 170 in January 1645: JHC iv, 26.
10. Gentles reads the first letter as containing a hint that Sir Thomas would succeed the Earl of Essex, but I read it differently. It informs Lord Fairfax that he will not be exempt from the provisions of the Self-Denying Ordinance. It then implies very strongly that Sir Thomas Fairfax will be his successor as general in the north: Gentles, *New Model Army,* 17-19: Bell, *Memorials* i, 142-3.
11. Maseres, *Tracts* i, 210.
12. See below 117-19.
13. Firth and Rait, *Acts and Ordinances* i, 625-6; Bell, *Memorials* i, 165. It was not to include the new colonels. They had been named by the Commons a month earlier on the same day as they appointed Sir Thomas as commander-in-chief.
14. Markham, *The Great Lord Fairfax*, 194; Gibb, *The Lord General*, 91; Hopper, *Black Tom*, 63; Gentles, 'Choosing officers', 265.
15. In the end filling the gap was delegated to the county committee for Kent, which paid the regiment's wages and was most likely to know who was alive and who dead.
16. Whitelock, *Memorials*, 134-7; JHC iv, 63, 64, 77; JHL vii, 259, 264, 271.
17. Maseres, *Tracts* i, 208.
18. Rushworth, *Historical Collections* vi, 37; *Old Parliamentary History* 13, 470.
19. BL, Thomason Tracts, E 314 (21), p. 46.
20. The information on which the analysis is based can be found in collated form in Wanklyn, *Reconstructing* i, 43-64, 147-52. Additional material alone is referenced from here onwards. Some basic analysis is to be found in ibid, 23-7. Wanklyn, 'Choosing officers' covers some of the same ground in considerable detail, but there the focus is on the changes the House of Lords wanted to make to the February list.
21. The fifth regiment, William Davies's, was probably disbanded because it was the smallest.
22. See for example Stoyle, *Soldiers and Strangers*, 130-1; Gentles, 'Choosing of officers', 270; Hopper, *Black Tom*, 62, 64. According to Hopper, Fairfax and his father resented plundering by Scottish soldiers in the north of England and their obtaining resources that should have gone to the army of the north: *Black Tom*, 62.
23. Wanklyn, 'Choosing officers', 120-1.

24. Juxon, Journal, 73. For the officers of the armies of Essex, Waller and Manchester see Wanklyn, 'Reconstructing' i, 147-52; Spring, *Waller's Army* and *Army of the Eastern Association*.
25. CSPD 1644-5, 246.
26. Journal, 76.
27. This point was made very forcibly in Kishlansky, *Rise of the New Model Army*, on page 43.
28. *ODNB* 58, 346-8.
29. Kishlansky, The case of the army, 67-8.
30. This conclusion is somewhat different from that in my 'Choosing officers', but underpinning the argument there was the assumption based on the work of others that the February list was entirely Fairfax's own work.
31. Hopper, *Black Tom*, 63.
32. Ibid; Gentles, Choosing officers, 267.
33. CSPD 1644-5, 461, 453; Firth and Davies, *Regimental History* i, 116; Wanklyn, *Reconstructing* i, 62.

Chapter 10

1. This murky episode, often described as the Saville affair, is examined in great detail in MacCormack, *Revolutionary Politics*, 77-81.
2. He left for the Continent immediately afterwards: Sprigg, *Anglia Rediviva*, 20-3, 29, 32; CSPD 1644-5, 536. 539.
3. CSPD 1644-5, 555, 567, 572, 580.
4. JHL vii, 411-12; CSPD 1644-5, 38-40, 556-7.
5. Rushworth, *Historical Collections* vi, 38: CSPD 1644-5, 567.
6. JHC iv, 166.
7. CSPD 1644-5, 573-4. Only two pieces of business were completed in the morning. It met again in the afternoon, which was unusual, and on the following day, which was a Sunday, and that was almost unprecedented.
8. Ibid 1644-5, 578-9.
9. CSPD 1644-5, 510.
10. Sprigg, *Anglia Rediviva*, 32-4; JHC iv, 169; JHL vii, 421. The decision seems to have been almost unanimous. The eleven colonels who signed were all who were present on that day, and they had previously commanded regiments in all three armies that had gone to make up the New Model. Colonel Harley, one of those missing, was probably absent due to a war wound, while another, Sir Hardress Waller, was still in London drumming up recruits: Firth and Davies, *Regimental History* i, 359, CSPD 1644-5, 592. The rest were either with Vermuyden or at Taunton.
11. CSPD 1644-5, 533; JHC iv, 138, 169; JHL vii, 364, 421, 433.
12. Gentles, *English Revolution*, 266.
13. Sprigg, *Anglia Rediviva*, 52-3; Bulstrode, *Memoirs*, 114-15. A newspaper report claims that news of the letter arrived in London on 13 June, the day before the battle. In 1647 Fairfax himself stated that he received the letter at Naseby on the

14th and that it did not influence the way he fought the battle. BL, Thomason Tracts, E 262 (10); Bodleian, Tanner MS 59, 750.

14. Orrery, *Art of War,* 154.
15. Hopper, *Black Tom,* 45.
16. Using pay warrants for early June 1645, Blackmore estimates that the two flanking regiments were 1,500 and 1,400 strong, while the three regiments in the centre were 1,100, 1,000 and under 600 strong: Counting the New Model Army.
17. Foard, *Naseby,* 276. Fairfax's only other contribution to the opening phase of the battle concerned the artillery. Unlike at Marston Moor, fighting was not preceded by a lengthy artillery duel, which he may have regarded in retrospect as having been a complete waste of time. Pushing a forlorn hope into the shallow valley between the two armies indicates that Fairfax was as keen as the royalists were for fighting to begin as quickly as possible. It is also possible in the case of the king's army and possibly of the New Model that they did not have their heavier pieces in position at the start of the battle. For some interesting speculation about this based on problematic evidence see ibid, 250.
18. Sprigg, *Anglia Rediviva,* 43; Whitelock, *Memorials,* 151.
19. CSPD 1644-4, 610, 617; JHL vii, 463-4; JHC iv, 187. His dilemma, however, was a political rather than a military one. It will be discussed in the next chapter.
20. CSPD 1644-5, 585.
21. JHL vii, 463; CSPD 1644-5, 569-85, 593.
22. CSPD 1644-5, 617, 62 1. For Goring's attacks on Waller's brigade see Bodleian, Clarendon Ms 24, 103-13; Whitelock, *Memorials,* 140, 141.
23. JHC iv, 152-3; JHL vii, 393.
24. BL, Thomason Tracts, E292 (14).
25. Ibid, E 292 (28).
26. Wanklyn, *Warrior Generals,* 170-1.
27. According to an eyewitness the contribution of the second cavalry squadron was crucial, but they got none of the thanks because the officers were not of Cromwell's religious persuasion: Baxter, *Reliquiae,* 54-5.
28. Sprigg, *Anglia Rediviva,* 64-6; BL, Thomason Tracts, E292 (30); ibid, E 293 (3), (8).
29. There were nine brigades of royalist horse in Cornwall in March 1646: Rushworth, *Historical Collections* vi, 109.
30. BL, Thomason Tracts, E 293 (3), (8), (17), (18).
31. Sprigg, *Anglia Rediviva,* 74, 75.
32. Ibid, 103, 121.
33. Carte, *Original Letters* i, 112-14, 140-2; BL, Thomason Tracts, E 324 (6), (15).
34. Carte, *Original Letters* i, 119.

Chapter 11

1. BL, Thomason Tracts, E 343 (8), pp. 3, 4, 13, 64.
2. God's Doings and Man's Duty, 4,7,22.

3. Rushworth, *Historical Collections* vi, 110.
4. Sprigg, *Anglia Rediviva*, 323-5; Peter, *God's Doings, Man's Duty*, 25; Peter, Message to Parliament, BL, Thomason Tracts, E 318 (6).
5. BL, Thomason Tracts, E 292 (28); ibid, E 293 (3), (6).
6. Sprigg, *Anglia Rediviva*, 116, 140. 181-2.
7. BL, Thomason Tracts. E 292 (28); ibid, E 293 (3); ibid, E 317 (14); Sprigg, *Anglia Rediviva*, 104-5, 118.
8. Hopper, *Black Tom*, 69; Gentles, *New Model Army*, 45-6.
9. See below 111-12.
10. Kishlansky, *Rise of the New Model Army*, 63; CSPD 1645-7, 235, 244, 263; Sprigg, *Anglia Rediviva*, 122.
11. Ibid, 22
12. *Black Tom*, 184 citing J. Peacey, *Politicians and Pamphleteers* (2004).
13. Luke, Letter Books, 322-3,328, 582.
14. CSPD 1645-7, 351.
15. *Rise of the New Model Army*, 61-5. Firth opted for merit tempered to some extent by seniority, but he drew exclusively on evidence from Cromwell's time as lord general: *Cromwell's Army*, 49-53. Fairfax claimed that it was the practice in the army to reward antiquity (seniority) and merit, thus making it hard to place a stranger, but this was in a letter trying to gently let down a father trying to secure a place for his son: BL, Additional Ms 18976, 205.
16. Wanklyn, *Reconstructing* i, 59-60.
17. Ibid i, 69, 79, 154-5.
18. Ibid i, passim.
19. CSPD 1645-7, 89-128 passim.; HMC, Portland Mss i, 265-6.
20. There is a very full account of Massey's entire military career in D.S. Evans's Ph.D. thesis.
21. HMC, Portland Mss i, 242, 262, 269-70.
22. Roe, *Military Memoir*, 15, 21-3; Sprigg, Anglia Rediviva, 77, 116; Hopper, *Black Tom*, 75. This is an excellent illustration of Fairfax using the power to issue orders to garrison troops belonging to another command granted to him in his commission against the wishes of the Earl of Essex: JHL vii, 298.
23. *Memorials*, 162; Sprigg, *Anglia Rediviva*, 77.
24. JHL viii, 113-16; JHC iv, 415-18.
25. Evans, 'Civil war career of Massey', 203, 209-10.
26. Browne was elected as a member of parliament in late 1645, but did not have to resign his military command: JHC iv, 418.
27. See below 105-7.
28. CSPD 1645-7, 2-3; HMC, Portland Mss i, 270.
29. For the circumstances surrounding its surrender see below 108.
30. Baillie, *Letters* ii, 283, 292, 298, 315; Rushworth, *Historical Collections* vi, 68.
31. See above, chapters 5 and 6.
32. Bell, *Memorials* i, 228, 264-85; CSPD 1645-7, 221.

33. The proposal to increase the size of Massey's brigade in January 1646 probably began with anxiety among West Country MPs. For this see above XXX.
34. Gentles, *New Model Army*, 76-81, but especially 79.
35. Firth and Rait, *Ordinances* i, 204, 298-9; CSPD 1644-5, 578-81; JHC iv, 182.
36. Wanklyn, *Warrior Generals*, 167.
37. Sprigg, *Anglia Rediviva*, 133-38; CSPD 1645-7, 152-3.
38. Sprigg, *Anglia Rediviva*, 139-59.
39. Fairfax had written a letter to the Committee dated 17 October. This was discussed on the 24th and it was decided that two of its members should ask the Commons how to frame the reply: CSPD 1645-7, 204. They failed to do so. As the letter has not survived, its contents are unknown, but it is most likely that it contained details of his future plans. It was not Fairfax's letter reporting the capture of Tiverton, which is dated 20 October.
40. Sprigg, *Anglia Rediviva*, 149-50; JHC iv, 309, 323; CSPD 1645-7, 196.
41. Ibid 1645-7, 221.
42. Bell, *Memorials* i, 258-9; Whitelock, *Memorials*, 180; JHL vii, 713; CSPD 1645-7, 235.
43. JHC iv, 250-1.
44. Bell, *Memorials* i, 261; Whitelock, *Memorials*, 182, 183.
45. HMC, Portland Mss i, 340; CSPD 1645-7, 271, 330; Whitelock, *Memorials*, 188, 191.
46. Bell, *Memorials* i, 282.
47. Ibid i, 283; CSPD 1645-7, 283-4, 341. For the trouble in Dorset see Whitelock, *Memorials*, 192
48. CSPD 1645-7, 325, 340-1. For evidence of Parliament's generosity see Whitelock, *Memorials*, 182-9.
49. Bell, *Memorials* i, 282.

Chapter 12

1. JHL viii, 308-9.
2. BL, Thomason Tracts, E 341 (23).
3. Cary, *Memorials* ii, 30.
4. See above 32-5, 55-62.
5. JHL ix, 112-13.
6. Morrill, 'Mutiny and discontent'
7. BL, Thomason Tracts, E 341 (16).
8. Firth, *Regimental History* ii, 632, 643, 649,650; JHL viii, 424.
9. JHC v, 577, 581, 615, 630; JHL viii, 380.
10. JHC iv, 631.
11. BL, Thomason Tracts, E 458 (3) Firth, Clarke Papers i, 424.
12. W. Dell, *Several Sermons and Discourses* (1652), 65-112; JHL viii, 397, 403, 418-19.

13. JHL viii, 392, 414.

14. Bell, *Memorials* i, 295; JHL viii, 386. The officer was Colonel William Herbert, who was in London on personal business.

15. Whitelock, *Memorials*, 225. He had been elected as MP for Wootton Bassett in June 1646: *History of Parliament 1660-90* website.

16. Sprigg, *Anglia Rediviva*, 314-5; Ludlow, *Memoirs* i, 142; Gardiner, *Great Civil War* iii, 147-8; JHL viii, 530, 544, 563.

17. BL, Thomason Tracts, E 360 (2).

18. See for example, Hopper, *Black Tom*, 75; Gentles, *New Model Army*, 143; Braddick, *God's Fury, England's Fire*, 477-8.

19. Gentles mistakenly claimed that only three New Model Army officers attended the funeral: *New Model Army*, 143. Seven colonels and between seven and nine field officers did so. The number of captains cannot be ascertained as too many were listed by surname alone: BL, Thomason Tracts, E 360 (2); Wanklyn, *Reconstructing* i, 65-73.

20. Whitelock, *Memorials*, 225.

21. Sprigg, *Anglia Rediviva*, 314-15; Rushworth, *Historical Collections* vii, 388-9.

22. Sprigg, *Anglia Rediviva*, 317-19;-BL, Thomason Tracts, E 360 (2).

23. *Memorials*, 227; *Journal*, 139-41.

24. Bodleian, Fairfax Ms 36, 2.

25. JHC v, 21; *Old Parliamentary History* xv, 222-3, 231.

26. JHC v, 34, 90, 91.

27. Bodleian, Fairfax Ms 36, 2-3.

28. For the complaints of Massey's former officers and men in early 1647 see JHC v, 65-7; JHL viii, 705.

29. JHC v, 106-8.

30. JHL ix, 114.

31. JHC v, 127; JHL ix, 111-16; *Old Parliamentary History* xv, 334.

32. Hopper, *Black Tom*, 76.

33. Cary, *Memorials* i, 187.

34. Gardiner, *Great Civil War* iii, 226; BL. Harleian Ms 166, 174. William Cowell, William Goffe and John Mill, captains in 1644, were field officers by 1647: Wanklyn, *Reconstructing* i, 78-9, 149-50.

35. JHL ix, 114; BL, Thomason Tracts, E 385 (19).

36. JHL ix, 115; Gentles, *New Model Army*, 154. For Cromwell see above XXX.

37. Woolrych, *Britain in Revolution*, 351-65; Gentles, *New Model Army*, 150-69.

38. JHC v, 137. The regiments to be disbanded were not those presumed to be radical. Four of those to be sent to Ireland were formerly from the Eastern Association Army and one from the Earl of Essex's.

39. CSPD 1645-7, 531, 534, 540; JHC v, 140.

40. Bell, *Memorials* i, 343; Rushworth, *Historical Collections* vi, 457-61.

41. Gentles, *New Model Army*, 157; Wanklyn, *Reconstructing* i, 153-6.

42. JHC v, 173, 181, 183-4; Firth, Clarke Papers i, 430-2; Bell, *Memorials* i, 348.

43. Woolrych, *Britain in Revolution*, 361-2.
44. Cary, *Memorials* i, 217-18.
45. JHL ix, 226-8; Firth, Clarke Papers i, 112, 117-22.
46. *Old Parliamentary History* xv, 411-12; JHL ix, 241; Cary, *Memorials* i, 228.
47. Woolrych, *Britain in Revolution*, 369-70
48. Firth, Clarke Papers i, 217, 223-4.
49. JHC v, 248; Bell, *Memorials* ii, 16.
50. Firth, Clarke Papers i, lviii- lix.
51. For a sympathetic view of a Fairfax fearful of causing even more deaths if he used his authority in the army to try and save the king's life, see Gibb, *The Lord General*, 205-16.
52. The fullest account of what is now the dominant narrative is to be found in Hopper, *Black Tom*, 83-89, 93-103.
53. Firth, Clarke Papers i, lxxv, 417-18.
54. See appendix 1 for my reasons and for the very tentative conclusions there and in Chapter 17.
55. *Great Civil War* iv, 305.
56. CSPD 1648-9, 27, 86, 177.
57. Ibid, 61, 62, 87, 97.
58. Bell, *Memorials* ii, 32-5.
59. See above 128-31 and Wanklyn, *Warrior Generals,* 196-7, 282.
60. Gentles, *New Model Army,* 331-46.
61. JHC vi, 430; Whitelock, *Memorials,* 460-2.
62. Hopper, *Black Tom,* 114-15, 198-9.
63. For the attempts to persuade him to change his mind, see Ludlow, *Memoirs* i, 242-4; Whitelock, *Memorials,* 460-2.
64. As far as I can ascertain, Major John Barber was the only company or troop commander who refused to serve in Scotland for reasons of conscience: Whitelock, *Memorials,* 466; Wanklyn, *Reconstructing* ii, 43-59.
65. Gardiner, *Commonwealth and Protectorate* i, 207-8; JHC vi, 344, 423, 427-8.

Chapter 13

1. Ludlow, *Memoirs* i, 144-5 Clarendon, *Great Rebellion* 5, 91; Hutchinson, *Memoirs,* 288.
2. JHC iv, 34; ibid, v, 34.
3. MacCormack, *Revolutionary Politics,* 144, 145.
4. Bell, *Memorials* i, 248, 252.
5. 'We are full of faction and worse': Firth, *Cromwell,* 159.
6. Ashley, *Greatness of Oliver Cromwell,* 178.
7. Gardiner claimed that in March Cromwell swore a fearful oath in God's name that the army would peacefully disband: *Great Civil War* iii, 222. His source was Clement Walker but Walker's narrative would allow for it to be part of a speech delivered in

late April or May either before the commissioners left for the army headquarters or on their return: *History of Independency,* 5.Given Walker's bias against Cromwell Woolrych had doubts about the speech's provenance: *Britain in Revolution,* 361.

8. There was some optimism in the commissioners' report to the House on 20 May: Firth, *Clarke Papers* i, 99. For the problematic sources for Cromwell's speech see Gardiner, *Great Civil War* iii, 258-9.

9. See, for example, Gardiner, *Great Civil War* iii, 257-8, 264-5; Firth, *Cromwell,* 160-2; Ashley, *Greatness of Oliver Cromwell,* 180-82; Howell, *Cromwell,* 92, and more recently Marshall, *Oliver Cromwell Soldier,* 168-9,and J.C. Davis, *Oliver Cromwell,* 142, and Woolrych, *Britain in Revolution,* 364-5.

10. Walker, *History of Independency,* 31-2; Maseres, *Tracts* i, 243, 247; Clarendon, *Great Rebellion* 4, 223.

11. BL, Thomason Tracts, E 458 (3).

12. Huntington's evidence is largely ignored by historians, the principal exception being Ashton who describes it as 'prejudiced and slanted' and Gardiner who sees him as 'trying to damage Cromwell as much as possible: *Counter-Revolution,* 168-9; *Great Civil War* iii, 246.

13. For Fairfax's behaviour see above 116-18.

14. Wanklyn, *Reconstructing* i, 76-96.

15. The best most recent narrative is in Braddick, *God's Fury, England's Fire,* 493-537.

16. For a balanced assessment of the army's mood, see Woolrych, *Britain in Revolution,* 408-9.

17. BL, Thomason Tracts, E 522 (26); JHC v, 566; CSPD 1648-9, 112, 140, 199.

18. See for example, Carpenter, *Military Leadership,* 164-6; ODNB 32, 325.

19. Hill and Watkinson ask the question, but do not provide an answer: *Cromwell has the Honour,* 91.

20. Cromwell estimated that he had 5,600 foot and 3,000 horse: Abbott, *Writings* i, 634. However, he failed to mention several cavalry regiments that were with him. I have therefore added 1,000 to his estimate. Much larger figures have been proposed, but they ignore regiments left behind in Yorkshire.

21. Wanklyn, *Decisive Battles,* 190-2.

22. Bodleian, Clarendon Ms 2862.

23. Carlyle, *Letters* i, 336-7.

24. Marshall, *Oliver Cromwell Soldier,* 187.

25. Hodgson, *Original Memoirs,* 117; Bodleian, Clarendon Ms 2862.

26. Carlyle, *Letters* i, 338-9; BL, Thomason Tracts, E 267 (21).

27. Hodgson, *Original Memoirs,* 117-18; Bodleian, Clarendon Ms 2862; Carlyle, *Letters* i, 338-9. The path taken by the English regiments has been identified as Watery Lane, but that is incorrect as it would have taken them straight to the bridge, which had to be captured later in the battle. Instead they used a lane that joined the A6 about a quarter of a mile north of the bridge, which can be seen on early maps of the town.

28. HMC, Portland Mss iii, 175; Turner, *Memoirs*, 64; Burnet, *Memoirs*, 360; Hodgson, *Origina l Memoirs*, 120.
29. Carlyle, *Letters* i, 329-30, 336.43.
30. Firth, Clarke Papers ii, 62-3; Ludlow, *Memoirs* i, 211-12; Gentles, *New Model Army*, 140-2.
31. Hutchinson, *Memoirs*, 305-6.

Chapter 14

1. Scott, *Politics and War*, 171-2, 183-5; CSPD 1649-50, xlix, lxi.
2. Ibid 1650, 253, 258, 288, 419; ibid 1651, 302-395.
3. *Britain in Revolution*, 437; CSPD 1650, 412, 419, 424; ibid 1651, 350, 354-5, 361, 364.
4. Woolrych, *Britain in Revolution*, 445-9.
5. For the consequences of the suppression of the uprising on regiments and officers see Wanklyn, *Reconstructing* i, 97-8, 108-9; ibid ii, 53, 191.
6. Gentles, *New Model Army*, 253-4; Wheeler, *Irish and British Wars*, 209-11.
7. Wanklyn, *Warrior Generals*, 211-13.
8. Burke, New Model Army, 1-29.
9. Wanklyn, *Reconstructing* ii, 188.
10. Gardiner, *Commonwealth and Protectorate* i, 155; Carlyle, *Letters* ii, 55.
11. Wanklyn, *Warrior Generals*, 286; Wanklyn, *Reconstructing* i, 55-64; ibid ii, 179-89.
12. BL, Thomason Tracts, E 778 (7); Wanklyn, *Reconstructing* ii, 23, 53-66 69-83.
13. Stevenson, *Revolution and Counter Revolution*, 148.
14. Wanklyn, *Warrior Generals*, 216-17. Cromwell estimated that he was outnumbered by two to one: *Old Parliamentary History* xix, 342.
15. BL, Thomason Tracts, E 612 (4).
16. Hodgson, *Original Memoirs*, 143-4. Carte, *Letters* i, 383 shows that the English were facing the right wing of the Scottish horse.
17. Hodgson, *Original Memoirs*, 147; Carlyle, *Letters* ii, 105-7; Carte, *Letters* i, 382-3.
18. This is shown by a letter he wrote towards the end of the 1648 campaign: Thurloe, *Collection of State Papers* i, 101.
19. Cary, *Memorials* ii, 292-3.
20. Marshall, *Oliver Cromwell Soldier*, 255; Davis, *Oliver Cromwell*, 105.
21. See his letters of 24 and 26 July printed in *Old Parliamentary History* xix, 497-8.
22. Concerns about this can be read between the lines in a letter Cromwell wrote before the invasion of Fife: Gardiner, *Commonwealth* ii, 30.
23. Cary, *Memorials* ii, 291-5. Within a day or so of the battle of Worcester he had ordered four of his regiments of foot to leave for Scotland via Hull and Kings Lynn: CSPD 1650-1, 416.
24. Not Lichfield as I claimed in *New Approaches*, 60.

25. Gardiner, *Commonwealth and Protectorate* i, 40-1; Carpenter, *Military Leadership*, 162.

26. Wanklyn, *New Approaches*, 60-1.

27. Cary, *Memorials* ii, 354; CSPD 1650-1, 407; BL, Thomason Tracts, E 640 (5), (23); ibid, E 641 (4).

28. Wanklyn, *Warrior Generals*, 223-5.

29. Cary, *Memorials* ii, 353-5; Whitelock, *Memorials*, 507. See also Wanklyn, Some Further Thoughts, 65-71 for a full account of the bridging operation.

30. Wanklyn, *Warrior Generals*, 226.

Chapter 15

1. See above 89.

2. This was in the spring of 1648 when he was appointed as major general in charge of the defences of London, as the corporation would not permit him to hold two posts: JHC v, 563. I am most grateful to Dr Ismini Pells for this information.

3. He continued to hold the office of lieutenant general of the horse in the New Model.

4. Woolrych, *Britain in Revolution*, 492-3.

5. Carlyle, *Letters* ii, 203-5.

6. BL, Thomason Tracts, E 632 (6); JHC vi, 428, 592.

7. *ODNB* 29, 346-9, 351.

8. BL, Thomason Tracts, E 126 (38).

9. See TNA, SP28/136, pt. 11 for the wounded. I am grateful to Simon Marsh for this information.

10. CSPD 1644, 271; Wenham, *Siege of York*, 100.

11. Wanklyn, *Decisive Battles*, 156; CSPD 1644-5, 158

12. Wanklyn, *Reconstructing* i, 51, 54, 61, 64.

13. Sprigg, *Anglia Rediviva*, 41-2; BL, Thomason Tracts, E 288 (38).

14. Sprigg, *Anglia Rediviva*, 229; CSPD 1645-7, 238, 314, 351; *ODNB* 29, 345.

15. BL, Thomason Tracts, E 445 (27), (30); Wanklyn, *Reconstructing* ii, 191.

16. Gardiner, *Commonwealth and Protectorate* ii, 107-8.

17. BL, Thomason Tracts, E638 (13); Moody ed., *New History* iii, 347; Ludlow, *Memoirs* i, 274-8, 283-6.

18. Ludlow, *Memoirs* i, 278, 293-4; TNA, SP 28/62-97.

19. Gardiner, *Commonwealth* ii, 108-12. There is no doubt that Gardiner's stereotype of Ireton was a literary device designed to allow Cromwell's military genius to shine out by comparison.

20. Hopper, *Black Tom*, 45.

21. BL, Thomason Tracts, E 71 (22); Rushworth, *Historical Collections* v, 302.

22. Bell, *Memorials* i, 85-91, 95.

23. CSPD 1644, 85, 87-8; Cooke, *Road to Marston Moor*, 201; *Old Parliamentary History* xiii, 172-3.

24. Even though Lambert seems to have been in the reserve at Selby, one London paper could not resist mentioning that Colonel John Bright, who led one of the assaults on the town, was Lambert's brother-in-law: Cooke, *Road to Marston Moor*, 201.
25. BL, Thomason Tracts E 54 (19); Maseres, *Tracts* i, 434.
26. At about that time Lambert was promoted to commissary general, though he was still described as colonel in the report of an engagement in Yorkshire in October 1644: Ibid; BL, Thomason Tracts, E 256 (28).
27. JHC iv, 26; BL, Thomason Tracts, E 273 (2), (5).
28. This account is based almost entirely on a royalist report written when Langdale returned to Newark a few days later: BL, Thomason Tracts, E 274 (20).
29. The London journals blamed treachery, faulty intelligence and Colonel Forbes, who was a Scot, while most did all they could to absolve Lambert and Lord Fairfax from any blame: ibid, E 273 (2), (5), (6), (7), (10).
30. He may have joined the New Model Army on the day after the battle of Naseby: Hill and Watkinson, *Cromwell hath the Honour*, 2. However, the evidence is too imprecise to be convincing: BL, Thomason Tracts, E 289 (3).
31. Sprigg, *Anglia Rediviva*, 182, 229; BL, Thomason Tracts, E 319 (4).
32. Wanklyn, *Reconstructing* i, 90. His appointment was before 16 August: Whitelock, Memorials, 152.
33. Hill and Watkinson, *Cromwell hath the Honour*, 39-97; Hodgson, *Original Memoirs*, 118.
34. CSPD 1648-9, 148, 150, 159; HMC, 10th report appendix 6, 171-2; Hill and Watkinson, *Cromwell hath the Honour*, 114-15, 126-35; Wanklyn, *Reconstructing* i, 161-4.
35. This was the regiment that rejected Monck. See above 160.
36. There is a single example of his acting in an administrative capacity in relation to the supply of arms early in the campaign: CSPD 1650, 208.

Chapter 16

1. *ODNB* 15, 638; Deane, *Life of Richard Deane*, 70-1.
2. Marsh, *The Train of Artillery of the Earl of Essex*, 23, 28, 47, 69, 71, 79, 81, 96, 112, 117, 167, 198.
3. Rushworth, *Historical Collections* v, 709.
4. HMC, appendix to the 6th report, 37.
5. Spring, *Army of the Eastern Association*, 86-7; Sprigg, *Anglia Rediviva*, 96.
6. JHC v, 176.
7. Wanklyn, *Reconstructing* i, 88. 101; Deane, *Life of Deane*, 357-60.
8. BL, Thomason Tracts, E 632 (6); Wanklyn *Reconstructing* ii, 70.
9. For a discussion of the reasons see below 161.
10. Gumble, *Life of Monck*, 4-25; *ODNB* 38, 578-81; CSPI 1647-60, 9.
11. Stevenson, *Revolution and Counter Revolution*, 42-6; Wheeler, *Irish and British Wars*, 145, 175.

12. CSPI 1647-60, 27, 30.
13. Gardiner, *Commonwealth and Protectorate* i, 73.
14. For the best short modern narrative see Woolrych, *Britain in Revolution*, 466-7.
15. HMC, Ormonde Mss os ii. 90-1; Gardiner, *Commonwealth and Protectorate* i, 80-2; Ludlow, *Memoirs* i, 228; Gilbert, *Contemporary History* ii, 207.
16. BL, Thomason Tracts, E 562 (1), (15); Gilbert, *Contemporary History* ii, 216-20.
17. BL, Thomason Tracts, E 562 (2), (6), (10).
18. Ibid, Thomason Tracts, E 532 (7).
19. Ibid; HMC, Ormonde Mss os ii, 91.
20. Ludlow, *Memoirs* ii, 228-9.
21. Gumble, *Life of Monck*, 27-9; JHC vi, 263-4, 277; BL, Thomason Tracts, E 562 (1), (2), (15).
22. Wanklyn, *Reconstructing* ii, 210 citing TNA, SP28/69, 488.
23. Monck's hold over Cromwell was stated most clearly by Lord Clarendon: Clarendon, *Great Rebellion* 4, 145-6.
24. *ODNB* 20, 17-18; Spring, *Army of the Eastern Association*, 67, 81. As far as I am aware, Fleetwood did not protest at what he might have regarded as a slur on his honour, possibly because Ireton had been quartermaster-general in the earl of Manchester's Eastern Association army.
25. *ODNB* 20, 18; Wanklyn, *Reconstructing* i, 51, 93.
26. *ODNB* 25, 528-30; BL, Thomason Tracts, E 574 (26).
27. For an assessment of his performance see above 148-9.
28. Hodgson, *Original Memoirs*, 143-4; Gumble, *Life of Monck*, 34-8.
29. Carlyle, *Letters* ii, 213.
30. CSPD 1648-9, 208. Accounts of campaigning in the Clyde valley in late 1650 have been written in such a way as to suggest that there was a second front there managed by John Lambert, but it was only by accident that Cromwell was absent from the skirmish at Hamilton, which dispersed the small Western Association army, and the pacification of the south-west of Scotland that followed was achieved by negotiation, not by armed occupation. Moreover, Lambert's victory was not of his own making, but the outcome of a misconceived night attack on the town by the Scots: BL, Thomason Tracts, E 619 (1).
31. This was in May 1651, but he had probably been acting in Hammond's absence from late 1650 onwards.
32. Wanklyn, 'Cromwell's generalship', 42-4.
33. Cary, *Memorials* ii, 345-7, 350-2, 365.
34. *Old Parliamentary History* xix, 494, 497; Wanklyn, 'Some further thoughts', 65-71; Atkin, *Cromwell's Crowning Mercy*, 88, 90, 98.
35. Cary, *Memorials* ii, 291-303; *Old Parliamentary History* xix, 498, 502, 506-11; ibid, xx, 10-16.
36. CSPD 1651, 341, 345, 347, 350, 355-6, 361; Whitelock, *Memorials*, 502-3.
37. Cary, *Memorials* ii, 355; *Old Parliamentary History* xx, 40-1.
38. Wanklyn, *Reconstructing* ii, 151, 161, 163, 270.

Chapter 17

1. Experiences, 125-6.
2. *Great Rebellion 6*, 91.
3. According to Thomas Juxon, the day before Cromwell denounced Manchester in the House of Commons Lady Manchester tried unsuccessfully to convince him that her husband held him in high regard. Her foreknowledge that an attack was imminent could have been due to an informant on the Committee of Both Kingdoms, but it could also have been in response to a warning from the earl that he had been threatened and was about to be denounced: Juxon, Journal, 67.
4. Maseres, *Tracts* i, 308.
5. BL, Thomason Tracts. 669/f10 (32); ibid, E362 (6).
6. The evidence for this is brought together in MacCormack, *Revolutionary Politics*, 211.
7. CSPD 1644-5, 157-8.
8. See above 37,51.
9. See L. Scrimshaw, 'Oliver Cromwell and The English Revolution', *Cromwell Four Centuries On*, P. Gaunt ed., (2013), 53.

Appendix

1. Markham, *Life*, 392-3.
2. Bodleian, Fairfax Ms 36, 1-14.
3. Hopper, *Black Tom*, 224-30.
4. Worcester College, Oxford, Clarke Mss 66, 67. Fairfax may have had a veto, however, as Joyce was not promoted to captain, but there is no reason for dismissing out of hand Fairfax's claim that he did not have advance knowledge of Pride's Purge, as the decision to expel members of the House of Commons was not agreed until the evening before and by a cabal of officers and like-minded war party MPs.
5. Gardiner, *Commonwealth and Protectorate*, 294. Hopper cites the contemporary evidence for Fairfax falling within the clutches of the Presbyterian ministers through his wife's influence, but seems to prefer other explanations: *Black Tom*, 114-15.

Bibliography

Manuscript Primary Sources
National Archives, Scotland
PA 11/1-16, 13/6

British Library
Additional Mss 11692, 18778-9, 18976, 31116-17
Harleian Mss 163-6, 483, 2224, 3783.

Bodleian Library, University of Oxford
Carte Ms 80
Clarendon Ms 24, 2862
Fairfax Ms 36.
Firth Mss C6-8
Tanner Mss 54-63

House of Lords
Main Papers 177
Nalson Papers microfilm iii

Wadham College Library, Oxford
Ms A18. 14

Worcester College, Oxford
Clarke Mss 65, 67, 69

Staffordshire County Record Office
D868.2

Printed Primary Sources

Abbott, W. ed. (1937) *The Writings and Speeches of Oliver Cromwell*, Harvard, Mass.: Havard University Press.
Acts of the Parliaments of Scotland (12 vols., 1814) T. Thomson and C. Innes eds.

Anon, (21 vols. 1751–61) *The Old Parliamentary History (The Parliamentary or Constitutional History of England)*, London.

Archer, Elias, *A True Relation of the Trained Bands of Westminster, the Green Auxiliaries of London and the Yellow Auxiliaries of the Tower Hamlets under the command of Sir William Waller 16 October to 20 December 1643*, London.

Atkyns, Richard (1967) 'The Vindication of Richard Atkyns Esquire', published in *Military Memoirs of the English Civil War*, P. Young ed., London: Longman.

Baillie, Robert (1841) *Letters and Journals 1637–1662*, D. Laing ed., Bannatyne Club 72, 73, 77, Edinburgh.

Baxter, Richard (1696) *Reliquiae Baxterianae*, London.

Bell, R. ed. (1841) *The Fairfax Correspondence*: *Memorials of the Reign of Charles I*, 2 vols., London: Richard Bentley.

Bruce, J. & Masson, D. eds. (1875) 'Manchester's Quarrel: documents relating to the quarrel between the Earl of Manchester and Oliver Cromwell', *Camden Society*, new series xii.

Bulstrode, Sir Richard (1721) *Memoirs and Reflections on the Reigns of King Charles I and King Charles II*.

Burnett, G (1677) *Memoirs of the Dukes of Hamilton*, London.

Calendar of the Clarendon State Papers (1869), Oxford: Oxford University Press.

Calendar of State Papers Domestic 1644, 1644-45, 1645-47, 1648-9, 1650-51, 1625-49 addenda, London: HMSO.

Calendar of State Papers Ireland 1647-60.

Calendar of State Papers Venetian, 1642-3, 1644-7.

Carlyle, T. (3 vols., 1904 ed.) *Letters and Speeches of Oliver Cromwell*, ed. by S.E. Lomas and C. Firth, London: Methuen.

Carte, T. ed. (1739) *A Collection of Original Letters and Papers concerning the Affairs of England (1641-1660) found amongst the Duke of Ormonde's Paper*, 2 vols. London: J. Buttenham.

Cary, H. ed. (1842) *Memorials of the Great Civil War in England*, 2 vols. (London).

Clarendon, Edward, Earl of (1888) *The History of the Rebellion and Civil Wars in England*, W. Macray ed., Oxford: Oxford University Press.

Codrington, Robert (1646) *The Life and Death of the Illustrious Robert, Earl of Essex*, London.

Cowley, H. (1788) *The Poetry of Anna Matilda*, London.

Dell, William (1652) *Several Sermons and Discourses*, London.

Dore, R. ed. (1983-4 and 1990) Sir William Brereton, Letter Books i-iv, *Lancashire and Cheshire Record Society*, 123, 128.

Firth, C. ed., (1891-1901) The Clarke Papers, *Camden Society* new series 49, 54, 61, 62.

Firth, C. and Rait, R. eds. (1911) *Acts and Ordinances of the Interregnum 1642-1660*, London: HMSO.

Gilbert, J. (1879) *A Contemporary History 1641-52*, 3 vols. Dublin: Irish Academic Press.

Green, M. ed. (1857) *Letters of Queen Henrietta Maria,* London: Richard Bentley.

Gumble, Thomas, (1671) *The Life of General Monck, Duke of Albemarle,* London.

Historical Manuscripts Commission (HMC): London: HMSO.

6th Report (House of Lords), 8th Report Part II (Duke of Manchester), 10th Report V (Marquis of Ormond), 10th Report VI (Bouverie, Lord Braye), 13th Report I, III (Duke of Portland), 15th Report R.R. Hastings II.

Hodgson, John (1809) Original Memoirs in Sir Walter Scott, *The Diary of Sir Henry Slingsby,* London.

Hopton, Ralph, Lord Hopton (1902) Bellum Civile, C. Chadwyck-Healey ed., *Somerset Record Society* 18.

Hutchinson, Lucy (1808) *Memoirs of the Life of Colonel John Hutchinson,* London: Longman.

Journals of the House of Commons ii, iii, iv, v, vi.

Journals of the House of Lords v, vi, vii, viii, ix, x.

Juxon, Thomas (1999) Journal 1644-47, K. Lindley and D. Scott eds, *Camden Society* 5th series 13.

Ludlow, Edmund (1894) *Memoirs 1625-1672,* 2 vols., C.H. Firth ed., Oxford: Oxford University Press.

Luke, Sir Samuel (1947, 1950, 1952-3) Journals, I. Phillip ed., *Oxfordshire Record Society,* 29, 31, 33.

Luke, Sir Samuel (1963) Letter Books, H. Tibbutt ed., *Historical Manuscripts Commission Joint Publications* 4, HMSO.

Marsh, S. (2016) *The Train of Artillery of the Earl of Essex,* The Pike and Shot Society.

Maseres, Francis, Lord ed. (1815) *Select Tracts relating to the Civil Wars in England,* vol 1., London: R. Wilkes.

Meikle, H.W. ed. (1917) 'Correspondence of the Scottish Commissioners in London', *Roxburghe Club.*

Orrery, Roger Boyle, Earl of (1677) *Treatise of the Art of War,* London.

Peter, Hugh (1646) *God's Doing: Man's Duty,* London.

Roe, Henry (1873) Military Memoir of Colonel Birch, J. Webb (ed.), *Camden Society* new series,vii.

Rushworth, J. ed. (1721) *Historical Collections of Private Passages of State,* vols. V and VI, London: D. Browne.

Scott, Sir Walter ed. (1809-15) Somers Tracts, IV.

Slingsby, Sir Henry (1836) *Diary of Sir Henry Slingsby* D. Parsons ed., London: Longman.

Smith, Sir Thomas (1906) *De Republica Anglorum,* L. Alston ed., Cambridge. Cambridge University Press.

Spalding, R, ed. (1990) *The Diary of Bulstrode Whitelock*, Oxford, Oxford University Press.

Sprigg, Joshua (1844 ed.) *Anglia Rediviva*, Oxford: Oxford University Press.

Thurloe, John (1742) *A Collection of State Papers of John Thurlow Esquire, Secretary to the Council of State*, London.

Turner, Sir James (1829) *Memoirs of his Own Life and Times*: Edinburgh: Bannatyne Club.

Vicars, John (1647) *Jehovah-Jireh*, London.

Walker, Clement (1648), *A History of Independency*, London.

Walker, Sir Edward (1705) *Historical Discourses upon Several Occasions*, London: S. Keble.

Warburton, E.B.G., (1849) *Memoirs of Prince Rupert and the Cavaliers*, London: Richard Bentley.

Warwick, Sir Phillip (1701) *Memoirs of the Reign of King Charles I etc.*, London.

Washbourne, J. ed. (1825) *Bibliotheca Gloucestrensis*, Gloucester.

Whitelock, Bulstrode (1732) *Memoirs of the English Affairs etc.*, London: J. Tonson.

Young, P. ed. (1953) Sir John Byron's Relation of the Late Western Action, *Journal of the Society for Army Historical Research* xxxi.

Collections of Newspapers and Pamphlets
British Library
Thomason Tracts.

Printed Secondary Sources
Books

Adair, J. (1997 2nd ed.) *Roundhead General: The Campaigns of Sir William Waller*, Stroud: Sutton.

Adamson, J., (2007) *The Noble Revolt: The Overthrow of Charles I*, London: Weidenfeld and Nicolson.

Ashley, M. (1957) *The Greatness of Oliver Cromwell*, London: Hodder & Stoughton.

Ashton, R. (1995) *Counter Revolution: The Second Civil War and its Origins*, London: Yale University Press

Atkin, M. (1998) *Cromwell's Crowning Mercy: the Battle of Worcester 1651*, Stroud: Sutton.

Atkin, M. (2004) *Worcestershire under Arms: An English County during the Civil Wars*, Barnsley: Pen & Sword.

Braddick, M. (2008) *God's Fury, England's Fire: A New History of the English Civil Wars*, London: Allen Lane.

Burne, A. and Young, P. (1959) *The Great Civil War*, London: Eyre and Spottiswood.

Carpenter, S.D.M. (2005) *Military Leadership in the British Civil Wars, 1642-1651: 'The Genius of this Age'*, London: Frank Cass.

Cooke, D. (2007) *The Road to Marston Moor*, Barnsley: Pen & Sword.

Cotton, R. (1877) *Barnstaple and the Northern Part of Devonshire during the Great Civil War 1642-1646*, Exeter.

Davis, J.C. (2001) *Oliver Cromwell*, London: Arnold.

Deane, J. (1870) *The Life of Richard Deane, Major-General and Admiral-at-Sea*, London: Longman.

Farr, D. (2003) *John Lambert. Parliamentary Soldier and Cromwellian Major General*, Woodbridge, Suffolk: Boydell and Brewer.

Firth, C.H. (1962 ed.) *Cromwell's Army*, London: Methuen.

Firth, C. H. (1904) *Cromwell*, London: Putnam's.

Firth, C.H. and Davies, G. *The Regimental History of Cromwell's Army*, Oxford: Oxford University Press.

Foard, G. (1995) *Naseby: the Decisive Campaign*, Whitstable: Prior Publications.

Gardiner, S.R. (1901) *Oliver Cromwell*, London: Longman.

Gardiner, S.R. (1991 ed.) *History of the Great Civil War*, 4 vols., Moreton in the Marsh: Windrush Press.

Gardiner, S.R. (1903) *The Commonwealth and the Protectorate*, 3 vols., London: Longman.

Gaunt, P. ed. (2013) *Cromwell Four Centuries On*, The Cromwell Association.

Gaunt, P. (2014) *The English Civil War: a Military History*, London: Taurus.

Gentles, I. (1992) *The New Model Army in England, Ireland and Scotland 1645-1653*, Oxford: Blackwell.

Gentles, I. (2007) *The English Revolution and the Wars in Three Kingdoms 1638-1652*, Harlow: Longman, Pearson.

Gibb, M. (1938) *The Lord General, A Life of Sir Thomas Fairfax*, London: Lindsay Drummond.

Grainger, J.D. (1997) *Cromwell against the Scots: The Last Anglo-Scottish War 1650-1652*, East Linton, East Lothian: Tuckwell Press.

Hexter, J.H. (1968 ed.) *The Reign of King Pym*, Cambridge, Mass.

Hill, Christopher (1970) *God's Englishman: Oliver Cromwell and the English Revolution*, Weidenfeld and Nicolson.

Hill, J. and Watkinson, P. (2012) *Cromwell hath the Honour*, Frontline Books, London.

History of Parliament 1660-1690

Holmes, C. (1974) *The Eastern Association in the English Civil War*, Cambridge: Cambridge University Press.

Hopper, A. (2007) *Black Tom: Sir Thomas Fairfax and the English Revolution*, Manchester: Manchester University Press.

Howell, R. (1977) *Oliver Cromwell*, London: Hutchinson.

Hughes, A. (1987) *Politics, Society and Civil War in Warwickshire, 1620-1660,* Cambridge: Cambridge University Press.

Kenyon, J. (1988) *The Civil Wars of England,* London: Weidenfeld & Nicolson.

Kenyon, J. and Ohlmeyer, J. eds (1998) *The Civil Wars: A Military History of England, Scotland and Ireland 1639-1660,* Oxford: Oxford University Press.

Kishlansky, M. (1979) *The Rise of the New Model Army,* Cambridge: Cambridge University Press.

Kitson, Sir Frank (1994) *Prince Rupert: Portrait of a Soldier,* London: Constable.

Kitson, Sir Frank (2004) *Old Ironside; the Military Biography of Oliver Cromwell,* London: Weidenfeld & Nicholson.

Little, P. ed. (2009) *Oliver Cromwell, New Perspectives,* London: Palgrave Macmillan.

MacCormack, J. (1973) *Revolutionary Politics in the Long Parliament,* Cambridge, Mass.: Harvard University Press.

Markham, Sir Clements (1870) *A Life of the great Lord Fairfax,* London: MacMillan.

Marshall, A. (2005) *Oliver Cromwell Soldier: The Military Life of a Revolutionary at War,* London: Brasseys.

Moody, T., Martin, F. and Byrne, F. eds. (1991) *A New History of Ireland, Vol. 3 1534-1691,* Oxford: Oxford University Press.

Morrill, J., (1976) *The Revolt of the Provinces,* London.

Morrill, J. ed. (1990) *Oliver Cromwell and the English Revolution,* London: Longman.

Oxford Dictionary of National Biography (2004) Matthew, H. and Harrison, B. eds., Oxford: Oxford University Press.

Porter S. and Marsh, S. (2010) *The Battle for London,* Stroud, Glos.: Amberley.

Reece, H. (2016) *The Army in Commonwealth England 1649-1990,* Oxford: Oxford University Press.

Scott, C., Turton, A. and Von Arni, E. (2004) *Edgehill: the Battle Reinterpreted,* Barnsley: Pen & Sword

Scott, C. and Turton, A.(2016) *Hey for Old Robin: The Campaigns and Armies of the Earl of Essex during the First Civil War,* Solihull: Helion & Co.

Scott, D. (2004) *Politics and War in the Three Stuart Kingdoms,* London: Palgrave MacMillan.

Snow, V. (1970) *Essex the Rebel: The Life of Robert Devereux, the Third Earl of Essex,* Lincoln, Nebraska: University of Nebraska Press.

Spring, L. (2007) *Waller's Army,* Pike and Shot Society.

Spring, L. (2016) *The Army of the Eastern Association: Officers and Regiments,* Pike and Shot Society.

Stevenson, D. (2003) *Revolution and Counter Revolution in Scotland 1644-51,* Edinburgh: John Donald.

Stoyle, M. (2005) *Soldiers and Strangers: an Ethnic History of the English Civil Wars,* London, Yale University Press.

Terry, C. (1899) *Life and Campaigns of Alexander Leslie, Earl of Leven,* London: Longman, Green.

Wanklyn, M. (2006) *Decisive Battles of the English Civil Wars,* Barnsley: Pen & Sword.

Wanklyn, M. (2010) *Warrior Generals: Winning the British Civil Wars,* London: Yale University Press.

Wanklyn. M. (2015–16), *Reconstructing the New Model Army,* 2 vols. Solihull: Helion & Co.

Wanklyn, M. and Jones, F. (2004) *A Military History of the English Civil Wars: Strategy and Tactics,* Harlow: Pearson Longman.

Wedgwood, C.V. (1958) *The King's War,* London: Collins.

Wenham, P. (1970) *The Great and Close Siege of York,* Kineton, Warwicks.: Roundwood.

Wheeler, J.S. (2002) *The Irish and British Wars 1637-1654: Triumph, Tragedy and Failure,* London: Routledge.

Woolrych, A. (1961) *Battles of the English Civil Wars,* London: Batsford.

Woolrych, A. (2002) *Britain in Revolution 1625-1660,* Oxford: Oxford University Press.

Young, P. (1967) *Edgehill: the Campaign and the Battle,* Kineton: Roundwood Press.

Young, P. (1970) *Marston Moor 1644,* Kineton: Roundwood Press.

Young, P. and Holmes, R. (1974), *The English Civil Wars,* London: Eyre Methuen.

Essays and Journal Articles:

Adamson, J.S.A. (2002) 'The triumph of oligarchy: the management of war and the Committee of Both Kingdoms, 1644-1645', *Parliament at Work,* C. Kyle and J. Peacey eds., Woodbridge: Boydell Press.

Beats, L. (1977-8) 'The East Midlands Association 1642-1644' *Midland History* IV.

Blackmore, D. (2005) 'Counting the New Model Army' *English Civil War Times,* 5

Burke, J. (1990) 'The New Model Army and the problems of siege warfare, 1648-51, *Irish Historical Studies,* XXVII.

Firth, C.H. (1900) 'The battle of Dunbar', *Transactions of the Royal Historical Society,* new series, 14.

Gentles, I. (1994) 'The choosing of officers for the New Model Army', *Historical Research,* 67.

Kishlansky, M. (1978) 'The case of the army truly stated: the creation of the New Model Army', *Past and Present,* 81.

Morrill, J. (1972)'Mutiny and discontent in English provincial armies 1645-1647, *Past and Present,* 56.

Wanklyn, M. (1981) 'Royalist strategy in the south of England 1642-1644' *Southern History* 3.

Wanklyn, M. (2007) 'A general much maligned: the generalship of the Earl of Manchester, July to November 1644', *War in History* 14.2.

Wanklyn, M. (2011) 'Oliver Cromwell and the performance of Parliament's armies in the Newbury campaign 20 October to 21 November 1644', *History* 96.

Wanklyn, M. (2014) 'Choosing officers for the New Model Army February to April 1645', *Journal of the Society for Army Historical Research*, 92.

Wanklyn, M., 'Cromwell's generalship and the conquest of Scotland 1650-1651', *Cromwelliana*, ser.3, 4.

Wanklyn, M., (2016) 'Some further thoughts on Oliver Cromwell's last campaign', *New Approaches to the Military History of the English Civil Wars*, I. Pells ed., Solihull: Helion.

Theses

D.S. Evans (1995) 'The civil war career of Major-General Edward Massey', Ph.D. London.

Postscript

Professor Martyn Bennett's military biography of Cromwell, *Oliver Cromwell at War* (LB Tauris) was published after I had signed off the final version of the proofs of *Parliament's Generals*. I have therefore been unable to take account of its contents but, although we occasionally have similar insights, Bennett's assessments of his command of strategy and tactics and of his behaviour towards the earl of Manchester in the Newbury campaign sit firmly within the dominant narrative tradition of Cromwell the military colossus.

Index

Earle, Sir Walter 29, 30

East Anglia 16, 25, 27, 66, 67, 87, 89, 113, 181

Eastern Association, the 35, 40, 55, 59, 66, 69, 87, 89, 101, 181

Edgehill, the battle of 7, 10, 14-16, 18-21, 23, 25, 27, 32, 66, 67, 146, 172

Edinburgh 137, 139, 153

Essex, Robert Devereux, Third Earl of 2, 5, 6-26, 29, 31-54, 56-57, 59-62, 65, 66, 69, 74, 75, 77, 78, 81, 87, 88, 89, 101-05, 108, 109, 112, 115, 124, 159, 169, 170-79, 182-83, 186

Essex House 8, 52, 53, 179

Exeter 25, 30, 34, 44, 95, 96, 101, 103, 105-07, 176

Fairfax, Anne Lady 118, 169

Fairfax, Brian 168

Fairfax, Ferdinando, Second Lord 23-24, 68, 77, 78, 79, 104, 107, 111, 116-17, 124, 151-52, 182-83, 193

Fairfax, Sir Thomas, later Third Lord Fairfax 2, 24, 38, 48, 60-62, 64-65, 69, 77-85, 86-96, 97-107, 108-12, 114-21, 124, 126-27, 132, 133, 135, 137, 145, 147-51, 159, 166, 168-69, 180, 182-87, 189, 195

Fenlands, the 66, 67

Fiennes, Nathaniel 29

Fife 139, 140, 153, 161, 162, 191

Fincher, Richard 75

Firth, Sir Charles 12, 57, 65, 119, 186

Fleetwood, Charles 113, 116, 138, 142-3, 145-46, 148, 153, 159, 160, 162-63, 169, 194

Forbes, Colonel 151-2, 193

Forbois, Mr. 154

Fortescue, the foot regiment of Richard 96

Forth, the Firth of 137, 139, 140, 141, 161, 162

Forth, the river 139

France 4, 44, 95, 140

Gainsborough, the engagement at 68, 147

Gardiner, S.R. 2, 55, 60, 65, 89, 119, 148-9, 168-69, 179, 189-90, 192

Gell, Sir John 173

Gentles, Ian 12, 59, 61, 79, 85, 104, 177, 183, 188

Gerard, Sir Gilbert 88

Glenham, Sir Thomas 73-4

Gloucester 9, 11, 18, 24, 27, 34-5, 42, 43, 84, 102, 173

Goffe/Gough, William 127, 188

Goring, George Goring, Lord 86, 91-95, 102, 105, 185

Gough/Goffe, William 127, 188

Grantham, Lincs. 67, 68, 146

Greaves, Richard 125

Grenville, Sir Bevil 31

Grey, Thomas, Lord Grey of Groby 67, 173

Grey, William, First Lord Grey of Wark 25, 27, 66

Gumble, Thomas 160

Hamilton, the battle of 140, 153, 160, 194

Hamilton, James, 2nd Duke of Hamilton 120, 127-31, 136, 141, 156

Hammond, Robert 84, 89, 126, 133

Hammond, Thomas 115, 126, 145, 154, 194

Harley, Edward 114, 184

Harrison, Thomas 70, 85, 118, 135, 141, 142-5, 146, 159, 160, 162-63

Haselrig, Sir Arthur 35, 43, 53-54, 56, 75, 79, 83-84, 134, 179

Heads of Proposals, the 126

Helmsby Castle, Yorkshire 151

Henrietta Maria, Queen 16, 17, 44, 176

Herbert, Lord 27, 29